DERAIN

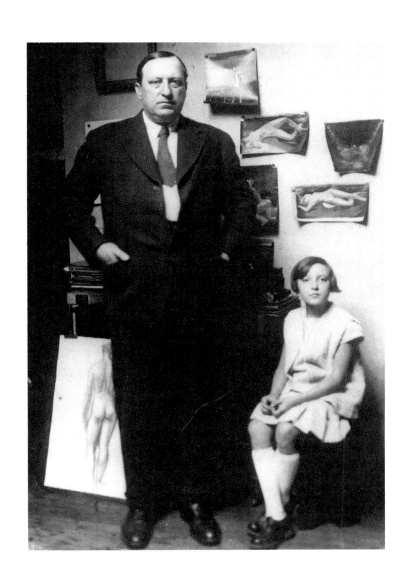

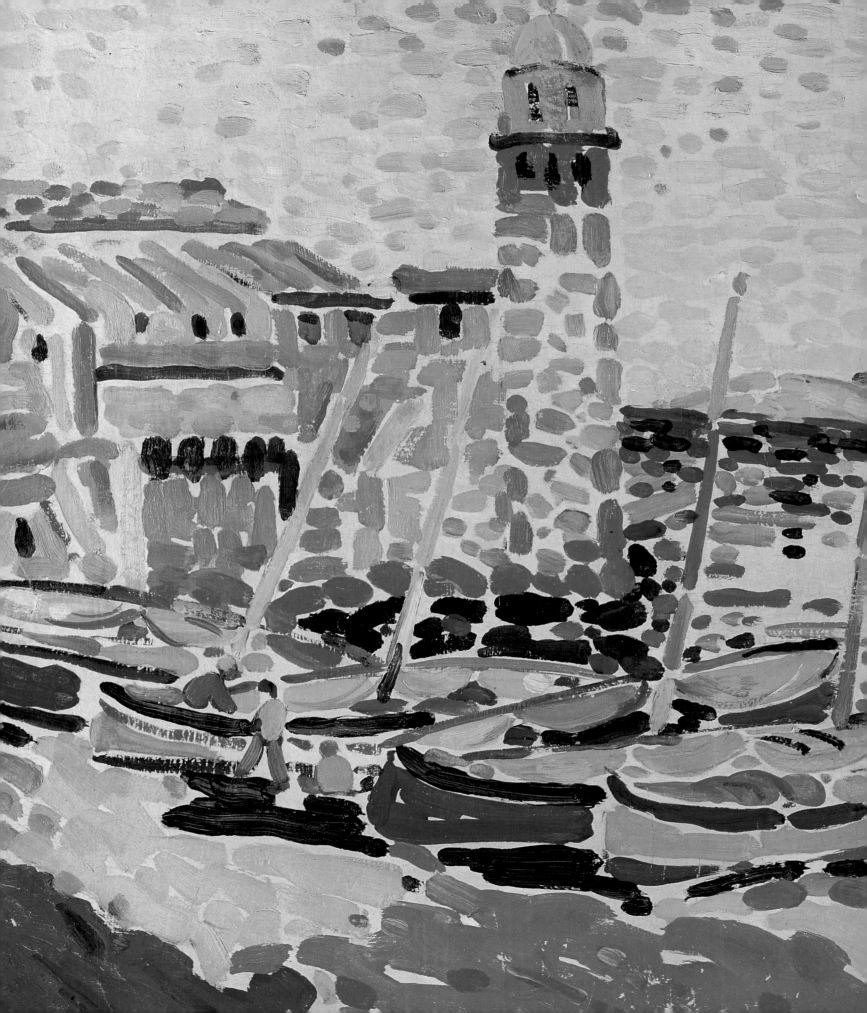

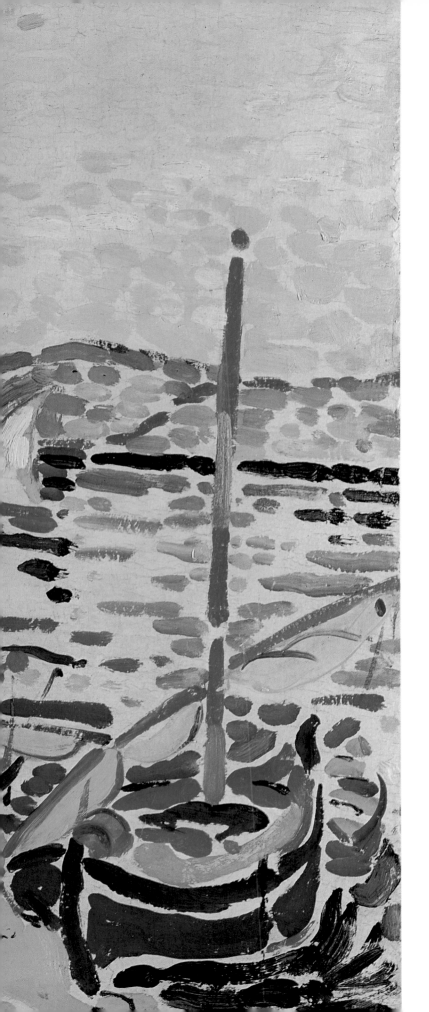

DERAIN

JANE LEE

PHAIDON · OXFORD
UNIVERSE · NEW YORK

To Geneviève Taillade

Published in Great Britain by Phaidon Press Limited, Musterlin House, Jordan Hill Road, Oxford, OX2 8DP

ISBN 0 7148 2649 9

A CIP catalogue record for this book is available from the British Library

Published in the United States of America by
Universe, 381 Park Avenue South, New York, N.Y. 10016

ISBN 0–87663–605–9

Cataloging-in-Publication Data for this book is available from the Library of Congress

First Published 1990

Typeset and printed in Great Britain by
Butler & Tanner Ltd, Frome and London

1. (*half title*) Derain in his studio with his niece, Geneviève Taillade, 1927, Private collection.
2. (*title*) *Boats in Collioure*, 1905, Staatsgalerie, Stuttgart.
3. (*opposite*) Study for *Arlequin et Pierrot*, Private collection (cat. 87).

Published for the exhibition *André Derain* held at the Museum of Modern Art, Oxford, 16 December 1990–18 March 1991, and at the Scottish National Gallery of Modern Art, Edinburgh, 27 March–27 May 1991 and the Musée d'Art Moderne de la Ville de Troyes, 22 June–16 September 1991.

Exhibition organized by the Museum of Modern Art, Oxford.
Exhibition curated by Jane Lee with Chrissie Iles.

The organizers wish to thank le Ministère de la Culture, de la Communication et des Grands Travaux; la Région de Champagne-Ardennes; la Ville de Troyes; British Airways Cargo; SNVB, (Groupe CIC); and the Horaco W. Goldsmith Foundation for their support of the exhibition *André Derain*.

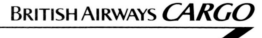

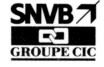

The organizers are grateful to Her Majesty's Government for agreeing to indemnify the exhibition under the National Heritage Act 1980 and to the Museums and Galleries Commission for their help in arranging this indemnity.

The Museum of Modern Art, Oxford, receives financial assistance from the Arts Council of Great Britain, Oxford City Council, Oxfordshire County Council, Visiting Arts and Southern Arts.

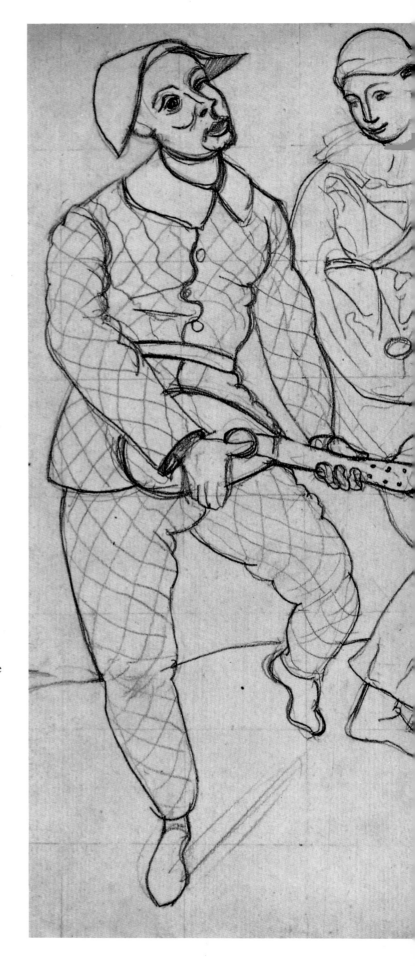

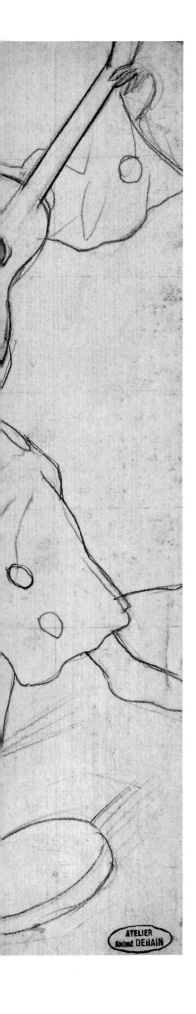

CONTENTS

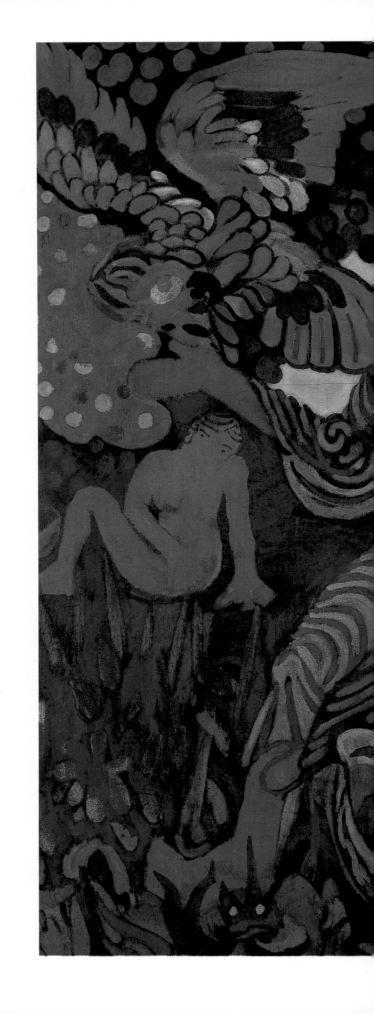

4. *La danse*, 1906, Courtesy Fridart Foundation.

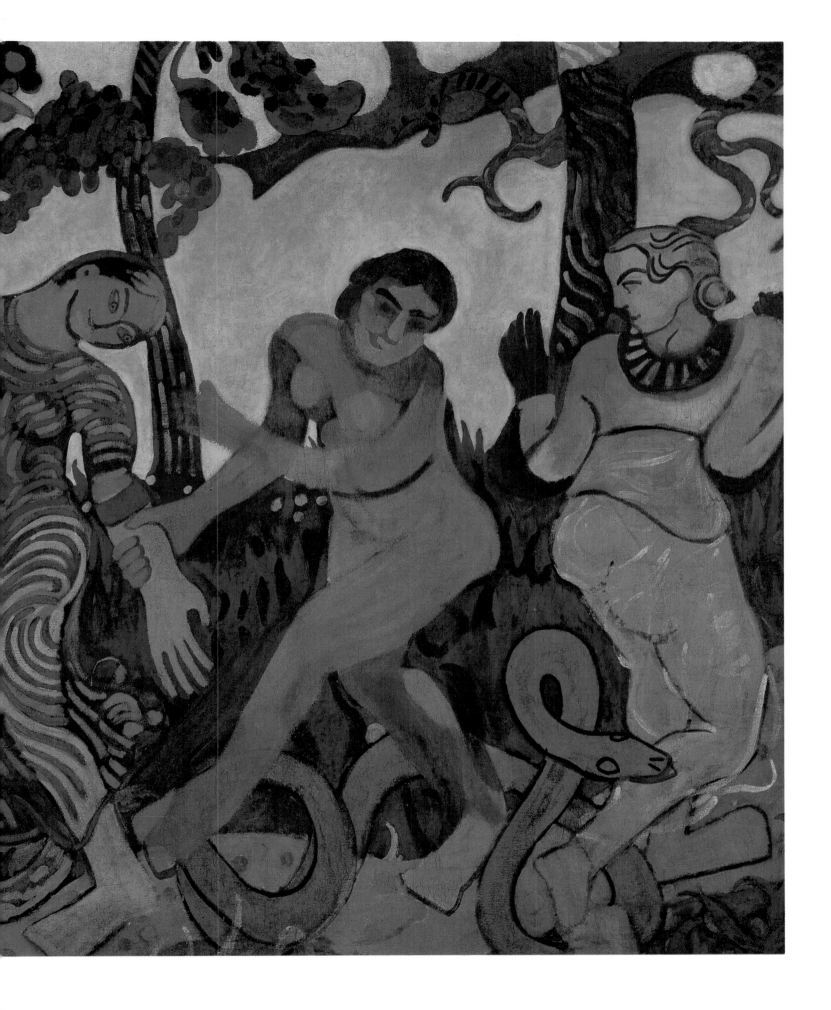

A SUMMARY BIOGRAPHY

1880   Born 17 June.

1899   Frequents Linaret, Matisse, Puy, Marquet. Paints at Académie Camillo corrected by Eugene Carrière.

1900   Meets Vlaminck, shares studio 'La Baraque' with him at Chatou.

1901   Copies Biagio d'Antonio's *Road to Calvary* in the Louvre. Introduces Vlaminck to Matisse at the Van Gogh exhibition at the Galerie Bernheim Jeune. Military service begins.

1904   Returns from military service to Chatou. Attends Académie Julien. Meets Apollinaire.

1905   Sells nearly complete contents of studio to Ambroise Vollard. Paints with Matisse at Collioure. Exhibits in 'fauve' Salon d'Automne. Painting trip to London financed by Vollard.

1906   Second trip to London. Summer: at L'Estaque with Matisse. Associates with Picasso in Montmartre.

1907   Picasso introduces Derain to Alice Princet (née Géry) who becomes Derain's wife. Moves to Montmartre (22 Rue Tourlaque).

1908   May to November: to the south of France. Joined by Braque, Dufy and Friesz.

1909   January and February: paints in Le Havre. Summer: painting on the North coast of France and then around Marseilles. Illustrates Apollinaire's *L'Enchanteur pourrissant*. Death of Derain's father.

1910   To Boulogne and England with his mother. Winter: painting in and around Marseilles and Cagnes. Summer and autumn: in and around Cadaquès and Beauvais. Moves to 13 Rue Bonaparte.

1911   Summer: painting in Crécy-en-Brie and environs, and in Boulogne.

1912   Summer: painting in Cahors and Vers (Lot). Illustrates Max Jacob's *Les oeuvres burlesques et mystiques de Frère Matorel mort au couvent de Barcelone*.

1913   Summer: at Serbonne, Lyons, Martigues, Sausset, joined by Vlaminck.

1914   At Avignon and Montfavet (near Avignon) with Picasso and Braque.

1914–18   Serves in Champagne, Somme, Verdun, L'Aisne, march to Mainz.

1916   Illustrates André Breton's *Mont-de-Piété* (published 1919).

1918   Sets for Claudel's *L'Annonce faite à Marie* for Duroc theatre company.

1919   Summer: in London. Designs sets and costumes for *La boutique fantasque*, Diaghileff's Ballets-Russes. Paints decorations for Halvorsen's rooms. Illustrates Vlaminck's *A la Santé du Corps* and René Dalize's *Pauvre Macchabé mal enterré*.

1920   Paints in and around Cahors. Illustrates André Salmon's *Calumet* and Georges Gabory's *La Cassette de Plomb*.

1921   Trip to Rome and the Campagna. Summer: painting in Sanary and La Ciotat, joined by Kisling and Mondzain.

1922   Summer: painting at Sanary, Les Lecques and St Cyr-sur-Mer (as he would every summer through the 1920s).

   Illustrates Georges Gabory's *Le Nez de Cléopâtre*.

1924   Designs décor for the ballet *Gigues* (Soirées de Paris). Buys house at Chailly-en-Bière in the Fontainebleau forest.

1926   Designs décor for ballet *Jack in the Box* (Etienne de Beaumont). Illustrations for Georges Coquiot's *En suivant la Seine*.

1927   Set of lithographs *Metamorphoses* published by Les Quatre Chemins.

1928   Carnegie Prize. Moves to 5 Rue du Douanier near Parc de Montsouris, next door to Braque.

1929   Illustrates Vincent Muselli's *Les Travaux et les Jeux*. Buys Château Parouzeau.

1930   Paints at Saint Maximin, Var and Bandol.

1932   Designs ballet *La Concurrence* (Ballets-Russes de Monte Carlo). Paints at St Rémy.

1933   Conceives and designs two ballets, *Les Fastes* and *Les Songes* (Les Ballets 33). Paints at St Rémy.

1934   Paints at Gravelines, Dunkirk and at St Rémy. Illustrates Antonin Artaud's *Héliogabale*, Petronius's *Le Satyricon* (published 1951) and La Fontaine's *Contes et Nouvelles* (published 1950). Designs the cover of the surrealist journal *Minotaur*. Death of Derain's dealer, Paul Guillaume.

1935   Buys 'La Rosarie', a house at Chambourcy. Sells the houses in Paris and Chailly-en-Bière and the Château Parouzeau. Shares Léopold-Lévy's studio in Rue d'Assas near the Jardin de Luxembourg. Designs the cover of the classicist journal *Voyage en Grèce*.

1936   Paints on the northern coast of France. Designs sets for ballet *Epreuve d'Amour* (Ballets-Russes de Monte Carlo).

1937   Trip to London.

1938   Illustrates Oscar Wilde's *Salomé* and Ovid's *Les Héroïdes*.

1940   Leaves Paris in the *exode*.

1941   Paints at Oussons-sur-Loire. In Paris lives in the Rue de Varenne. Taken into Germany.

1943   Paints at Donnemarie-en-Montois. Illustrates Rabelais' *Pantagruel*.

1947   Illustrates Héron de Villefosse's *Eloge des Pierreries*. Designs décor for ballet *Mam'zelle Angot* (Sadlers Wells). November: in London.

1948   Designs décor for ballet *Le Diable l'Emporte* (Ballets Roland Petit). Illustrates *Le Génie du Vin* for Etablissements Nicholas.

1950   Illustrates Antoine de Saint Exupery's *Citadelle* in the Oeuvres Complètes of that author. Illustrations for *Amie et Amille* (published 1957) may also have been done in this year.

1951   Designs décor for ballet *Il Seraglio* (Festival d'Aix-en-Provence).

1953   *Anacréon* published for which Derain's numerous lithographic illustrations may have been done some time earlier. Designs décor for ballet *The Barber of Seville* (Festival d'Aix-en-Provence).

1954   8 September: death of Derain at Garches, Seine-et-Oise.

André Derain died thirty-six years ago at the age of seventy-four from complications following a car crash. Since that time he has become a neglected, almost peripheral figure in the history of European art. His work seems to have had little internal consistency; he had turned his back on the notion of the avant-garde, and his devotion to the traditional genres and subject matter of art appeared old-fashioned.

To the casual observer, therefore, the life and work of Derain presents an enigma. Ostensibly he seems to have been an artist who, instead of forging ahead to create new forms of expression like his friends Matisse or Picasso, chose rather to stand back in the shadows of tradition, entering a dialogue with the art of the past. It is only recently that a more judicious view has prevailed in which the celebration of tradition can, paradoxically, be seen as a revolutionary force for change.

Derain was part of that group which constituted the first generation of Fauves and Cubists, yet by 1910 he had destroyed much of the early work which was still in his possession and had started to distance himself from the deconstructions of Cubism, in a move towards a kind of painting which was at the same time both evocative and architectonic. He now began to combine the spiritual references of medieval art with the Quattrocento and the more corporeal classicism of the sixteenth and seventeenth centuries, in a synthesis of tradition with modernity which had been implicit, although not directly stated, in the work of Cézanne.

Derain's *rappel à l'ordre* took place in the years immediately before the First World War, and anticipated what was to be the mood of many of his colleagues throughout Europe in the early 1920s.

The exhibition, the catalogue of which is incorporated in this book, focuses on Derain's later work and traces the ways in which the artist redefined modern painting, not in terms of existential agony or of the reconstruction of perceived and known data, but in a living and evolving dialogue with the art and culture of the Western tradition.

In pursuing this, Derain employed no easy formulae; some paintings are constructed through colour, while others depend upon a strict architecture of chiaroscuro and subtle modulation of form. The art of the past became a never-ending stimulus to the creativity of the present in a practical demonstration of how art did not have to scream, to turn somersaults or to destroy itself to be born anew in order to be a challenging, invigorating and beautiful element in modern life.

Both the exhibition and this book, by Jane Lee, analyse and celebrate this achievement – Derain's velvet revolution.

David Elliott, Director
Museum of Modern Art, Oxford

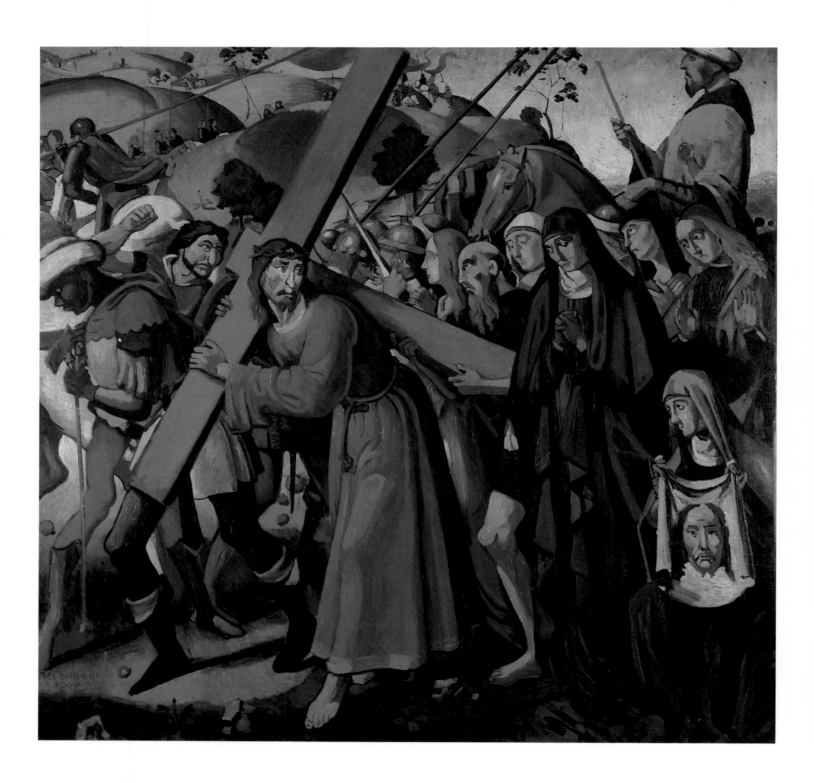

Derain was born on 17 June 1880, the son of a well-to-do *cremier*, in Chatou, a small town on the banks of the Seine just outside Paris. Chatou was a favourite haunt of the Impressionists, the site of Renoir's *Déjeuner des canotiers* (Phillips Collection, Washington, D.C.), and Derain later referred to his birthplace as a 'sort of Barbizon at the gates of Paris'. His first master was a local landscape painter, Jacomin, who, when Derain was about fifteen years of age, took him for lessons with his own two sons. Nearly half a century later Derain, reminiscing in the journal *Comoedia*, recalled that Jacomin had thought him a rebel. Nevertheless, as he had left the Lycée Chaptal in Paris with the drawing prize as well as the prize in natural science, his parents recognized that painting might become one of their son's accomplishments and looked kindly on Derain's long rambles along the banks of the Seine for sketching and landscape painting. As a profession, however, they chose engineering and in 1895 sent their son to a preparatory college to be trained to enter one of the great technical schools.

The engineering college to which Derain was sent was in the Rue Jacob in Paris, not far from the Ecole des Beaux Arts and the several 'free' academies and painting classes which surrounded it. From the Rue Jacob it is a short walk to the banks of the Seine and across the river to the Louvre. Derain ignored his engineering studies. When he was not painting river landscapes, he was in the museum. His attention was fastened at this time on the 'primitives', that is, on painting before Raphael in Italy and Dürer in the north. This was not an unusual interest at the end of the last century when European connoisseurship was re-evaluating the fifteenth-century painting of both Italy and the regional schools. This re-evaluation affected both hanging and acquisitions in the Louvre. For Derain's generation it was the leading Symbolist artists, particularly Maurice Denis and his circle, who sustained the avant-garde interest in early Renaissance painting.

In 1899, while prowling the Louvre, Derain met Georges Florentin Linaret (1878–1905), an old friend from his days at the Lycée Chaptal, painting a copy after Uccello. Linaret's copy, painted in vivid, pure hues, straight from the tube, exemplified the young painter's adherence to a Symbolist attitude to colour espoused in Paris since 1889. In that year the painter Paul Sérusier had brought to the Académie Julien a small landscape which he had painted on the back of a cigar box under Gauguin's direction. Gauguin had insisted on his using pure colours – the strongest ones – on his palette. This work became known as the *Talisman* (Private Collection, Paris), and within a year Sérusier's friend Maurice Denis had published a statement which began with a much-repeated remark, that a painting is primarily an 'arrangement of colours on a flat surface'.

5. *The Road to Calvary* (copy after Biagio d'Antonio), 1901, Kunstmuseum, Berne.

Linaret introduced Derain to his friends, the painters with whom he had studied in the studio classes of Gustave Moreau at the Ecole des Beaux Arts, including Georges Rouault and Henri Matisse. Matisse, who was eleven years older than Derain, had begun to exhibit with the Société Nationale des Beaux Arts, and at the death of Moreau in 1898, he and others from the Moreau studio had moved to the studio in which the painter Eugène Carrière, one of the founder members of the Société Nationale, regularly offered criticism and advice. Derain became a dedicated member of Eugène Carrière's studio in the Rue de Rennes and developed his ambition to devote himself entirely to painting.

There is no work by Derain which can be securely dated before 1899. *The Road to Carrières St Denis* of 1899 and *The Funeral* of about the same time (both in a Private Collection, Paris) may both have been done before he met Matisse, although they share with Matisse a community of interest in the work of Cézanne and Monet, and *The Funeral* was at one time in Matisse's collection. When Derain met him, the focus of Matisse's work was on a series of still-life paintings with sharp diagonal compositions, abruptly limited viewpoints, and heightened colour which expressed the fall of light (such as *First Orange Still Life*, Paris, Musée Nationale d'Art Moderne). Although no clear example of Matisse's influence upon Derain's very early work survives, it is likely that Derain took an immediate interest in the work of the older painter. By 1904 Derain had a highly developed understanding of Matisse's painting and of the investigation of local and reflected colour that had occupied Matisse at the turn of the century.

When Derain decided to undertake a large and ambitious copy in the Louvre, it may have been with Matisse's encouragement. To copy from a major work in the national collection was, and still is, an integral part of the training a painter receives at the Ecole des Beaux Arts, but Matisse had made copying an important part of his painterly practice for some years. While Linaret had been copying Uccello, Matisse had been copying, in an adjacent room, the colourful Signorelli fragment, the *Man with a Striped Sleeve*. On 24 January 1901 Derain signed into the Louvre permission book for the first time to copy a picture by Biagio d'Antonio which was then thought to be by Ghirlandaio. He continued to renew this permission ticket until his work was finished on 28 April of the same year.

Derain's transposition of Biagio, like Linaret's Uccello, is more vivid than the original but retains Biagio's range of colour, just as it retains his overall composition. The simplification of the tonality of the painting and of the structure of the figures flattens the composition into the front plane. His treatment of Biagio's *The Road to Calvary* (fig. 5) indicates Derain's interest in the Nabis group of Symbolist painters – Bonnard, Denis, Sérusier, Vallotton, Vuillard – who were increasingly visible at the turn of the century, with exhibitions in the Durand-Ruel Gallery and Galerie Bernheim Jeune. Beyond this, however, Derain created a linear tension and expressive attenuation reminiscent of the German primitives. The work was so strikingly expressive that it offended passers-by in the Louvre, who accused Derain of 'caricature' (Derain, 1942, p. 6).

The expressive qualities of Derain's work may also have been affected by the Van Gogh exhibition at the Galerie Bernheim Jeune which was held that March, while Derain was still painting his Louvre copy. This exhibition of seventy works was the first great display of Van Gogh's painting. It was an important exhibition for Derain and the formative inspiration for the work of his closest friend, another Chatou painter, Maurice Vlaminck. At the Van Gogh exhibition Derain introduced Vlaminck to Matisse and thereby assembled the future Fauve group for the first time. Derain and Vlaminck, later called by Maurice Denis the 'geniuses from the suburbs', had met accidentally in June 1900 on a train between Paris and Chatou. They had soon begun to paint together, sharing the dining room of a derelict restaurant 'La Baraque' on an island in the Seine as a studio and living a bohemian life-style in the circle of the decadent poet, La Noé. They were physically alike, tall and robust, but in other ways an unmatched pair. Unlike Derain, who was still supported by his parents, Vlaminck had been independent of his family for some time and was already married. Derain was well educated, both classically and scientifically, had read extensively, and had gained immeasurably from his hours in the Louvre. Vlaminck was intelligent but largely self-taught, and coming from a family of very limited resources, he earned a precarious living as a labourer, an author, a street musician, a racing cyclist, and occasionally as a postman. Derain had a well-developed habit of reflection and a cutting edge to his wit; Vlaminck had courage and energy. Each young man greatly admired the other.

Derain's family must have been despairing by this time, and Vlaminck began the younger painter's initiation into self-sufficiency. The author of money-spinning, sentimental, mildly pornographic little books of a kind which abounded in Paris at the turn of the century, Vlaminck had by 1903 commissioned Derain to do illustrations for two of his novelettes. It seems from Derain's letters to Vlaminck that he too intended to write such works for money, as he asks Vlaminck to end him 'des livres baths', 'crummy' books, as an example of style (Vlaminck, 1955). Derain would count on Vlaminck occasionally to find him ways of making money until he inherited from his father in 1909.

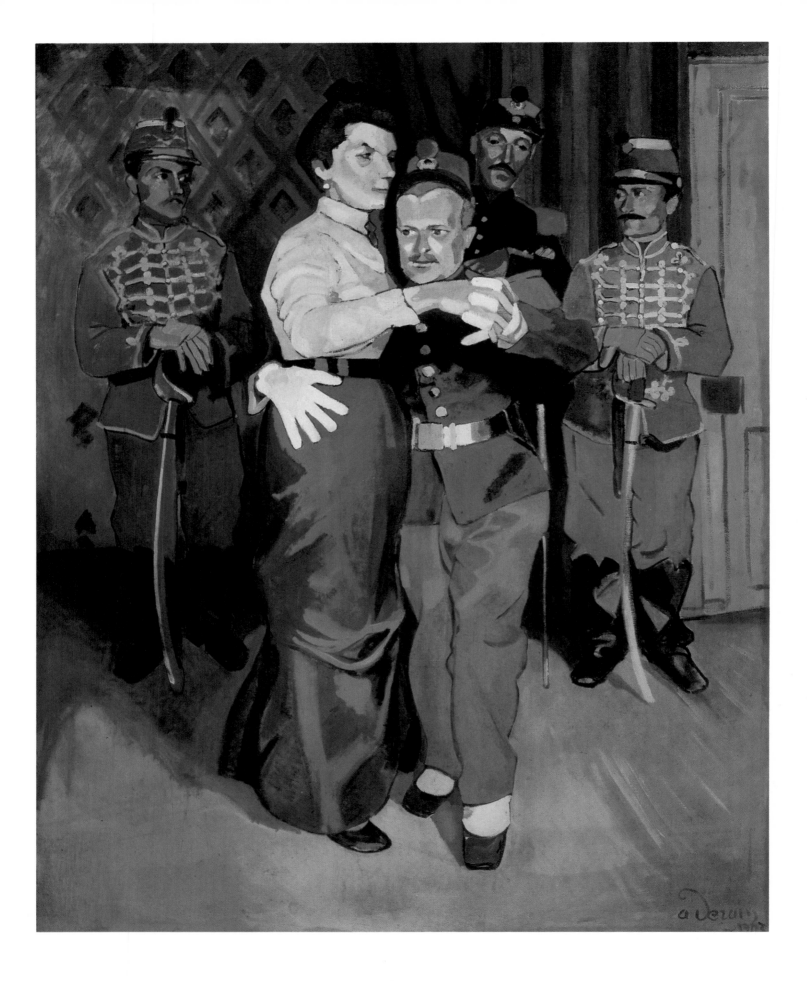

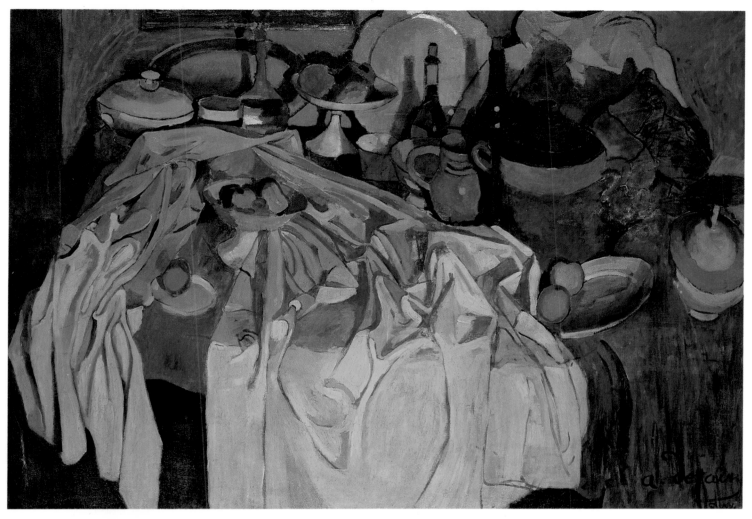

7. *Still Life*, 1904, Private collection.

6. (opposite) *Bal des soldats à Suresnes*, 1903, The Saint Louis Art Museum.

THE YEARS AT COMMERCY

The relationship between the two Chatou painters is documented by the correspondence which sustained their friendship during Derain's three years of compulsory military service. Derain spent the summer of 1901 in Belle Ile, a well-known painting spot in Brittany where Matisse had recently been, and then, in September of that year, reported to his barracks. His frustration at leaving his painting and particularly at leaving Paris is apparent in the plaintive evocation in his first letter to Vlaminck: 'La tête mijote dans les rues de Paris, comme dans un bouillon continuel. Un rien, un journal, une revue vous intéressent . . .' which marks the 'flaneur des deux rives' who was forced into uniform at Commercy that year (Vlaminck, 1955, p. 18). Derain had little hope of painting but intended to use his barracks life as the basis of a novel, as Vlaminck had done. The novel did not materialize, but hoping to supplement his small military stipend, he sent short works to Vlaminck who tried to have them published. Vlaminck also helped him by placing his illustrations with comic journals under the pseudonym of Bouzi.

Derain's letters to Vlaminck are full of despair at the systematic brutalization which was army life. Among his serious reflections on painting, however, and a few fantastic and poetic literary passages, are the 'slice of life' vignettes expected in 'naturalist' or 'realist' novels of the sort he was attempting to write. Only one of these vivid images seems actually to have resulted in a painting. Derain wrote: 'I'm writing to you from the back of a smoky little restaurant full of soldiers, where these blokes from the north are playing the accordion and dancing. It might interest you and maybe amuse you. Lots of infantrymen and hussars with long swords under a hazy light.'

Bal des soldats à Suresnes (St Louis Museum of Art) resulted from this initial observation (fig. 6). It was painted in 1903, presumably during a long leave. While Derain sat at the café table reporting the ball to Vlaminck, he also made a pencil drawing which was the first step towards this painting (now among Derain's manuscripts in the Bibliothèque Littéraire Jacques Doucet). The drawing shows the same dancing couple and is accompanied by detailed notes which Derain made of the scene. These notes describe a wider view than either the painting or the drawing as he records his observations of all corners of the room, of the soldiers and musicians and dancers, of the changing activity and movement around him, and even of his view out into the courtyard where a cockerel struts among his hens.

The painting is something of a résumé of the recent history of 'realist' painting in France, from Manet to Vuillard and Vallotton. It also pays homage to a painting by one of Matisse's friends from the studio of Gustave Moreau, Henri Evenepoël.

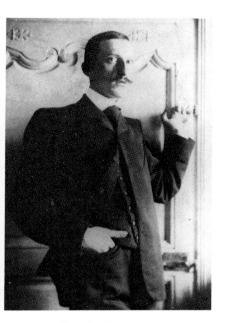

8. Derain after his military service, 1904, Private collection.

Evenepoël's *Fête aux Invalides* (Musées Royaux des Beaux Arts de Belgique, Brussels), with its similar low viewpoint, dancing couple, and row of watching soldiers, was exhibited in the Société Nationale des Beaux Arts in 1899, the year of the artist's death at the age of twenty-seven, and at that time it was criticized in the militarist press as an insult to the army. An anti-heroic view of soldiers at leisure among the people offended the conservative revanchist concept of a 'sacred' army, and if Evenepoël had been taken by surprise at this interpretation of his work, Derain, after the event, was not so innocent. Throughout the period of Derain's military service France was gripped by the ideological divisions raised by the Dreyfus case, and both Derain and Vlaminck were staunchly Dreyfusard and anti-military.

In the barracks Derain read widely, particularly the works of Zola, Balzac, Daudet, and Paul Adam. Derain's predicament and his long hours of reflection combined to sharpen his philosophical demands. He and Vlaminck were heirs to the 'realism' of Zola as well as to that of the draughtsman of Parisian daily life, Steinlen. In his letters to his friend, Derain criticized literary realism continuously, making a sharp distinction between what was of comfort to him and what was useful philosophically and artistically. He declared that he was bored, not only with Vlaminck's interminable lifting of a woman's skirt but with Steinlen and with the whole turn-of-the-century obsession with daily life and the need to '*chiffoner un sentiment ordinaire*', to work to shreds an ordinary feeling. Derain did not want to be 'of his time', he declared in his letters to Vlaminck; he wanted to be 'of all time'. In opposition to the sense of something formless and facile, in which any observation of life would do, he demanded a rigorously organized and disciplined thought which he identified specifically as 'scholastic' (Vlaminck, 1955, p. 92).

Derain preferred the 'fixed and eternal' over the shifting and momentary, and the letters in which he expressed this to Vlaminck document the equivocation with Impressionism which was at the heart of avant-garde painting at that time. Derain decries the cult of observation (*regardisme*) and the cult of the motif and of nature. He used the language of the current journals and centred his arguments largely on Van Gogh and Cézanne. He variously embraced the symbolist 'synthesis', based on a direct correspondence between lines, colours, and human emotions, and a more 'constructive' responsibility for the eternal and complex nature of the work he wanted to produce, based on principles of painting deduced from the works of great painters.

In all this he kept pace with Paris, despite the separation imposed by his military service. He had found another soldier in the barracks, a sculptor, with whom he could share the cost of a subscription to the *Revue blanche*. What distinguishes Derain is the philosophical depth he brought to these contemporary aesthetic arguments. Prolonged equivocation and a certain scholasticism remained with him throughout his life.

His impatience with Vlaminck seems to have evaporated quickly after he left the army. In September 1904 he returned to Chatou and began to paint with both Vlaminck and Matisse (fig. 8). Vivid landscapes painted in Chatou and the nearby village of Vésinet Le Pecq that autumn and winter, works such as *Barges at Chatou* and *Snowscape at Chatou* (Private Collection, Paris), were painted in Vlaminck's company. He returned to the Louvre regularly, not painting a copy but making drawings after Renaissance and Baroque paintings and after Delacroix, as well as after Egyptian sculpture. He roamed again with Vlaminck along the Seine and through Paris, collecting *curiosités* and French folk art. This was the beginning of a diverse and excellent collection to which Derain added throughout his life and which occasionally proved to be of the utmost importance to his own art and that of his friends.

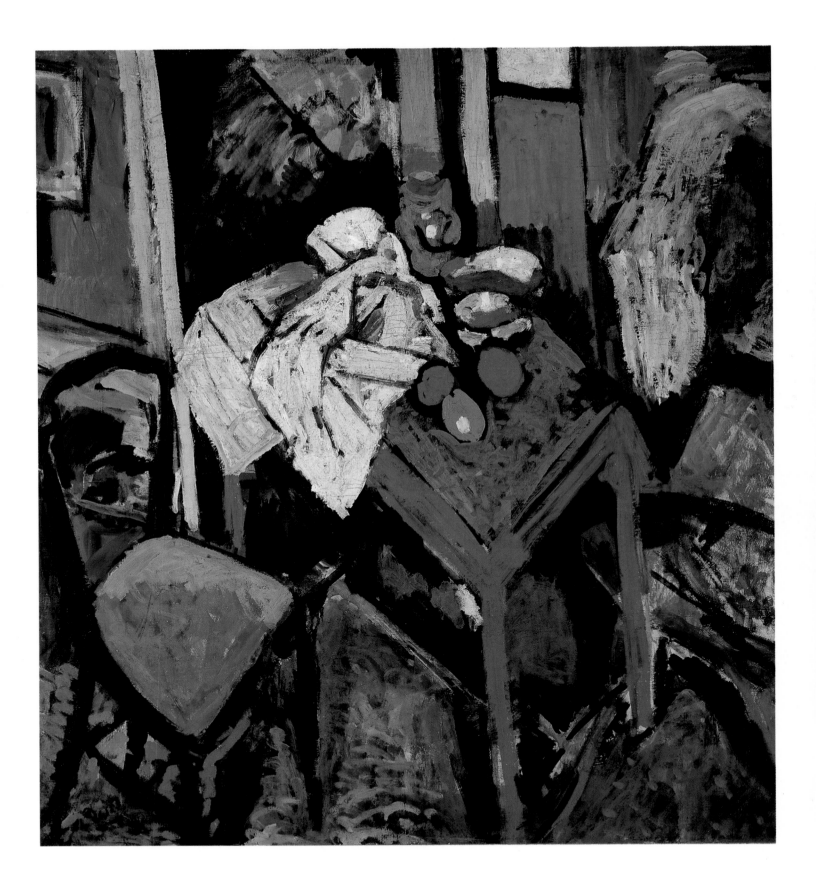

Soon after Derain's discharge from military service, Matisse visited the young painter's father and argued successfully for a small allowance to support him. Derain then began to attend the Académie Julien where fifteen years earlier the Nabis group of Symbolists had formed. Since Ambroise Vollard's exhibition of fifty works by Gauguin in the spring of 1903, there had been a strong revival of Symbolism in the galleries and studios, and this coincided with the founding of 'Neo-Symbolist' journals such as Guillaume Apollinaire and André Salmon's *Le Festin d'Esope* and Paul Fort's *Vers et Prose*. Derain and Vlaminck were well aware of this revival of literary Symbolism, as at this time they became friends with Apollinaire who lived in Vésinet near Chatou. While Derain had been at Commercy, Matisse had moved closer to the Nabis group, and particularly to those who were known as the Intimiste painters, Vuillard and Bonnard. Matisse and his close friend Marquet were founder-members of the Salon d'Automne, which had opened for the first time in 1903 with the participation of Vallotton, Vuillard, and Bonnard and with a dozen works by Gauguin, who had recently died in the Marquesas Islands.

Derain's major works of the winter of 1904–5 reflect the concerns of this group of painters, and particularly of Matisse to whom Derain, still a young man, looked for direction. Derain's large *Nature morte* of 1904 (Paris, Private Collection) is dependent on Cézanne's several *Nature morte au pot de gingembre* paintings, and it has, like the still lifes of Cézanne, the architectonic majesty of sixteenth-century Dutch still life (fig. 7). The intense local colour, the drawing, and the handling of paint are all derived, however, from a Symbolist tradition of still-life painting which began with Gauguin's still lifes at Le Pouldu. Furthermore, the complex play of reflected colour across the white cloth refers directly to the investigation of reflected colour and ambient light that Matisse undertook in his still-life paintings just before Derain began his military service. Derain recognized that this still life was one of the finest works he had painted. It is one of the very few pieces that he dated, and a year later, when the dealer Vollard came to his studio, he refused to sell it, retaining it, with his copy after Biagio, as a point of reference.

In another painting of the same year, the *Nature morte à la table rouge* (fig. 9) which is now in the Bührle Collection in Zurich, Derain created that corkscrew entry into a close interior space which is characteristic of Intimiste painting. The space seems all the smaller as the entry is cut off by the trapezoidal shape of the bright red table which pushes forward to the front plane of the picture. The green and red of the chair and table against the dazzling white of the cloth are redolent of the palette and

9. *Nature morte à la table rouge*, 1904, Foundation E. G. Bührle Collection, Zurich.

handling of Delacroix. Delacroix was an important source for Symbolist colour theory, particularly among the painters with whom Matisse had been most recently affiliated. Paul Signac had published a treatise, *D'Eugène Delacroix au Néo-Impressionisme*, in serial form in the *Revue blanche* in 1898, a work which was quickly republished as a book. Matisse had spent that summer with Signac painting in the south of France and had brought back highly coloured works influenced by Signac and Henri-Edmond Cross. Both of these artists were devoted to the divisionist techniques of Seurat, and this manner of painting is apparent in several of Matisse's canvases of that summer and the following autumn and winter.

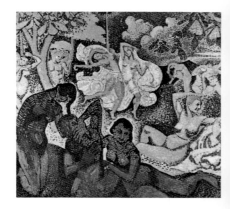

10. *L'Age d'or*, 1905, Museum of Modern Art, Tehran.

In March 1905, in the Salon des Indépendants, Matisse showed a divisionist work, a study of bathers by the sea with the Baudelairian title, *Luxe, calme et volupté*. Derain quickly responded to this, as though to a new challenge, with a larger canvas *L'Age d'or* of 1905 (now in Tehran) (fig. 10). Matisse's composition was inspired by Cézanne's bathers pictures, such as those now in Philadelphia and Stuttgart, and by the works of Puvis de Chavannes, such as *Girls by the Sea* now in the Louvre. In response to this tranquil 'Apollonian' classical composition, Derain struck a distinctly 'Bacchanalian' chord.

With none of the simplicity or order of Cézanne's compositions, Derain's *L'Age d'or* is complex and theatrical. The space is organized as a series of stage flats, and the dramatic differences in lighting add to its artificial and decorative character. Michael Parke-Taylor has shown in his study of Derain's sketches of this period (Parke-Taylor, 1980, pp. 366–7) that both the composition and the lighting of this work are influenced by Derain's study of Rubens's *Reconciliation of Louis and Marie* (Musée du Louvre, Paris). Another close compositional source is the picture on a *L'Age d'or* theme that Signac painted in 1894, *In a Time of Harmony* (Hôtel de Ville, Montreuil-sous-Bois).

The general theme of the Golden Age is handled in a manner close to that of Ker-Xavier Roussel. Dithyrambic, in the spirit of Nietzsche's *Birth of Tragedy*, Derain's painting is a work of Neo-Symbolism. The central group of dancing figures is based on the elaborate arabesques of Denis' works, such as *L'Echelle parmis les feuilles* (Musée du Prieuré, Saint-Germain-en-Laye). Several of the figures are distinctly Gauguinesque, and those in the foreground are painted as a dark 'bas-relief' in response to Gauguin's carvings. There is also a woodcut by Derain, now in the Rupf collection, Berne, which is closely related to this painting; in it the gouges of the knife have made a pattern like that of the directional strokes of the brush in the painting. The overall flecked and divided surface marks Derain's attraction to the recent work of Matisse, to the close mosaic of brilliant colour which he was developing with Signac in the south. In the summer of 1905 Derain joined Matisse in the South of France at Collioure (fig. 2), and he was able to travel every year thereafter. In February of that year Matisse had led Ambroise Vollard into Derain's studio, and the dealer had bought everything pinned to the walls, thus vindicating the confidence which Matisse had urged Derain's father to place in him, and leading him to increase his allowance.

Derain was versed in Neo-Impressionist painting before he arrived in Collioure. Although Signac lived in St Tropez, he showed every year in the Salon des Indépendants, and his work was included in exhibitions in which Matisse was shown. It was with Signac that Seurat had developed his refined analysis of the breakdown of light into colour and his theories of perception and human emotion. Without rejecting the emotive and allusive issues of Symbolism, Signac's theories put the constructive, compositional values of colour into the forefront. He had, in fact, long seen composition in painting as a parallel to musical composition.

Derain was prepared for Signac's limpid colour and constructive brushwork. What took him by surprise in the south, however, was the effect of the strong light which eradicated tonal contrasts, narrowing the gap between artificial composition in intense colour and observed reality. He wrote immediately and with emotion to Vlaminck of the orange and chrome yellow, of the bronze skin and the blue-black beards of the people, of the red, green, and grey pottery, of the donkeys, the boats with their white sails, and the multicoloured skiffs in the harbour. 'More than anything', he related to his friend in Chatou, 'it is the light. The blonde, golden light which suppresses shadows . . . there is so much to do . . . everything I've done until now seems stupid' (Vlaminck, 1955, p. 148). Once painting, he soon began to analyse his new position. 'I'm taking advantage of the rain to write to you', he told Vlaminck from Collioure, 'because normally the sunshine is so radiant that it makes me desperate the way it increases my "synthetic" difficulties and complicates my acrobatic exercises on the subject of Light . . .' (Vlaminck, 1955, pp. 154–5).

Derain offered Vlaminck the two points he had already gained by his trip, and they are revealing of the Symbolist attitude to painting with which he had left Paris for the south of France.

> First, a new conception of light which consists in this: the negation of shadow. Here the light[ed surfaces] are very strong, the shadows very light. Shadow is a whole world of light and a luminosity which opposes itself to the light of the sun: what one calls reflections. We've both neglected this so far, and in the future it might add expression to the composition. Second, around Matisse [I] know how to get rid of everything that the division of tone entails. He goes on, but I've come around from it completely and almost never make use of it any more. It's logical in a luminous and harmonious panel, but it ruins those things which get their expression from intentional disharmonies (Vlaminck, 1955, pp. 154–5).

Among the Symbolist followers of Gauguin and the Neo-Impressionist followers of Seurat, there was a great deal of common ground philosophically. To find a rationale on canvas, however, was still a difficult project, and Derain worked beside Matisse with increasing self-doubt and discomfort, finding it difficult to hold to both the Symbolist composition of flat areas of colour in relation to colour's direct correspondence with states of mind and the Neo-Impressionist vision in Collioure of colour which could evoke real space and light. 'It is terrible', he wrote to Vlaminck, 'to be constantly bothered by one school or another, one influence or another . . . I'm fed up with myself for still not feeling I've got there, not being something absolutely, something well defined . . . I find myself regretting the soldier of last year who made his footprints on the road in such a precise fashion' (Vlaminck, 1955, p. 159).

Nevertheless, he brought back with him thirty finished canvases, twenty drawings, and about fifty sketches. From among these canvases Derain chose those which would hang in the Salon d'Automne among those of Matisse, Vlaminck, Marquet, Rouault, the talented Norman painter Othon Friesz, the Dutch painter Kees Van Dongen, and the Russians Jawlensky and Kandinsky. It was at this 1905 exhibition that the critic Louis Vauxcelles christened them 'Fauves', that is, wild beasts. The works of painters in the Fauve group had already been and continued to be shown together in commercial galleries. Derain exhibited in two such shows between the Salon d'Automne and the end of the year, and the Fauves were also shown in the Salons of 1906. The critics distinguished them from late Symbolism as a 'movement', and Vauxcelles placed Derain at the head of the campaign with Matisse.

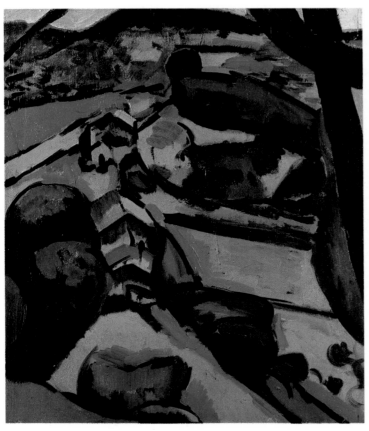

11. *Martigues Landscape*, 1908, Kunsthaus Zurich, Donation of Eduard von der Heydt.

12. (opposite) *Blackfriars*, 1906, Art Gallery and Museum, Kelvingrove.

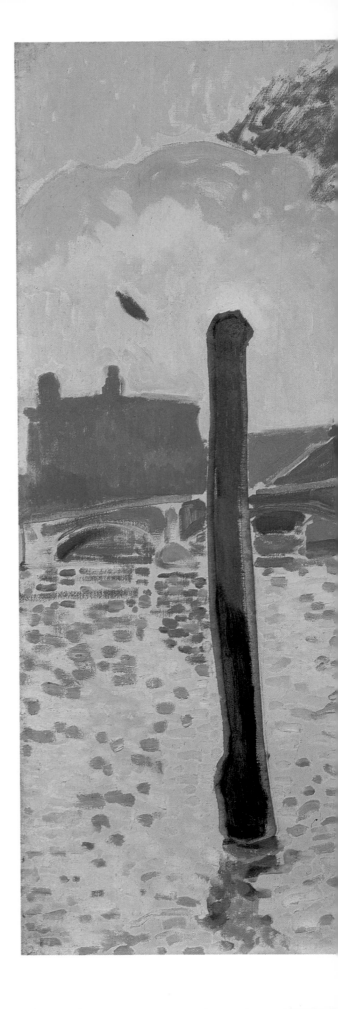

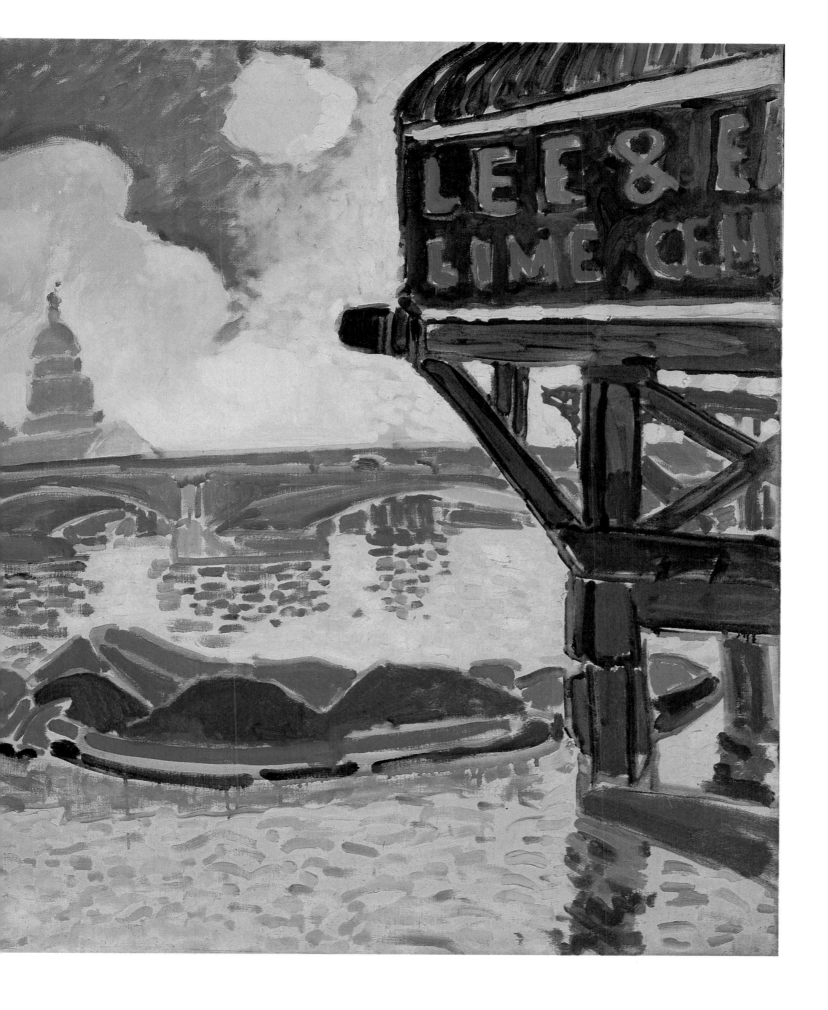

Vollard, impressed with Monet's *Thames* series, shown at the Durand-Ruel Gallery in 1904, sent Derain to London in the autumn of 1905 and the spring of 1906 (fig. 12). Then in the summer of 1906 Derain returned to the South of France, this time to the Bouche du Rhône. The term 'Fauvist' masks the technical variety in Derain's painting in the year between the two Salons d'Automne of 1905 and 1906. Derain had adopted Signac's block-like standard touch of the brush, applying pure colours to a white-primed canvas, often leaving a white reserve between the colour blocks to throw the colour forward in a dazzling mosaic. He adapted this, however, with the utmost agility to the needs of his painting, from discrete blocks of cadmium, chrome yellow, and cobalt laid out in Collioure like notes of music, to a close grid of changing hues from blue through violet to red, for example, in some of his London paintings.

The relationship between colour and white reserve which Derain constructed was influenced by his frequent use of watercolour, a habit he began with Signac and Matisse. The white reserve was sometimes bounded by blocks of colour in such a way as to give it shape and relief itself, a constructive manner which Derain perfectly understood in Cézanne. Sometimes, however, it remained the white priming which, surrounding a block of colour, clarified it, lit it, gave it éclat. It often disappeared entirely, and broad areas of a single colour abutted each other, colours in themselves evoking lighted surfaces, as Matisse explained in his 'Notes d'un peintre'.

Matisse was developing an idea of painting which recreated the initial effect of the motif upon the painter, not as a cypher for the motif itself but rather as an evocation of the emotional intensity of the particular visual experience which led to the painting. It is this synthesis of Impressionist dedication to the motif and Symbolist evocation of emotion which Derain attempted to accept in 1905. His analysis of this fusion and his final rejection of it is included in a letter to Vlaminck in the summer of 1906.

> I feel myself turning towards something better, where the picturesque counts less than it did last year and I'm only concerned with the question of painting ... If you don't add decorative qualities, the only tendency you can have is to purify more and more this transposition of nature ... I see no future except in composition because, in working after nature, I am enslaved to such stupid things that my emotion suffers an adverse reaction. I don't see any future at all in our tendencies: on the one hand we try to disengage ourselves from the objective world, and on the other we keep it as the cause and the end. No, really, viewing it objectively, I don't see what to do to make that logical (Vlaminck, 1955, pp. 146–7).

To Derain the opposite of Matisse's still fundamentally Impressionist position was no more acceptable: 'To make obtrusive compositions, that is to say, amuse ourselves composing paintings like Denis ... that's nothing but the transposition of a theatre set' (Vlaminck, 1955, p. 147). Derain's conclusion to these remarks in his letter to Vlaminck resounds with Bernard's conversations and correspondence with Cézanne which were current news in Matisse's circle and which informed Bernard's writings and reviews between 1904 and 1907. Derain wrote. 'I believe that the problem is rather to group forms in light and to harmonize them at the same time with the material one is using'. It is a conclusion which retains rather than resolves the dichotomy at the heart of painting.

From the 'Fauve' salon of 1905 through 1906 the influence of Gauguin upon Derain's work steadily increased. His Hyde Park paintings of the spring of 1906 refer directly to painting at Pont-Aven in 1889, and by the end of the year Derain had made wood carvings and twenty wood-block prints in the manner of Gauguin and Emile Bernard. The large painting of 1905, *L'Age d'or*, was the beginning of a highly decorative Neo-Symbolist phase of Derain's work which had been partly interrupted by his painting in the south. *La danse* (Josephowitz Collection, on loan to Tate Gallery, London) was probably painted in the autumn of 1906 at the time of the Gauguin retrospective at the Salon d'Automne and is associated directly with Derain's bas-relief friezes of dancing figures (fig. 4). In Tahiti, Gauguin had used photographs of Indian and Egyptian sculpture and Egyptian painting in the Louvre as models for his work. Derain adopted these and other exotic models in his carving and his painting. Of the three dancing figures in *La danse*, one is an ecstatic figure from a Romanesque cathedral sculpture, another is from Indian erotic sculpture, and the third is modelled on the maid in Delacroix's *Women of Algiers* (Louvre, Paris). The seated figure in the background is a quotation from Gauguin, and the colour, the exotic and emblematic beasts, and the 'decorative' space are all in the manner of Gauguin's late Tahitian paintings. The 'lyric' and 'theatrical' qualities of this work are outstanding; they may have been encouraged by stage design of the period.

It is likely that the theme of *La danse* is taken from Guillaume Apollinaire's long poem, first published in 1903, *L'Enchanteur pourrissant*, which Derain illustrated with woodcuts in 1909. The tenacity of Symbolism in the work of Derain owes a great deal to his relations with Apollinaire and the other Neo-Symbolist poets with whom he began to frequent the cafés and studios of Montmartre.

Derain also met Picasso at this time, and together in 1907 and 1908 they developed an interest in sculpture in both wood and stone, as well as an appreciation of the arts of non-European cultures. Derain had begun to collect African sculpture, and this added to the plastic values of an already highly eclectic aesthetic in Montmartre which celebrated classic Indian and Cambodian art, as well as naive art and the regional folk arts of France. Since the fall of Dahomey in 1893, great works of African art had been arriving in Paris, and the museum at the Trocadero exhibited this material in a more or less haphazard manner to the benefit of those like Derain who were developing as amateurs and collectors.

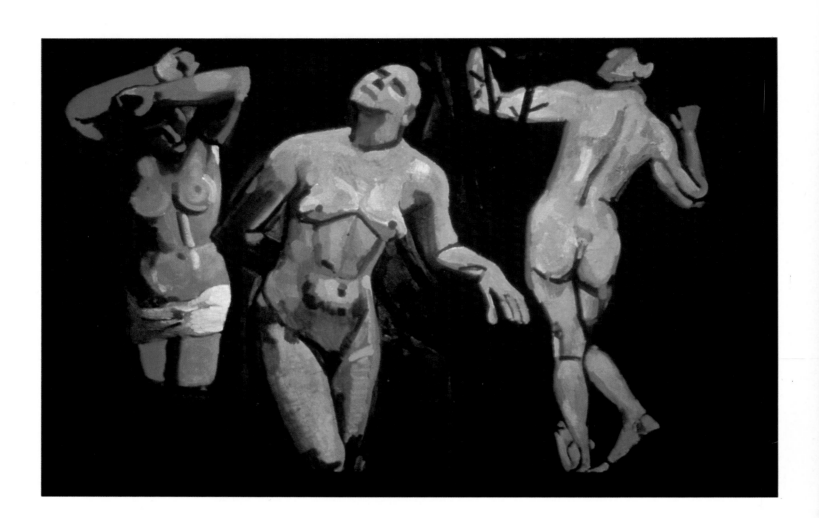

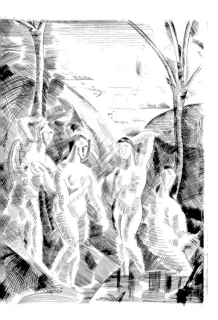

Derain continued to paint large figure pictures. *Les baigneuses* (Museum of Modern Art, New York) (fig. 13), which was shown at the Salon des Indépendants in the spring of 1907, was celebrated by his contemporaries in Paris, and Derain, whom Vauxcelles had classed as Matisse's 'deputy', found himself in the forefront of the avant-garde. The figures in *Les baigneuses* develop from those of *L'Age d'or*, particularly those on the far left of the earlier composition. The palette is a vivid version of Cézanne's blue, green, ochre, and terracotta used constructively, according to Matisse's habit of indicating a surface turned from the light in green or red. Light and shade are thereby sharply distinguished by colour. A strong directional light is indicated, and the central figure raises her face to the full light, reducing it to a nearly featureless mask, like the Fang tribal mask in Derain's collection. Not only colour but line has a constructive function in the making of these ponderous forms. The sharp angularity of the drawing, as well as the abrupt modelling, is reminiscent of Derain's sculpture and woodcuts. Derain had complained in the summer of 1906 to Vlaminck that they had been neglecting line altogether and, indeed, that 'there are many things which we lack in the general conception of our art' (Vlaminck, 1955, p. 146). *Les baigneuses* of the Salon des Indépendants made this good and followed directly from Derain's assertion to Vlaminck that what was needed in their painting were forms grouped in light and harmonized with the material at hand.

Derain painted at least two more large bathers panels at this time. One, which was bought by Kahnweiler in 1920, mixes the influence of Poussin with influences from Egypt and India. Another, now in the National Gallery in Prague, refers to Romanesque painting, as well as to African masks and perhaps also to a French folk sculpture in Derain's collection. In all of these, however, the prevailing influence is of Cézanne's bathers. Matisse, with whom Derain had painted many small bathers pictures, particularly in watercolour, painted in 1907 a large bather, *Nu bleu; Souvenir de Biskra* (Museum of Art, Baltimore). This was also associated with sculpture, not carving, as with Derain's *Les baigneuses*, but the modelling Matisse did in the studio of Antoine Bourdelle.

After the Salon des Indépendants exhibition of *Les baigneuses*, Georges Braque painted his large bather, *Le nu bleu* (Collection Alex Maguy, Paris). Picasso also admired Derain's work of that year, although he had begun his *Les demoiselles d'Avignon* (Museum of Modern Art, New York) before the Salon des Indépendants. Through 1907 Derain and Picasso saw one another a great deal, each of them making a considerable impact on the other's work. Picasso's painting was influenced by the mixing of visual and poetic references in the work of both Derain and Apollinaire. In return, Picasso's works of 1906 influenced Derain's painting of early 1908, *La toilette*, and the repeating and interlocking curves and angles of Picasso's still-life paintings of 1908 would continue to influence Derain's work as late as 1912. Derain may have painted many more bather paintings in 1907 and early in 1908, but during that winter he burned a substantial part of his work, to exorcize his feelings of dissatisfaction, according to his friend André Salmon (Salmon, 1956, p. 51).

The influence of Cézanne upon avant-garde painting had been continuous from the turn of the century. Matisse had in fact owned a small *Bathers* painting since 1898 (Musée d'Art Moderne de la Ville de Paris). Both Bernard and Denis had published their conversations with Cézanne in such a manner as to knit the sayings of the Aix master into the concerns of the moment. Cézanne's work was also seen more often in commercial galleries, as the prices rose and works passed from dealer to dealer. When Cézanne died in 1906, the directors of the Salon d'Automne planned a retrospective for 1907. This exhibition of October–November 1907 was the most significant display of Cézanne's painting to date, but it was preceded by an exhibition of watercolours in June at the Galerie Bernheim Jeune.

In the summer of 1907 Derain was in Cassis where his landscapes continued to show his 'grouping of forms in light' and his reduction of the Fauvist palette to that of Cézanne. A broad and self-consciously constructive attitude to composition simplifies Cézanne's refined adjustments of form and space. This massing of forms and simplification of composition had an important effect on the work of two 'Fauvist' friends of Derain, Georges Braque and Othon Friesz, who spent the summer nearby at Ciotat and visited Derain in Cassis. In the next year, 1908, Derain spent a full six months in the south of France, mostly at Martigues, and began a profound investigation into Cézanne's landscape paintings which he would continue until 1913 (figs. 11 and 16). Derain's works of these five years are among the finest landscape paintings of the pre-war avant-garde. At the same time they are the most serious and consistent review of the work of Paul Cézanne – the mainstay and the measure of all of the Cézannisme in Paris between 1908 and 1914.

In 1907 Derain had written to Vlaminck that he was considering settling permanently in the south of France, a temptation which is reflected in his extended summer painting period in 1908. He decided, however, to move to Paris from Chatou, and he settled in the Rue Tourlaque in Montmartre, where he stayed until 1910. It is likely that this decision was due to Alice Géry to whom Derain was introduced by Picasso; she was Derain's companion in October 1907 and became his wife soon after. Alice had been the wife of Maurice Princet, the Bergsonian mathematician who expounded on the fourth dimension and who frequented the artists' cafés of Montmartre. Many of Derain's friends lived in Montmartre or spent a great deal of their time there. Derain began to see Braque, Picasso, and the poets, André Salmon, Max Jacob, and Guillaume Apollinaire almost daily when he was in Paris. The group congregated not only in the cafés but in Picasso's studio in the Bateau Lavoir and became known as the 'bande à Picasso'. Derain was as close to the poets as he was to the painters. He had always been a bibliophile and took pleasure in their arcane references and poetic constructions, becoming, in Max Jacob's company, increasingly adept in many forms of mysticism.

The young German art dealer Daniel Henry Kahnweiler, who had opened a gallery in Paris in 1907, soon attached himself to this close-knit group of poets and painters, and by 1909 he was buying only the work of Derain, Vlaminck, Picasso, and Braque. Kahnweiler was an extremely active dealer who sent his artists' work to all the

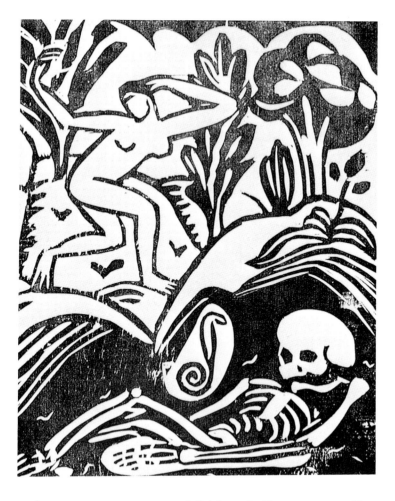

15. *L'Enchanteur pourrissant*,
1909, Kunstmuseum, Berne.

major contemporary art exhibitions in Europe, as well as to the Armory Show in New York. He co-operated with dealers in other countries, particularly in Germany, and in order to facilitate these business ties put his four artists under formal contract to the gallery in December 1912. Kahnweiler had an international clientele, and Derain's work eventually entered collections such as that of Kramar in Prague and Shchukin in Moscow. By 1909 Derain relied on Kahnweiler's continuous financial support, and by 1910 he had stopped showing in the salons.

The destruction of most of Derain's work in his crisis of 1908 seemed a catastrophe to Daniel Kahnweiler. 'The most important evidence for his development up to 1907 is now lacking', he wrote in 1920 (Henry, 1920) and regretted the loss of a whole series of life-size figure paintings, and particularly of a large painting of a bull. Paintings such as *Les baigneuses*, which had been purchased at the Salon, escaped the fire only because they had left the studio. There are enough survivors, however, to indicate that Derain was clearing the ground, as he would occasionally throughout his life, though normally without such melodrama. The woodcut illustrations for *L'Enchanteur pourrissant* (fig. 15) which Derain made through the summer of 1909 are the swan-song of his Fauvism. The bathers, the Golden Age themes of the Fauvist period, the overt exotic references, and the influence of Gauguin were all abandoned by 1910. The figure was almost entirely absent from Derain's work until 1913, and he did not return to painting the nude until after the First World War.

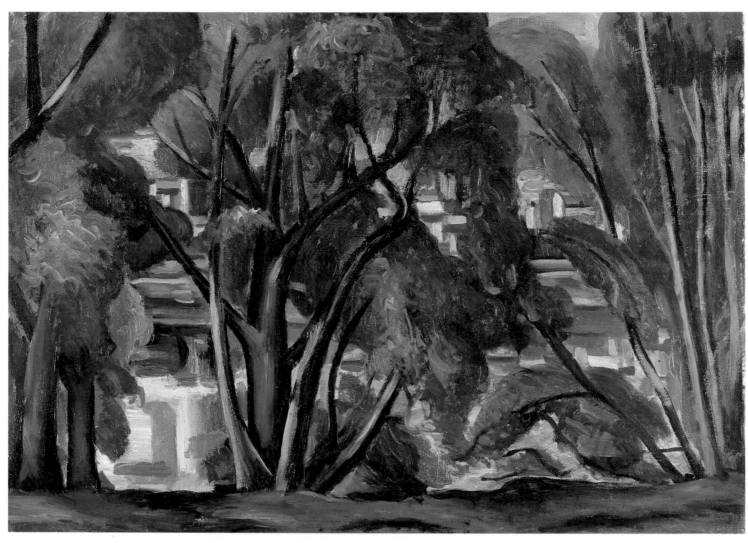

16. *Trees on the Banks of the Seine*, 1912, Staatsgalerie, Stuttgart.

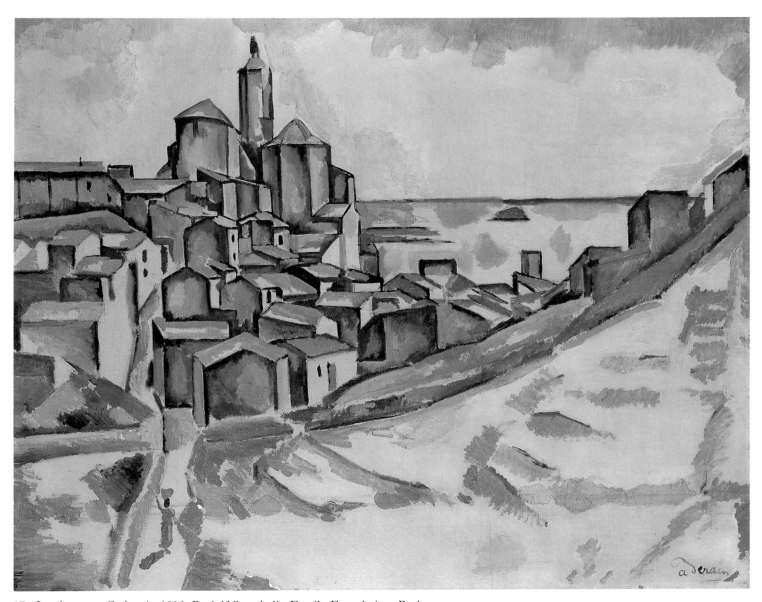

17. *Landscape at Cadaquès*, 1910, Rudolf Staechelin Family Foundation, Basle.

Derain became primarily a landscape painter. He extended his summer painting period in the South from May to November in 1908. He spent nearly the same amount of time away from Paris in 1909 and 1910, in winter as well as in summer. He spent January and February of 1909 in Le Havre and the whole summer, from early July to the end of October, painting both on the north coast of France and in the south around Marseilles. He spent the autumn of 1909 in Paris but was back in Marseilles by January 1910, and by February he was painting in Cagnes. That whole summer he spent on the French-Spanish border, principally at Cadaquès, returning to Paris for just a few weeks before he was off again to Beauvais. This peripatetic life-style was supported by Kahnweiler who sent Derain money as, when, and where he needed it. Derain turned over to Kahnweiler a number of paintings appropriate to his advances and against future demands, occasionally bundling Alice on to a train with several canvases from wherever he was painting so that Kahnweiler would not be kept waiting too long and could keep track of his development. Derain's periods away from Paris, however, were not always periods of isolation. He was sometimes joined by Braque, Picasso, and Vlaminck.

When, in February 1913, Apollinaire wrote of the beginnings of Cubism for the German journal *Der Sturm*, he claimed that 'Picasso's Cubism is the outgrowth of a movement originating with Derain' (Apollinaire, 1960, p. 281), and a year later in the French newspaper *L'Intransigeant* he wrote, 'There are two great currents, of which one issues from the Cubism of Picasso and the other from the Cubism of Derain; they both come from Cézanne' (Apollinaire, 1960, p. 371). By Derain's Cubism Apollinaire

18. *The Old Bridge at Cagnes*, 1910, Chester Dale Collection, National Gallery of Art, Washington, D.C.

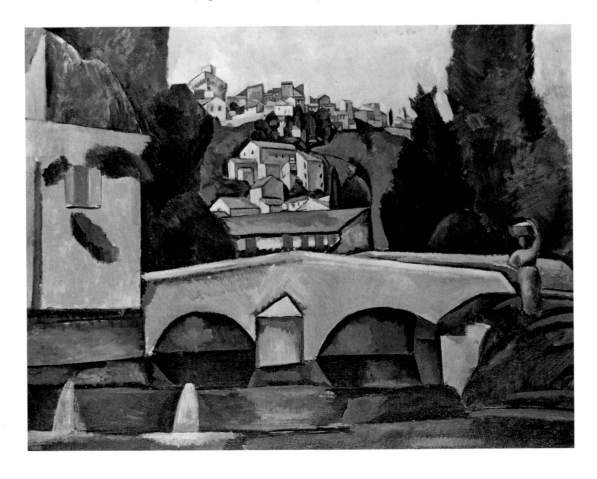

meant the landscape compositions of the summer of 1907, admired by both Picasso and Braque, and the imposing landscapes of the next summer at Martigues. The 1908 paintings were particularly admired by Apollinaire, who wrote of them at the time 'His plastic sincerity reveals itself ... by the terrible calm with which he dispassionately expresses himself in conformity with his passions' (Apollinaire, 1908, p. 88). Apollinaire saw in Derain the return to the classical mastery in modern painting for which he hoped and which was at the centre of the aesthetics by which he defined Cubism.

In February 1910 Derain painted *The Old Bridge at Cagnes* (National Gallery, Washington, D.C.) in which he parades the classicism of Cézanne's paintings of a similar motif (fig. 18). *The Old Bridge at Cagnes* refers to Poussin, and ultimately to Venetian painting, in constructing a parabola which floats above the bridge, containing the angles of walls and roofs. The figure at the side of the bridge acts as a key to admit into the painting memories of Giorgione and Titian. Cézanne's classicism allowed Derain to step back from the motif and compose in a Giorgionesque manner. This is the opposite of the stance taken by Braque and Picasso who were closing in on the motif, moving away from the classical allusions in Cézanne and towards a strongly abstract, highly ordered, geometrical composition.

A few months later Picasso and Derain were painting together in Cadaqués. While Picasso closed his shutters on the landscape and continued the Cubist series of figure paintings he had begun in Paris, Derain painted the landscape (fig. 17). Two years later the poet/critic André Salmon described these landscapes at Cadaqués as reviving El Greco's *View of Toledo* and congratulated Derain on restoring the glory of El Greco at a time when some still saw that painter as 'possessed' (Salmon, 1912, p. 23), a remark which may indicate Derain's involvement in the El Greco retrospective at the 1908 Salon d'Automne. From 1910 Derain's sensitivity to the deep affinity between the painting of his own day and the painting of the past became a more and more obtrusive element in his work. It is just this obtrusiveness of the historical sources of his work which divided his path from the Cubists.

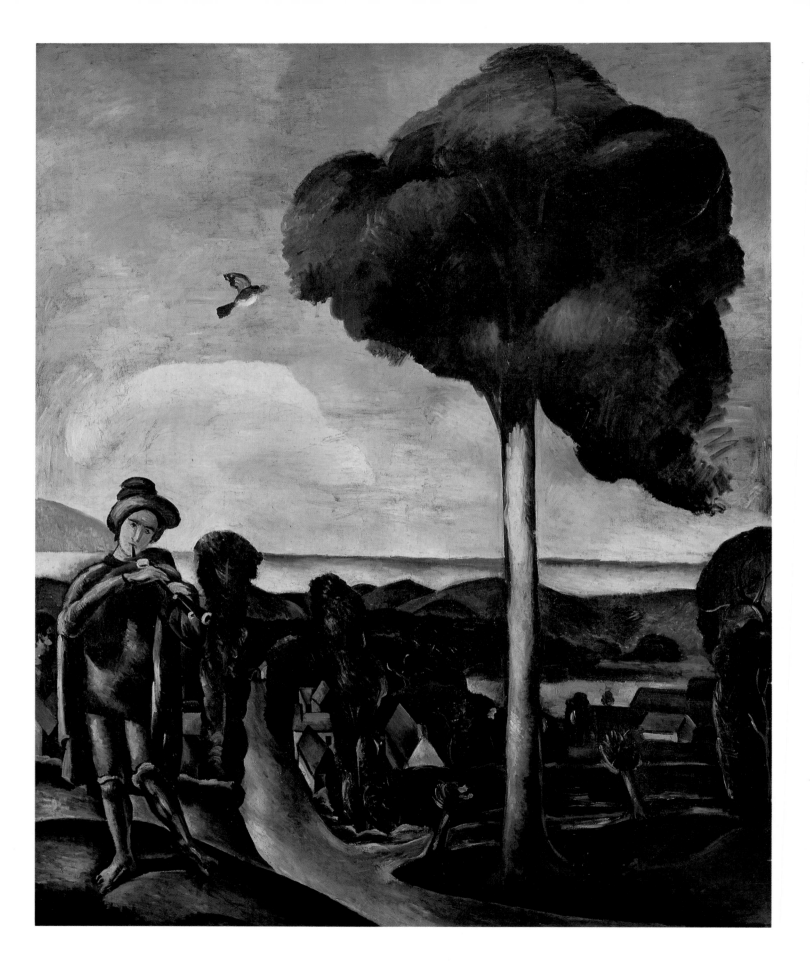

In 1911 Derain did not go to the south of France to paint in the summer but spent July in Serbonne (near Crècy-en-Brie), August in Boulogne and London, and September in Camiers. The landscapes of that year are a departure from the works of 1910, with the viewpoint shifted to allow a panorama with a long horizon and expansive sky which is lyrical rather than architectural. Among them, the key work is *Le joueur de cornemuse* (fig. 19) for which there are several related smaller works, the most important being *La route à Camiers* (location unknown). The landscape in *Le joueur de cornemuse* is not a study of a particular motif, as most of Derain's landscapes continued to be, but an 'artificial' landscape composed from studies of several motifs at Camiers and Serbonne and from his trip to Beauvais the year before. At the same time Derain produced an etching, *Paysage: Le Morin*, which incorporates the motifs of several of these paintings to create a work which might be compared with the contemporary lyrical and classically inspired work of Othon Friesz.

Le joueur de cornemuse* revives Derain's attachment to Renaissance painting and is inspired by a painting in the Louvre, Perugino's piping contest between *Apollo and Marsyas*. Its composition is based on a sharp division along the golden section, both horizontally and vertically, in the manner of Piero della Francesca. These references are not hidden but are as obvious as the references to early Renaissance painting in the works of Maurice Denis, the compositions of which 'can be seen', as Derain had remarked to Vlaminck in 1906. Derain, however, is more complex in his references than Denis, who aimed for a rhetorical clarity. His work is still consistent with works admired in Montmartre. The simplification of the figure in *Le joueur de cornemuse* is Cézanniste, extending the qualities of the landscape into the palette and drawing of the figure. The flat, wistful face of the bagpiper is reminiscent of the work of Marie Laurencin, and the air of detached poetic reverie recalls the work of 'Le Douanier' Rousseau. Derain's landscape is self-consciously archaic. The overlapping curves, the use of light and shade to create self-contained forms rather than a continuous spatial extension, and the conjunction of separate vignettes bring to mind the tradition of Franco-Flemish illumination.

Many of the landscapes of 1912 continue the storybook quality of *Le joueur de cornemuse*. *L'Eglise à Vers* (fig. 23) is as lyrical and allusive as the paintings of 1911, quoting the earliest French landscape traditions and the traditions of the early Renaissance. Tiny scenes of ploughmen recall the calendar pages of early fifteenth-century Books of Hours, just as the piping shepherd in *Le joueur de cornemuse* recalls the shepherd-musicians in *Annunciation to the Shepherds* scenes. Such images are an ancient

19. *Le joueur de cornemuse*, 1911, Minneapolis Institute of Arts.

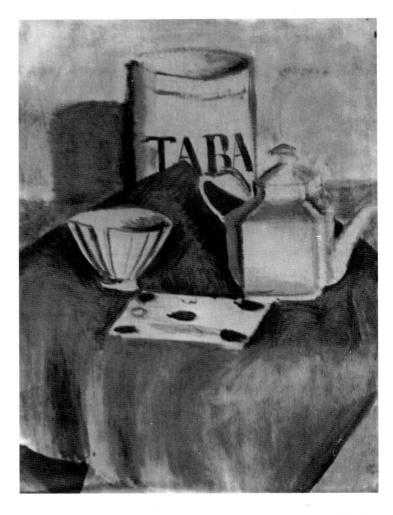

'source' of landscape painting in France and mark Derain's involvement with the poetics of Jean Moréas.

20. *Le pot de tabac*, 1912, Galerie Louise Leiris, Paris.

Moréas died in 1910 and the touching eulogy which Apollinaire published in the journal *Les Marges* in 1911 is a measure of the Symbolist poet's importance to Derain's milieu. Moréas presided over the Tuesday soirées at the café, Closerie de Lilas, which brought together the poets who contributed to the journals, *Vers et Prose* and *La Phalange*. According to Salmon, even Picasso was meek and respectful before Moréas. The publication of his *Pélerin passioné* had been the greatest of all Symbolist literary events. It followed ten years of study of ancient French poetry. Using the *chansonniers* of the Middle Ages as models and the vocabulary and syntax of early French, still heavy with Latin, Moréas wanted to 'climb back to the living springs of the language in order to give to French poetry [its] primordial character ... to evoke the modern spirit in its hereditary apparel' (Moréas, 1891). Looking back over Derain's work in 1925 André Salmon wrote of Derain that he had 'done as a painter what Jean Moréas had done as a poet and an impassioned pilgrim, climbing back to the origins to capture all the resources of his language' (Salmon, 1925, p. 571). In 1912, however, Salmon had been confused by Derain's painting, writing: 'The case of André Derain is rather unique. He lives on the edge of contemporary painting, and I'm not at all sure that his prolonged retreat doesn't carry with it some dangers' (Salmon, 1912, p. 21).

He recognized that Derain's wide-ranging tastes and learning had profoundly influenced his generation and the culture of Montmartre. He claimed for Derain a precocious understanding of that universal 'classical' art of which Charles Morice wrote in 1910 that it 'relates Mexico to Egypt, the Cambodians to the Gothics ... Giotto to Puvis de Chavannes' (Salmon, 1912, p. 22). The period of Montmartre, however, was over, and Derain's classicism was more precise. Rather than 'the classic', that is, work of transcendent excellence in the arts of all cultures, Derain was increasingly concerned with particular traditions of European painting.

Derain sent thirty-three still-life paintings to Kahnweiler in 1912, over half of his production. These works, thematically and iconographically, have an affinity with the works of Picasso and Braque, who concentrated almost entirely on still life in that year. The fatality of Cubist still life with its images of chance and change continued the tradition of *vanitas* painting. The *memento mori* symbols of musical instruments, snatches of music and broken words, clay pipes, glasses and bottles, cards and dice were associated with the 'fleeting life' of café and boulevard in modern French literature, from Huysmans' rambling on both sides of the Seine to Apollinaire's 'Zone' and Max Jacob's fragmentary poetry. All this is true of much of Derain's still-life painting, but his themes are more obviously consonant with that tradition in European painting which he identified as 'the pathetic, that is, the reciprocal relationship between life and death'.

In 1911 Kahnweiler acquired from Derain a still life, *La table* (Metropolitan Museum of Art, New York), which has a striking clarity of silhouette and a richness of colour which bring to mind Spanish Baroque still lifes. The isolation of the bowl from the jug and the window which divides the wall but offers no view give the work a stillness, a sobriety, and a meditative quality which reflect Derain's sensitivity to the elements which, in seventeenth-century still-life painting, encourage a spiritual interpretation. This seems to be the earliest of a series of still-life paintings of subtle pictorial metaphor and historical reference. Several of the works of 1912, such as the *Nature morte au crâne* (fig. 21) in the Hermitage, are tenebrist and add to the *memento*

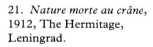

21. *Nature morte au crâne*, 1912, The Hermitage, Leningrad.

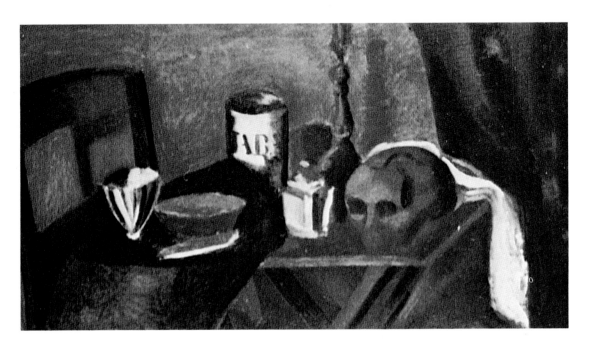

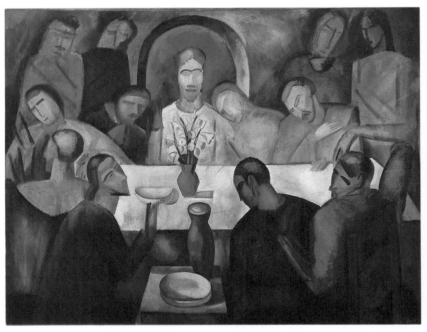

22. *Last Supper*, 1911, Art Institute of Chicago, Gift of Mrs Frank L. Lillie.

23. (opposite) *L'Eglise à Vers*, 1912, National Museum of Wales, Cardiff.

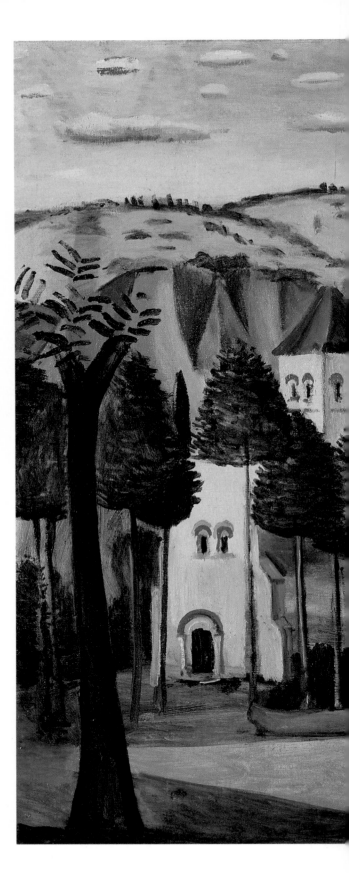

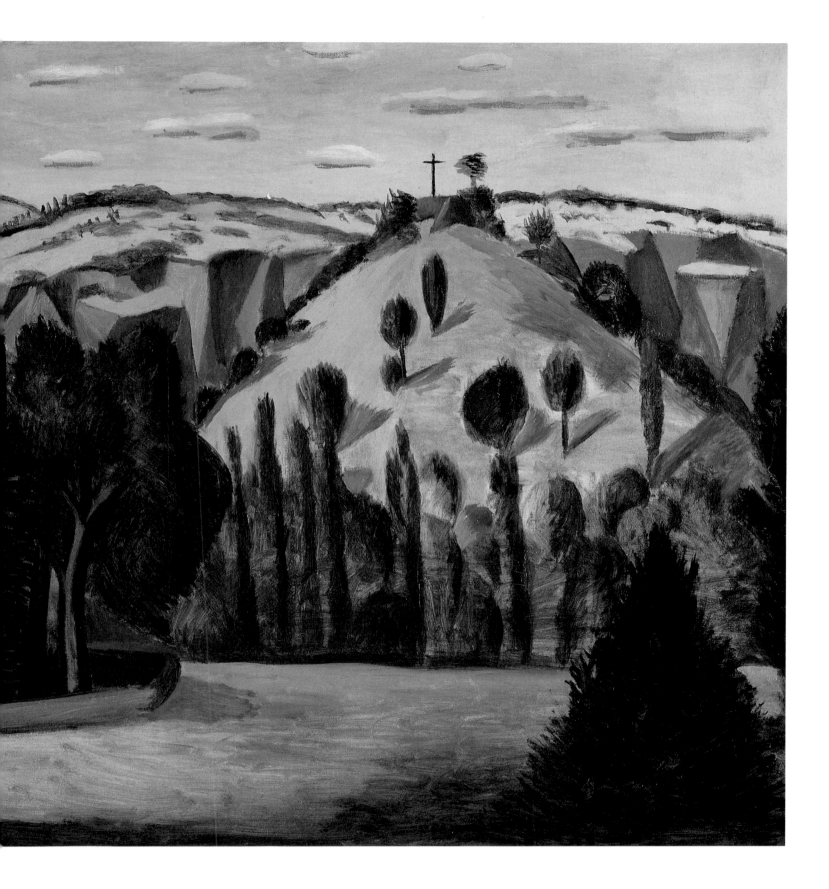

mori imagery the seventeenth-century symbolism of light and dark. The use of playing cards and the truncated word 'taba[c]' associate several of Derain's paintings with the current work of Picasso and Braque and with the imagery of Max Jacob's poetry. His tenebrism and his fluid handling of paint, however, relocate this Cubist imagery in the early work of Cézanne and the paintings of the seventeenth century on which it is based. The allusions intended in Derain's pictures are also more precise than those of his contemporaries. The points of Derain's playing cards, for instance, are more complex than the inevitable ace of Picasso or Braque and are clearly painted to be read in the 'language' of the cards, as in seventeenth-century painting (fig. 20).

In the summer of 1912 at Vers, in the region of the Lot, Derain rented the house of a curé, the windows of which provided a view of the church and a Calvary cross on a nearby hill. There Derain painted several still lifes in which a view through the window to the cross or the church infused the simple arrangement of vessels on a table with a eucharistic meaning (fig. 24). Association with the 'sacrifice' of the cross transforms the still life into the same sacrifice signified by vessels, that is, the eucharistic 'sacrifice' of the mass, and the still life becomes an altar table. This association through a window is ultimately based upon Renaissance painting, but it is a Renaissance characteristic which was taken up by Maurice Denis. The still lifes and the landscapes at Vers are painted in a spare, dry style, and the landscapes particularly recall the work of Piero della Francesca. The spare paint and light palette of still lifes such as *Le Calvaire* (Kunstmuseum, Basle) are also comparable with the handling in Matisse's contemporary work (fig. 25).

Derain's manuscript notes record not only his interest in divination through the cards but a metaphysics which is often expressed in Christological language. The eucharistic still lifes of 1912 reflect the importance in Derain's circle of the poet Paul Claudel. Claudel's poetry was greatly admired by Salmon and Apollinaire. His philosophical treatise, *Art Poétique*, of 1907 established a Platonic conception of time summarized by Jacques Rivière in his *Etudes* of 1912, 'Paul Claudel, poète chrétien'.

24. (left) *Still Life at Vers*, 1912, Galerie Louise Leiris, Paris.

25. *Le Calvaire*, 1912, Oeffentliche Kunstsammlung Basel, Kunstmuseum.

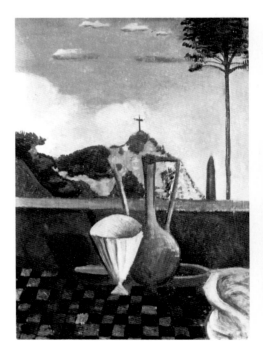

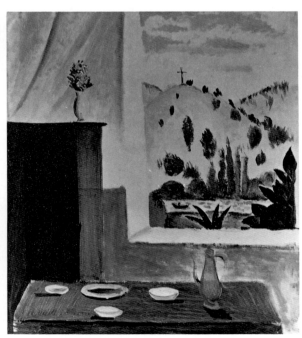

Many of the avant-garde poets had commented on the eucharistic reforms of the Catholic Church in 1905 and 1910, but Claudel, in *La Physique de l'Eucharistie*, took up the issue of the eucharist as a philosophical as well as a theological question. Transubstantiation, Claudel wrote, whether one believes or not, is an expression of Platonism which is deeply embedded in European thought.

It is likely that transubstantiation, that is, the changing of the 'real' substance of bread and wine into the 'real substance' of flesh and blood at the Catholic mass, became a part of the general theme of change and metamorphosis of the Cubist generation while they were together in Montmartre. Apollinaire made frequent oblique references to the liturgy and the gospel, and poems such as 'Zone' use imagery which is Christological and Gnostic. In 1912 Braque's paintings were reviewed in the Gnostic journal *Gnose*, although that journal rarely carried references to painting. The liturgy of the eucharist, and the Last Supper itself, has a history of alchemical as well as religious significance, and the theme should be considered in the wider context of mysticism, as well as in terms of Claudel's treatise of 1910.

Before his eucharistic still lifes Derain had painted a *Last Supper* (Art Institute of Chicago) (fig. 22). This is a major work which has never been securely dated, as it was not bought by Kahnweiler and was never exhibited in France. Judging by its Cézanniste blue palette and a figure style which is like that of the bathers canvases of 1907, it may have survived the 1908 fire. It could also be contemporary with Picasso's 1908–9 sketches in watercolour and pen and ink which show a Harlequin seated at the centre of a table among his followers like Christ. From these sketches Picasso began a large painting of Harlequin and his followers at a table. As he continued his work on this canvas, however, the figures were overpainted, and the composition was transformed into a sober and imposing still life (Kunstmuseum, Basle).

The lilies replacing the eucharistic meal in the *Last Supper* follow a specific iconography of the 'mysteries' of the church based on the commentaries of St Bernard of Clairvaux and appear in another *Last Supper* by Derain, an etching which dates from 1912–13. There is a painting exactly similar to this still life of lilies which was acquired by Kahnweiler in 1909, *Les lys* (location unknown). The still life of pots at the front of the table was added later, extending the iconography of the *Last Supper* to that of the mass by including the liturgical stage of the 'lavabo', the washing of hands. In a photograph taken of the *Last Supper* before it was restored after the First World War, two figures can clearly be seen drawn over the original painting in a style unlike the other figures but like those in the *Last Supper* etching. They seem to have been added, therefore, in 1912–13, and this dates the still life of vessels, as it is painted over them. Derain worked occasionally on this *Last Supper* painting, therefore, between 1908 and 1913, that is, while he was painting his mystical still lifes and his most complex and allusive painting before the First World War, *Le Samedi* (Pushkin Museum, Moscow).

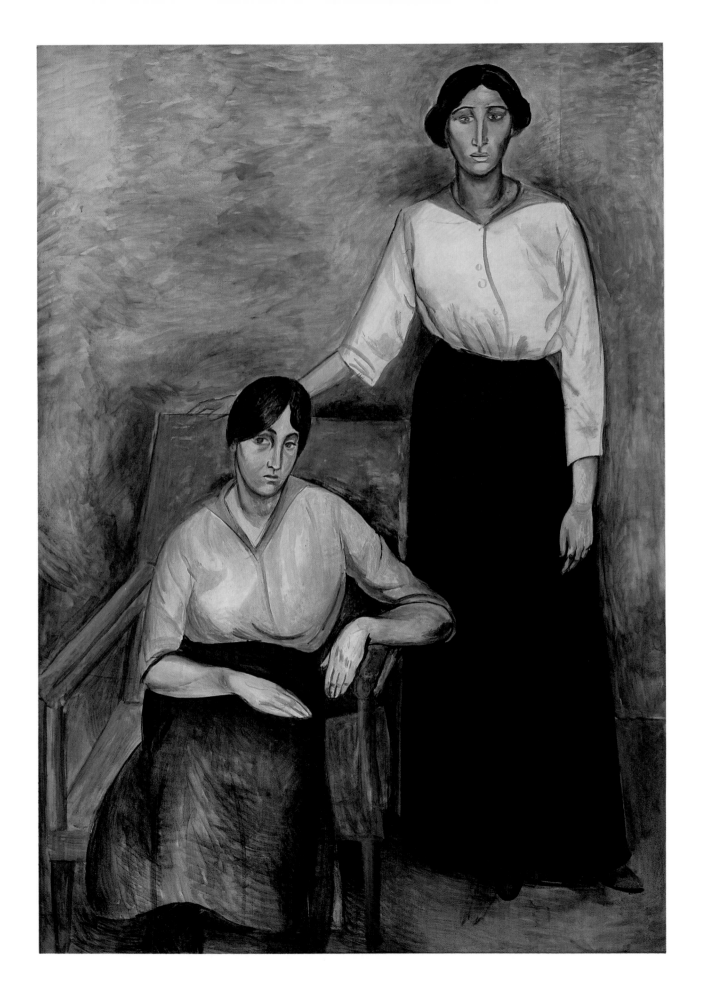

It is difficult to tell when Derain began the great canvas for which Apollinaire, it seems, provided the title, *Le Samedi* (fig. 28). It was bought by the Russian collector Sergei Shchukin in 1913 but seems not to have been removed from Paris until the next year. Salmon's remarks on this painting in 1925 suggest that it was in the studio for a long time and that it underwent several changes: '... famous Samedi, masterful work over which Derain the abundant, the joyous, laboured hard and didn't mind admitting it and about which he uttered a quip good enough to join the best of Picasso: "I've started my picture over again, the still life (it was in the first place a meal) has eaten the people!"' (Salmon, 1925, p. 572).

At an earlier stage it is likely that this work was closer in composition to the *Last Supper* and underwent changes like those which Picasso made to his painting. The three figures in *Le Samedi* are not far removed from those of Picasso's drawings, and the central figure of *Le Samedi* marks the centre of the picture with her hand on the table in precisely the same way as Picasso's *Harlequin* drawings. Derain may have begun *Le Samedi* in 1908 and continued with it until 1913. It is clearly the culmination of several years' work. The photographic records which Kahnweiler kept of his acquisitions reveal a smaller work for nearly every detail of this composition and for each of the separate still-life elements. The scene viewed through the window is that of the Vers landscapes of 1912. Only the figures themselves have no precise antecedents in Derain's work of the previous three years.

Chevalier X (Hermitage, Leningrad), a painting related to these dark and sober figures, which Kahnweiler acquired from Derain in 1914, indicates a link once again between the work of Derain and the current work of Picasso (fig. 27). *Chevalier X* combines the influence of the marionette figures which Derain collected with the stiff, flat, full-length portraits of English sixteenth-century painting. The newspaper in the hands of the figure was, in an earlier stage of the work, a real newspaper 'collaged' onto the canvas. *Chevalier X* could be compared with Picasso's flat, stiff, over-lifesize figures which, at one time or another, were partially newspaper. Similarly, Picasso's works of 1914, such as the dark *Man Leaning on a Table* (Private Collection, U.S.A.) might be compared with the dark, angular figures at the table in *Le Samedi*.

The figures in *Le Samedi* are heavily influenced by Romanesque sculpture and by both Romanesque and Gothic painting. A work of 1914 which has been called *Les buveurs* (Kubutoya Gallery, Tokyo) illustrates Derain's interest, before the First World War, in Gothic art, incorporating Cimabue angels into a painting which has a eucharistic theme (fig. 29). Between 1912 and 1914, Derain painted several pictures of melancholy,

26. *The Two Sisters*, 1913, Statens Museum für Kunst, Copenhagen.

43

anxious women, sometimes veiled (fig. 26). These works are done in a spare fresco-like style, and the faces are often based on late Gothic and early Renaissance models. It is this period of Derain's work which became known as his 'Gothic' or 'Byzantine' style. *Le Samedi* is an early statement of this medievalism of *c*.1914 and provides a link with the archaism of 1911 and the mysticism of the Montmartre period.

In 1916, in the catalogue to the Derain exhibition in the Galerie Paul Guillaume, Apollinaire spoke of the religious grandeur of Derain's works and associated it with the Avignon school (Paris, 1916, exh. cat.). Since the great exhibition of French 'Primitives' in 1904 and the purchase of the works of the Avignon master, Enguerrand Quarton, by the Louvre in 1905, this fifteenth-century school had been celebrated among Parisian artists. The greatest of Quarton's works, *The Villeneuve-lès-Avignon Pietà* was copied by several of Derain's contemporaries, and there is a Cubist copy of this painting by Van Rees which dates from 1913 (now in the Kunstmuseum, Berne). The spatial complications of the interior in *Le Samedi* are based on early Italian Renaissance paintings, particularly the antechambers and windowed rooms of Annunciation pictures, and on the interpretation of such works by Maurice Denis. The composition in the foreground, however, with the figures at the table, is based on *The Villeneuve-lès-Avignon Pietà*. The two paintings are virtually the same size, and *Le Samedi* resembles the *Pietà* in its light/dark divisions, in the angular expressiveness of the figures, and in the bold simplification of outlines. *Le Samedi* has the characteristic restraint of the Avignon school which shows itself not only in the interlocking of large simple shapes but also in the economy of gesture in which each sign or posture is an indispensable link in a chain of meaning. The gestures of the figures in *Le Samedi* are of this order, and *The Villeneuve-lès-Avignon Pietà* is an appropriate model for *Le*

27. (left) *Chevalier X*, 1912–14, The Hermitage, Leningrad.

28. *Le Samedi*, 1913, Pushkin Museum of Fine Arts, Moscow.

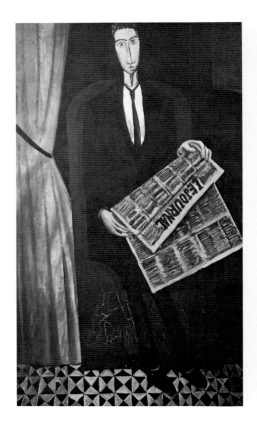

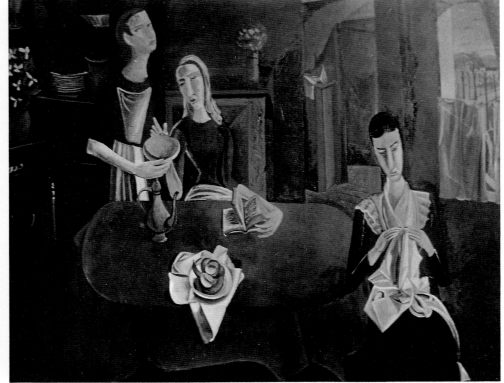

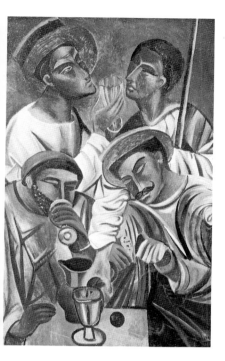

29. *Les buveurs*, 1913–14,
Kubutoya Gallery, Tokyo.

Samedi because the theme of Derain's painting is very close to a lamentation.

The central figure raises her right hand in benediction over the proffered bowl, while with her left hand she keeps the place in the sacramental text. This figure, who behaves exactly like a priest, is the only one who is veiled. Her gesture transforms the nature of the dish and jug in the same way that the Calvary cross through the window transformed the Vers still life, and by implication the still life on the now sacramental table becomes an 'offering'. If the blessing is of the eucharist and the painting is linked by the symbolism of the mass to the Last Supper, then the bowls and cloth in the alcove are a 'lavabo' like that included in both the painting and the print of *The Last Supper*. The window, which links an equally charmed exterior world to this quiet interior, reveals through a partly drawn curtain a steep-roofed church tomb and three bare trees among the leafy ones. The figure seated next to this window is sewing white cloth, and her juxtaposition with these references to the Crucifixion and Entombment makes of her sewing a sepulchral cloth, following the traditional iconography of the sewing basket of Mary.

Le Samedi refers to a particular Saturday. In Paul Claudel's 'Memento pour le samedi soir', published in the journal *La Phalange* in 1910, the meditations recommended for every Saturday actually commemorate the important liturgical Saturday, 'le samedi saint', in the Holy Week. It is the day of the Easter vigil and according to the Roman Missal: 'the day of the most intense sorrow, the day on which the Church tarries at the Lord's tomb, meditating about his Passion and Death'. The important figures in this vigil in the New Testament are the three Marys who ministered to Christ, and these are the three figures in Derain's painting. Although Holy Saturday was a day of quiet melancholy, it was also, at that time (before the 1951 liturgical reforms), the day on which all the Easter vigil liturgy was performed. This is a complex and primitive liturgy in which the world is symbolically re-created from the four elements. The new fire is created, the new water blessed, the winds are blessed and devils are cast out, the light is separated from the darkness, and finally the communion ritual is performed. Saturday afternoon is passed in a series of benedictions. The 'historical' moment of the original vigil of the Marys is made ahistorical by allowing the Holy Women to become the priest and acolytes who perform the liturgy which mystically re-creates the day before the Resurrection each year. Derain's *Le Samedi* is not without modern precedent. It follows a Symbolist tradition of liturgical rather than momentary time, established by Maurice Denis in his painting *Le mystère catholique* (Musée du Prieuré, Saint-Germain-en-Laye), in which the liturgical procession for Annunciation day replaces the Annunciate Angel. Theories of time were important to Derain and his contemporaries, particularly the philosopher Henri Bergson's *La Durée*, Claudel's *La Co-Naissance du Monde*, and Denis's recognition of the philosophical basis of the Catholic liturgy.

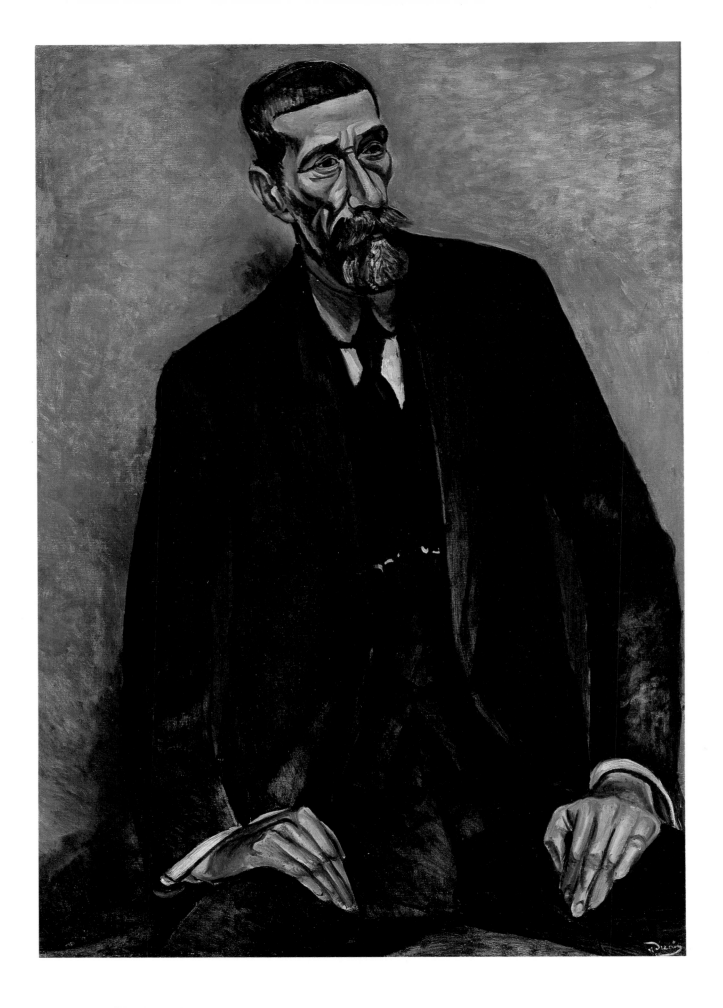

Before the First World War Derain's paintings showed an increasing sensitivity, not only to traditional iconography but to the subtle history of the genres of painting. *La gibecière* (Musée de l'Orangerie) of 1913 refers to the great 'natures mortes de la chasse' of Chardin and Oudry as well as to Cézanne (fig. 31). At the same time the obvious rhythm of echoing and opposing curves in *La gibecière* is developed from Derain's still lifes with clay pots of 1910, works which were themselves dependent on Picasso's still lifes of 1908. Like *Le Samedi,* this is a work which may have been in the studio for some time, as Derain refers to a *Nature morte au gibier* in a letter to Kahnweiler as early as 1911.

The *Portrait of Iturrino* (Musée National d'Art Moderne, Paris) of 1914 brings into view another tradition which, like the 'grand manner' of *La gibecière,* is made to hinge upon Cézanne (fig. 30). Cézanne's portrait of *The Watchmaker* (Guggenheim Museum, New York) and his late portraits of the gardener Vallier and of Choquet are poignant, dignified, and reflect a reverence for human life in the tradition of Rembrandt's portraits. Derain's aims are similar in the *Portrait of Iturrino,* and characteristics of Cézanne's portraits, such as an uneasy, assymetric pose, are exaggerated in this work. Derain had probably known the painter Francisco de Iturrino (1864–1924) since the turn of the century. A friend of Evenepoël, Iturrino was well known to Picasso and to Matisse, both of whom also drew his portrait. The Spanish painters of Iturrino's generation were noted in Paris for their sober dignity and disinterested manner, and Derain 'sanctifies' Iturrino with the conventions of the 'Byzantine' ascetic style of El Greco in the painting of the face and the characteristic leaf-like hands. Derain is referring to the several origins of 'pathetic' portraiture. In this he may have been influenced by the work of Iturrino's Spanish contemporaries in Paris, particularly Ignacio Zuloaga, who had been instrumental in bringing the El Greco exhibition to the Salon d'Automne in 1908 and whose ascetic portrait of his *Uncle Daniel* may have inspired Derain's *Portrait of Iturrino.*

Derain's overt references to paintings of the past override the formal similarities between his work and that of his contemporaries, and this made it difficult for his friends to write supportively of his art just before the First World War. In 1912 and 1913 Apollinaire was occupied with the formal changes which Futurism, Cubism, and Orphism had brought to painting and wrote that Derain had done his best work before 1910. Salmon, also, was worried about Derain's recent painting which seemed to be 'on the margin of modern art'. Some of this misunderstanding can be attributed to Derain's long absences from Paris, so that during these months the poets saw only the

30. *Portrait of Iturrino*, 1914, Musée National d'Art Moderne, Centre Georges Pompidou, Paris.

47

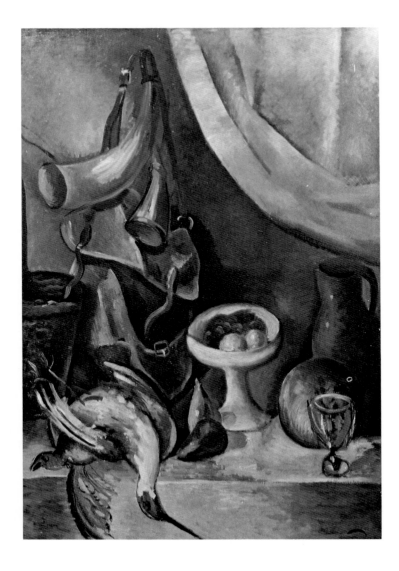

31. *La gibecière*, 1913, Musée de l'Orangerie, Paris, Collection Jean Walther and Paul Guillaume.

finished works as they were acquired by Kahnweiler. It is also due, however, to their sensitivity to the proper use of sources. Quotations of Indian or Javanese sculptures, of African masks, or of isolated motifs from European paintings of the past was entirely acceptable to the avant-garde critical spirit of the day. These elements, relocated into a new work, became formally and thematically submissive to the new whole. Derain upset this balance of power, submitting the new work to the source rather than the source material to the new work, when he situated his work in a particular tradition.

Style, in the modern sense of the individualistic material and formal construction of each artist's work, was of the greatest importance to the critics of the pre-war period as a mark of continuity and coherence in an artist's production. Derain subverted this, adopting the formal manner of works of other centuries, as he aligned his work with a thematic tradition such as 'pathetic portraiture' or '*memento mori* still life'.

Derain's *traditionisme* was celebrated, however, as soon as the rhetoric of war had reversed the respective values of the individual and the group. In his introduction to the catalogue of Derain's 1916 exhibition at the Galerie Paul Guillaume, Apollinaire leaves us in no doubt that Derain is proof of the superior French civilization in the face of 'the artistic impotence of contemporary Germany'. Apollinaire attributes to Derain the same qualities by which, according to the daily newspapers, the French were winning the war, a mixture of daring and discipline:

> Derain has passionately studied the masters. The copies which he has made of them in the Louvre show his concern to know them. At the same time, by an unequalled daring he has passed over all that contemporary art counts the most daring to retrieve, with simplicity and freshness, the principles of art and the discipline which springs from it (Paris, 1916; exh.cat.).

Derain is characterized with virtues which, by the end of the war, would become a new critical standard: 'After the truculence of his youth, Derain has turned towards sobriety and measure' (Paris, 1916, exh.cat.).

Derain's truculent, Fauvist youth had ended with the studio fire in the winter of 1907/8 when he had begun to paint sober landscapes very much in the manner of Cézanne. By 1912 Derain's *traditionisme* was well developed. It had been encouraged by contemporary poetry, in the wake of Moréas' reform of the Symbolist movement, and by the appeal to the early Renaissance in the circle of Maurice Denis. It was sustained both by his visits to the Louvre and by the theoretical arguments of his friends. The poet Max Jacob, for instance, whose essay on 'style' and 'situation' was first published in 1916 as the preface to *Le cornet à dés*, had a similar attitude toward the adoption of a historical style in order to make broad allusions to a thematic tradition. In his essay Apollinaire appropriated Derain's recent work to the cause of French identity as it is expressed in the critical construction of the 'French Tradition' (Paris, 1916, exh.cat.).

Apollinaire revealed the nature of the reassessment which allowed this appropriation: 'Derain's art is now stamped with that expressive grandeur which one could call antique . . . but archaism to order is entirely banished from his work. In literature, the classical art of a Racine who owes so much to the ancients nevertheless carries not a trace of archaism' Paris, 1916; exh.cat.). The long tradition of literary classicism was used to banish any thought of pastiche from the criticism of these works and the works of other painters in France who during and after the war based their works on the 'masters'. The Racinian model, however, would prove as insufficient to Derain's work as it was to Picasso's, and the subtle problem of the relation of Derain's painting to its historical sources would be taken up again in the early 1920s.

Apollinaire had begun to identify young painters in Paris, such as Moise Kisling, as 'followers of Derain' as early as 1912. In addition, Derain's relations with the young German painters who congregated at the Café du Dôme and the trade between Kahnweiler and Alfred Flechtheim ensured that he had many admirers in Germany. Thus, the works of Derain's 'Gothic' period were well known to the painters who constructed the early *Neue Sachlichkeit* movement after 1918. Similarly the Italians in Paris, in particular the circle of the poet Savinio, admired the poetic *quattrocento* manner of *Le joueur de cornemuse* of 1911. The Vers landscapes and the series of paintings of melancholic women of 1912 and 1913 influenced the development after the war of *Scuola Metaphysica* painting in Italy.

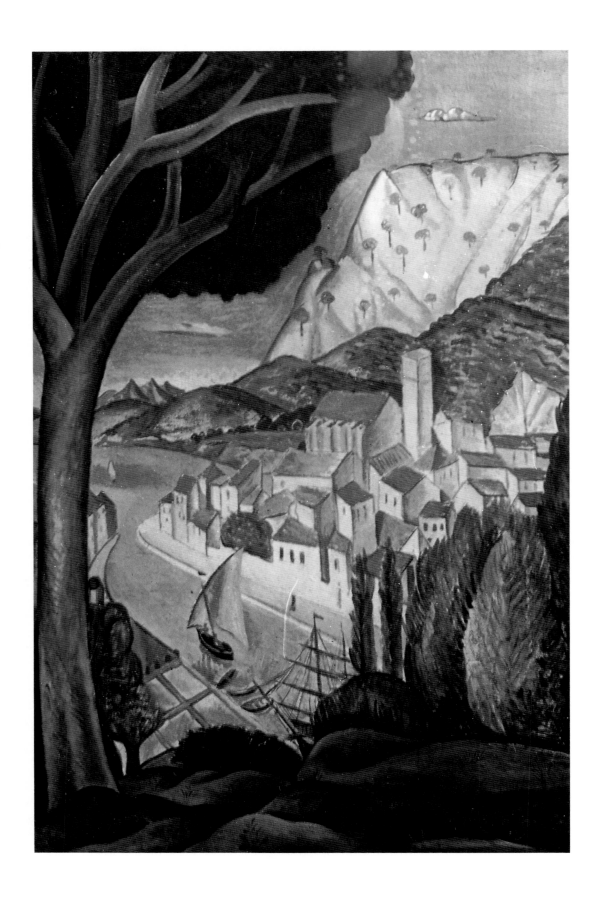

On 12 June 1914 Derain wrote to Kahnweiler from Avignon of 'that delicious crack of the whip which every year the Midi gives me' (Leiris archives). By 21 June when he next wrote to his dealer, Picasso had joined him in Monfavet, and the Braques were expected in a few days' time. Only in a postscript to this letter is there any indication that Derain had any thought of war that summer: 'The political situation looks pretty strange to me; I notice this evening the fall of a still-born minister, what do you think of that?'

The three painters were still together in the south when the order came to mobilize, and in the few days of forewarning and of anxious waiting, they had been inseparable. The moment is best expressed in a letter from Derain, still at the front on the 26 September 1918, answering, in the terse style acceptable to the military censor, a collector's enquiry about a work attributed to Picasso, now in the Yale University Art Gallery: 'The stone you ask me about resulted from something that happened at dinner in my house at Avignon a few days before the war. Some tiles in the kitchen fell down, and we decided to paint them in mutual homage, that is all there is to the story' (Leiris archives). By the end of August, Derain was in uniform.

Having had only a few days in which to report to his barracks in Lisieux, Derain left a studio full of works, finished and unfinished, from that spring, to which he had added as many of the Avignon landscapes as he and Alice could carry back to Paris. Kahnweiler, as Derain was not to know until 1919, had been in Bavaria when war became a certainty and only just managed to escape with his wife to Switzerland and so avoid conscription into the Kaiser's army. As a German citizen, all of Kahnweiler's goods including the stock of his gallery were forfeit to the French state. Eventually, because of the contract between Derain and Kahnweiler and the advance payments Derain had received from his dealer, even some of the works still in Derain's possession were sequestered.

In 1914 the art world momentarily collapsed, and Derain relied upon Alice and upon his friends. Matisse helped by authenticating the paintings Derain had left unsigned and in 1915 opening Derain's studio to Walther Halvorsen, the Norwegian painter and critic, who had briefly been Matisse's student and had become a dealer. Halvorsen wrote to his friend Sorensen on 24 October 1915 not only of the three Derain landscapes he had bought but also of the large painting of a dog which their mutual friend, another ex-pupil of Matisse, Werenskiold, had acquired (fig. 33) including in his letter a deft little drawing of the work (letter courtesy of Céline Wormdal, daughter of W. Halvorsen).

Within a year of the declaration of war the art world had begun to recover.

32. *Harbour in Provence*, 1913, The Hermitage, Leningrad.

Leave was short and infrequent, but because for much of the war the front was only two or three hours by train from Paris, even those in active service were not entirely exiled from the capital. Derain showed in the two mixed exhibitions which Paul Poiret's sister Madame Bongaard mounted in her fitting rooms in 1915 and 1916, and in 1916 Alice arranged a one-man show in the apartment gallery of Guillaume Apollinaire's protégé, Paul Guillaume. In the same year in 'Den Franske Ustillung', an exhibition mounted by the Kunstnerforbundet, the artists' union in Oslo, with the active assistance of Salmon and Apollinaire, two paintings by Derain were shown. One was a self-portrait and the other, the portrait of his close friend, the designer Paul Poiret, which Derain had painted in the barracks at Lisieux, where they both began the war. In the Norwegian catalogue this portrait, now in the Musée des Beaux Arts in Grenoble, was listed as an unfinished work.

Of the three introductory essays in the Kunstnerforbundet catalogue, by Jean Cocteau, Guillaume Apollinaire, and André Salmon, only the Salmon text was translated into Norwegian. Neutral Norway left in French Apollinaire's declaration of the 'sublime duty which the great French civilization imposes on artists'. With more tact, Salmon concentrated upon the recent developments in art in Paris and presented the war as a painful interlude in French artistic life. Derain's own opinions on the war, evident in his manuscript notes as well as his letters to Vlaminck, were in line with Salmon's rather than Apollinaire's.

Derain explained to the anarchist Vlaminck that he felt it was no good resisting the call to arms. He had no desire to fight, but he did not delude himself that he was a free man. Derain's resigned anti-heroic attitude distanced him from the ideals of both pacifists and warriors. Even under fire his detached observation remained the same. In the trenches he wrote:

> There are two sorts of heroes, the breakneck aviator who's only happy in danger, the sort who in peacetime is generally up before the magistrate but in time of war is decorated, just a matter of circumstances. But there's another, the well-educated young man, stupid and cold, a plant growing with no trouble in the flowerpot of history. Whether lay or clerical, it's the same barrel, all the stupidities that cold hearts have pushed out of themselves wish this specimen of humanity upon us. Deaf to all virtue and all vice but lost anyway, he throws himself at death out of despair that he'll never understand beauty, love, life ... There is a real hero, the real victim of war, the father of a family who thinks of his wife and children. He misses them but is not afraid because that's too stupid. The man who knows a life in which the heart lives knows that stupidity exists and that it sometimes rules everything, that it's the destruction of all that is the heart. You've just got to wait and hope for the chance to see once more those people and those things which replenish the human heart (Doucet MS 6913, f. 26v).

During the war Derain had little time for painting. 'I'm working', he wrote to Vlaminck in 1917, 'I draw as much as I can, and I'm planning works for whenever I get a chance' (Vlaminck, 1955, p. 228). According to Georges Gabory, whose poetry Derain illustrated at the end of the war, Derain had filled several sketchbooks with drawings at the front, but he sold them immediately after the war to Walther Halvorsen. They have not been located since. Derain also made some mask-like sculptures from the beaten metal of shell cases, and this led his enthusiastic friend André Salmon vainly to declare him in 1919 the new hope of avant-garde French sculpture. At the end of the war, while Derain was with the occupying troops at Mainz, he designed costumes and

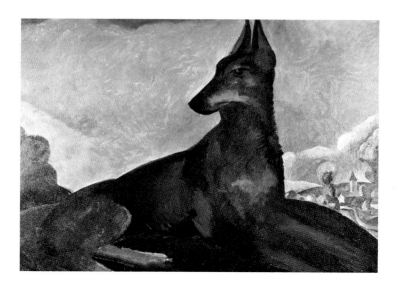

33. *Portrait of the Artist's Dog*, 1914, Musée d'Art Moderne de la Ville de Troyes, Donation Denise and Pierre Lévy.

sets for Paul Claudel's mystical drama *L'Annonce faite à Marie* for the Scandinavian Duroc Theatre Company. Derain's costume drawings show the inspiration as much of Brueghel as of Claudel's thirteenth-century setting. A small painting in the Musée d'Art Moderne de la Ville de Troyes, a study for the backdrop for Claudel's play, indicates the survival of the style of the 1912 Vers landscapes in Derain's decorations.

The several pages of war writings among Derain's surviving manuscript notes include descriptions of the countryside, particularly the wet and wasted land he marched through to Flanders and Mainz. There is also an account of a forge at work with precise details of light and shade. Derain also wrote poems during the war, among them '*Voici la mort*' and more than one poem entitled '*Vue du front*', in which his debt to his friends Max Jacob, Pierre Reverdy, and Guillaume Apollinaire is apparent. Remarkable among these poems is that hallmark of Neo-Symbolism, the 'mystery of life', in '*Voici la Mort*': '*Voici ses seins qui n'allaiteront plus, voici sa bouche ses cheveux ses bras, ses enfants s'accrochent à ses jambes inquiétés, affaré même du mystère de cette grande douleur.*' ('. . . here are her breasts which give no more milk, here her mouth, her hair, her arms, her children clinging to her legs, worried, frightened even of the mystery of that great pain.' Doucet MS 6913, f. 27r). And in '*Une vue du front*': '*Le cheval mange de l'herbe/son oeil voit c'est la lumière/du soleil son oreille entend/et son corps se deplace. L'herbe rentre dans les flancs qui se meurent/que de mystère, que de mystère dans tant/de douceur, de calme, de repos et d'azur.*' ('The horse grazes, his eye sees that it is the light of the sun, his ear hears and his body moves. The grass enters his moving flanks. Nothing but mystery, nothing but mystery in so much sweetness, calm, stillness and blue.' Doucet MS 6913, f. 28v).

The same conviction that what is important remains on the edge of our understanding inspired his ideas on painting at that time, and in 1917 he wrote to Vlaminck, 'I have some thoughts on what should preoccupy painters: the unknown only. No more mechanics, that is to say no more means of expression, colours, line, etc. but that which is inexplicable only' (Vlaminck, 1955, p. 227). On the other side of the page on which Derain had written '*Une vue du front*' he had written: 'God doesn't know how to make miracles, miracles are reserved for man. Avoid explaining his acts. Explanation is a destruction' (Doucet MS 6913, f. 28r).

AFTER THE WAR

After 1918 Derain wrote of his only memory of the war ('I don't count the horrors I saw as memories'). It was a tale of the difficult life of an African soldier at the front and was probably inspired by Apollinaire's 'Les Soupirs du servant du Dakar'. Another memoir written soon after the armistice, 'La Chute d'homme', indicates that at some point in the war Derain suffered those effects of disorientation which are the first stage of shell shock: 'lying on my back, that is, lying on my stomach on infinity, as I didn't know to what I should attribute the phenomenon, the centripetal force stopped holding me to the surface of the globe, and I suddenly flew off' (Doucet MS 6913, f. 19r).

Derain had spent more than four years at war, as he wrote to Vlaminck, 'always under fire, the mud, the rain or the dust, nothing to eat, nowhere to sleep, and always the same, always, with no let up . . .' (Vlaminck, 1955, p. 221), and he returned to Paris early in 1919 exhausted and demoralized. An invitation from the choreographer Massine to begin immediately the décor and costumes for a Ballets-Russes production *La Boutique Fantasque* was a great stroke of luck.

Derain spent three months in the late spring and early summer of 1919 in Vanessa Bell's London flat, as the ballet was to open at the Alhambra, in the lively company of Bloomsbury bohemia, and this softened his post-war trauma. In London he rejoined Picasso who was also working with the Ballets-Russes. Derain's sets for the ballet developed the decorative qualities of *Le joueur de cornemuse* of 1911 and the *Harbour in Provence (Martigues)* (fig. 32) of 1913. He quickly realized both his expertise as a decorator and the fascination which such projects had for him. He would continue to design for the ballet throughout his life.

Returning to Paris from London in August 1919 Derain received a letter from Kahnweiler who was still in exile in Berne. He wrote back: 'since the war I've had much more success, without doubt it is because I've painted very little; the world is inexplicable. At the moment I'm working a great deal. I've not left Paris; I'm still in the Rue Bonaparte where I've rented another studio which gives onto mine' (Kahnweiler, 6 September 1919). In his extended studio Derain may already have begun the series of large paintings and decorative *rinceaux* which the Norwegian dealer Walther Halvorsen commissioned for his dining room. They were well under way, if not finished, by 4 December 1919 when Kahnweiler wrote from Switzerland asking Derain if he would mind his photographer Deletang photographing them. It is likely that Halvorsen intended, once Derain had had time to produce enough work, to put him under contract, and as early as 1917 Derain had informed Vlaminck that Halvorsen had approached him but that nothing was to be formalized until after the

34. *Nu au chat*, 1923, Private collection.

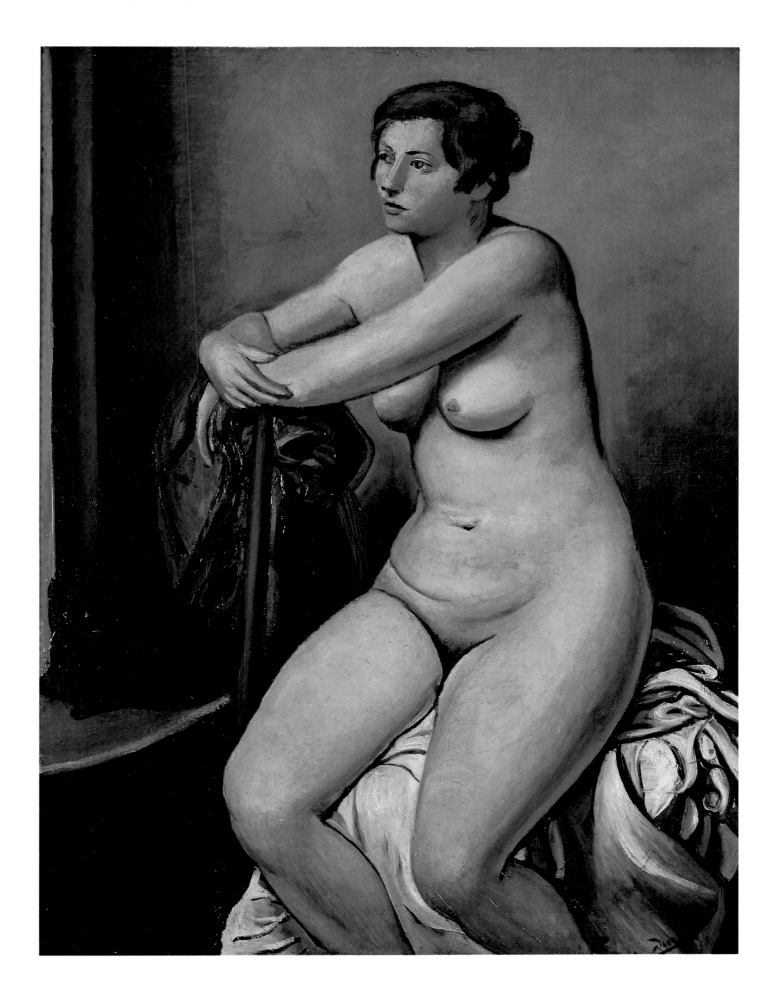

war. Now, however, Derain renewed his relations with Kahnweiler who, through his partner in Paris, Simon, not only bought Derain's paintings but published his etchings and engaged him again in book illustration.

The German dealers began planning their Derain shows as soon as the Treaty of Versailles was ratified, and in 1922 Derain showed in the Tannhauser Gallery in Munich, as well as in the Flechtheim Gallery in Berlin. Another associate of Kahnweiler's, Joseph Brummer in New York, also organized a Derain exhibition in that year. Derain continued to sell to Halvorsen, to other galleries, and to collectors who called at his studio, such as the American John Quinn, and Kahnweiler found it increasingly difficult to secure the best work. During the sales of Kahnweiler's sequestered goods in 1921 and 1923, Derain's pictures held their prices relatively well, and this sign of strength helped to sustain the price of his current work. Derain found himself courted on all sides by the dealers. He refused to sign a contract with Kahnweiler and by February 1924 had ended their special relationship. From this time his works seem to have been sold almost exclusively to Paul Guillaume. Guillaume devoted himself to Derain's practical affairs, running his every errand and leaving him to paint. This idyllic relationship lasted until Guillaume's death in 1934. An expert businessman, Guillaume turned to advantage the strength of the dollar in France in the 1920s, and both he and Derain became wealthy.

The argument with Kahnweiler, however, had not been over prices but over the dealer's position in the art world and his demand for a continuous flow of new works. From Kahnweiler's letter to Derain on 3 March 1924, it is clear that Derain did not want to be on either side of the argument over Cubism which was then raging in Paris. 'I understand your wish', wrote Kahnweiler, 'to hold your exhibition in a gallery "sans tendance".' More important than this, however, was Derain's freedom to keep his work in the studio as long as he wished. Kahnweiler assured him, 'You want to be free. You have every right to be ... you are keeping your works at the moment, good. You say that you will sell them to me when you go back to selling ...' This was not Kahnweiler's manner of dealing with an artist, but it is likely that it became Guillaume's. Guillaume published many Derain pictures in his gallery journal, *Les Arts à Paris,* or otherwise offered them for sale, some years after they were painted. Thus, since Derain's works are never dated, their date of execution is often difficult to determine.

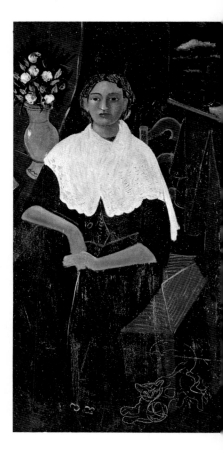

35. *Madame Derain in a White Shawl*, 1919, Tate Gallery, London.

Coming back to a 'cold' studio, Derain needed time to build his work around him. The works of 1919–20 are predominantly portraits and heads, rather than still lifes and landscapes. This continued the trend of the work he had left in 1914. He painted several related bust-length studies, heads, and portraits of women in these two years (fig. 37 and cat. 45), including several portraits of his wife (*Madame Derain in a White Shawl,* Tate Gallery; fig. 35). He also did portraits of his friends, such as *Paul Guillaume* (Musée de l'Orangerie) (fig. 36) and *Georges Gabory* (Private Collection, London), and of others, such as that of the explorer *Fridtjof Nansen* now in the Videnskaps Akademiet in Oslo.

These works are tender and direct, a reminder of the desire Derain expressed in a letter to Vlaminck from the trenches: 'I want to do nothing but portraits, real portraits with hands and hair; that's real life!' They are a reaction against his sense of alienation from others in the abnormal circumstances of war, 'all these brutes who are otherwise good people'. At the same time these pictures indicate a 'classicism' which ranges from the use of Renaissance, antique, or archaic sources, in both painting and sculpture, to allusion to Jacques Louis David's lively brushstroke and thin paint. The admiration for David among avant-garde painters had begun before the war, from the

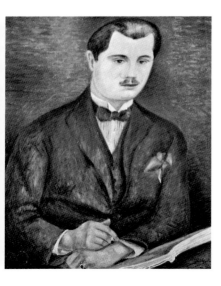

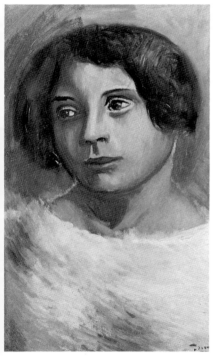

37. *L'Italienne*, 1920, Staatsgalerie, Stuttgart.

36. (top) *Portrait of Paul Guillaume*, 1919, Musée de l'Orangerie, Paris, Collection Jean Walther and Paul Guillaume.

time of the 1913 David retrospective at the Petit Palais, and was cultivated through the 1920s by critics such as Florent Fels and Waldemar Georges, both great apologists for Derain.

The new classicism of 1920 in Paris was equally an enthusiasm for the works of Camille Corot who, it was thought, had brought the Renaissance directly into the nineteenth century. Juan Gris, for example, made a Cubist study of Corot's *La femme à la perle*, a painting based upon Leonardo's *La Gioconda* in the Louvre. Derain's *La paysanne grècque* in the Raeber collection, Switzerland, and his *L'Italienne* in the Walker Art Gallery, Liverpool, are directly inspired by Corot's late studies of women in peasant costume such as *L'Italienne Agostina* of 1866.

Corot's influence did not stop at Derain's sudden interest in 'Mediterranean' figures. It also extended to his portraits, such as that of *Madame Kahnweiler* in 1922 (Musée Nationale d'Art Moderne, Paris), and eventually to his nudes (cat. 8 and 11). Nowhere was Corot's influence stronger, however, than in Derain's landscapes. In January 1921 Derain travelled to Rome, and he seems to have seen the Campagna in terms of the landscapes which Corot had painted there. In that year Corot's palette and his softly curving paths and masses of foliage begin to appear in Derain's work. Even a work such as *Woodland Scene at Ollioules* (Private Collection; Sutton, 1959, p. 51) which essentially continues the manner of pre-war works such as *Le bois* in the Hermitage, Leningrad, has the flowing rhythm of Corot's landscapes of the mid-1840s.

The influence of Corot was integral with Derain's resumption of landscape painting after the war. His first attempt, in the summer of 1920, had been fraught with difficulty. He wrote to Kahnweiler on 3 September 1920: 'I curse painting every day, it gives me so much trouble. The fact is it's been six or seven years now since I've faced the landscape, and I've been completely knocked off course.' The next summer he went down to Sanary (Var) intending to paint nudes, but he could not find a model and for a month did not paint. The trip to Rome, he told Kahnweiler, had spoiled him for the Côte d'Azur. He now had a horror of the French landscape and wanted to get back to the studio. On 5 November, however, he was still at Sanary and writing to tell Kahnweiler of the marvellous effects of the mistral upon the landscapes he was painting.

Derain's intention to work from the model during the landscape painting season in 1921 was a drastic change from his pre-war routines. Between 1910 and 1914 Derain had not painted a single nude, but by May 1922 Kahnweiler was complaining that Derain's nudes were to be seen everywhere in Paris except in his gallery, and he asked Derain to provide him with some. The number, scale, and variety of these works suggest that he had been planning such pictures during the war and that on his release he took up eagerly the breadth of possibilities in application, composition, drawing, and pose which are open to a painter with a wide knowledge of the traditions of painting the nude (fig. 48). He drew constantly from the model, and his drawings, as well as his paintings, show his concern with his *métier,* understandable in a painter whose powers had been pent up for some years (fig. 34).

Derain's sudden development as a painter of the nude, however, did not happen in isolation but was contemporaneous with Picasso's monumental classical bathers as well as his *Women at a Fountain* (Museum of Modern Art, New York) and with Braque's decorative *Canéphores* (Musée Nationale d'Art Moderne, Paris). Derain's grand nudes were quickly celebrated among the critics as worthy of comparison with Renoir and Courbet, two painters whom Derain much admired and whose work was widely exhibited at the time, due to the death of Renoir at the end of 1919 and the 'official' acceptance of Courbet with the purchase of his *Atelier du peintre* by the Louvre

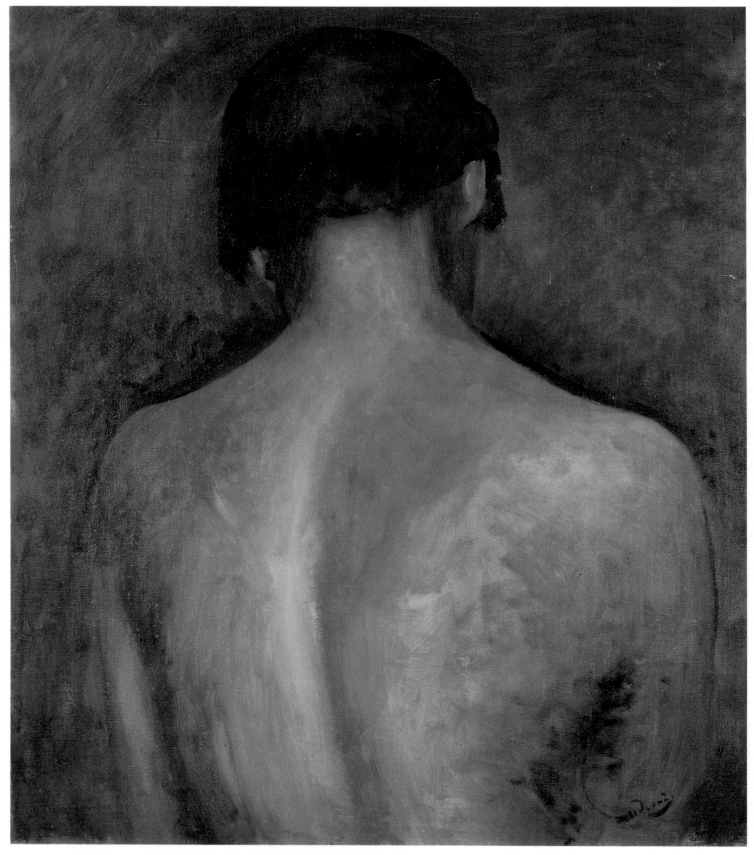

38. *Le dos*, c. 1923, Musée d'Art Moderne de la Ville de Paris (cat. 9).

39. (opposite) *Le beau modèle*, 1923, Musée de l'Orangerie, Paris, Collection Jean Walther and Paul Guillaume.

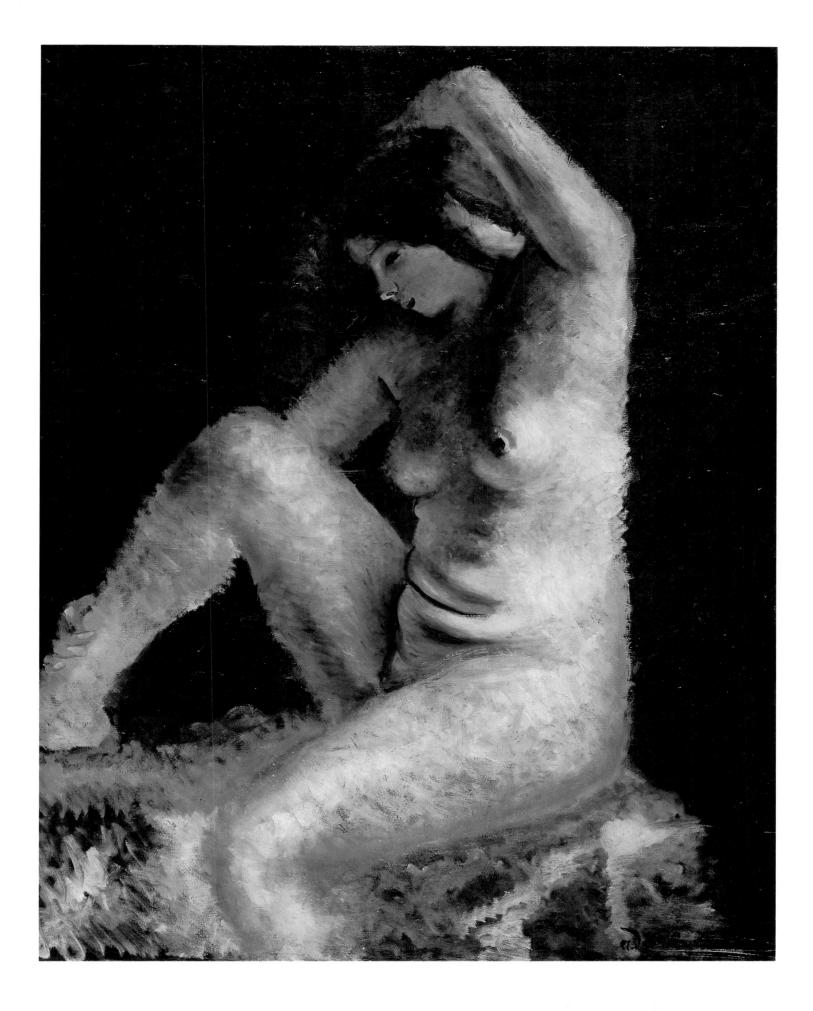

early in 1920. In 1923 Elie Faure wrote of Derain's nudes almost entirely in terms of Renoir's late paintings, an inspiration, according to Faure, which Derain shared with Picasso.

Le beau modèle (fig. 39) and Le modèle blond, both in the Musée de l'Orangerie, are clearly inspired by Renoir, but details such as the frothy treatment of Le beau modèle recall Renoir's own sources in Fragonard and Boucher. Derain wrote of him: 'Renoir goes back to the source, to the delightful, carnal eighteenth century, cultured but ardent, with its pleasant, melancholic, gentle, and voluptuous human nature' (Doucet MS 6889, f. 10r).

The 'earthy' qualities of Nu à la cruche (fig. 42) and related works (see Rey, 1925, p. 36) may well stem from Derain's interest in Courbet, stimulated perhaps by two major Courbet shows at the Galerie Bernheim Jeune, one in the winter of 1917–18, the other in 1919. The most ardent admirer of Courbet at this time was Dunoyer de Segonzac, whose studio was separated from Derain's only by a narrow courtyard. Derain wrote of Courbet: 'only one man remained perfect and pure at the beginning, without conventions or rules – Courbet, coming straight from nature, he is "homme peintre"'(Doucet MS 6889, f. 11r).

Together, Derain's opinions of Renoir and Courbet might express the union of skill and substance, of knowledge of painting and desire to 'étaler de la couleur' which he describes more than once in his manuscript notes. They also reflect, however, the broadly held opinion of the time, one might say the mystique, of these two painters. The appreciation of Renoir and Courbet at the end of the war was informed by the division between the 'classical ideal' (Renoir) and the 'folk or regional ideal' (Courbet). The combination of these, it was argued, had provided France with her cultural superiority. This idea was at least partly responsible for the increased visibility of Renoir and Courbet and hence their influence upon Derain and other painters.

There is no doubt that Derain was influenced at least by the 'classical' terms in which French culture had been described during the war, in opposition to the supposed barbarism of the Germans. He distinguishes, for instance, between the 'carnal' nature of Renoir, of which he approves, and that of Cézanne: 'Cézanne returned to the Mediterranean obsession, the magic line of the horizon which provides a base for the temples and, with that, the fire of antique man, painful creation' (Doucet MS 6889, f. 10r).

Derain was not, however, concerned with nationalist ideology. Wartime privation had led him, as it did others, to luxuriate in ambitious painting after the war and had sharpened his well-developed appetite for grandeur of conception and execution in painting. This ambition was shared by the collectors and patrons of the post-war period, as is shown by the fashion for elaborate murals and large canvases with complex, multifigured compositions. Added to this was Derain's conviction that in the museums the painter finds not only his inspiration but his measure. This is revealed in his notes on seeing the Caillebotte donation of Impressionist paintings hanging in the Louvre just after the war: 'I was bowled over when I saw the Impressionists exhibited in the Louvre beside Rembrandt, Rubens, Velázquez, Watteau, Poussin, Raphael. They looked, of course, like the work of semi-artistic little girls, but the colour of the canvas was very cold and the colours not at all supported. One completely grey Le Nain would demolish the Monets' (Doucet MS 6912, f. 3r/v).

During the war an aesthetic had developed within the avant-garde which accommodated Derain's particular involvement with the painting of the past. Where the current nationalist mystique of Renoir and Courbet, or of Corot or Fouquet for that matter, served his own mystique of great painting, Derain appropriated it, combining it indiscriminately with the lauding of Netherlandish, English, Spanish and Italian painting. It was a process similar to nationalism, as it defined a particular tradition of European art, but Derain did not speak of a French tradition as did Jacques-Emile Blanche, Florent Fels, Louis Vauxcelles, Yves Alix, or Waldemar Georges. His friend Clive Bell, however, was more sensitive to such matters and suggested in his book *Since Cézanne* in 1922 that young French painters were preponderantly influenced by Derain because they felt supported and protected by his 'unconscious nationalism', a remark that was quoted a year later by Salmon.

Derain, however, was considerably irritated at being seen as a 'chef d'école'. He was so incensed by Jacques-Emile Blanche's comments on what was needed, from Derain and others, for the good of French painting, that in 1921 he published a satiric piece in which the pedantic Blanche was tipped into the lake by Picabia (*Signaux de la France et de Belgique,* September 1921, reprinted in a shorter version in Lévy, 1976, pp. 142–7).

As one of the most celebrated artists of the 1920s, a great deal was written about Derain, and the fact that he was admired by a large number of young painters and established critics made him a larger target for the few who carped at his success, such as Maurice Raynal who wrote ironically of his work. To Derain, Raynal's accusations of eclecticism and facility were the mark of a critic who valued an artist by his adherence to a 'style' or a movement. Derain despised this idea and called it the 'aimez vous de la cannelle?' attitude to painting: 'Do you like cinnamon? If you do, it can be sprinkled all over the painting for you, little dabs for those who like Impressionist cinnamon, little lines for those who like Cubist cinnamon' (Doucet MS 6887, f. 25v). He did not publish this bitter *bon mot,* but it has the sound of something which had already been said with gusto over a café table. The slight was one against the critics. Although Derain's letters to Vlaminck and his notes both indicate that he thought Cubism a regrettable aberration, he had the greatest respect for Braque. Derain's *traditionisme,* on the other hand, was well understood by Braque and Picasso, who in the early 1920s shared many of his enthusiasms.

The rehanging of the Louvre and the quatercentenary of Raphael's death in 1920, with its attendant exhibitions, had brought the issue of continuity with the Renaissance to the fore, and the real nature of the relationship of modern painters with Raphael and other masters had been argued out in terms of 'imitation', 'pastiche', and the 'return to tradition'. Derain was among those whose comments had been printed on the front page of the newspaper *Le Matin* on 6 April 1920. 'Raphael,' declared Derain, 'c'est le plus grand incompris.' Raphael cannot be understood until a painter is very experienced, argued Derain; his influence, therefore, cannot touch a debutant. To Derain the question was not one of 'imitation' but of 'initiation' (repr. in Salmon, 1922, pp. 149–53).

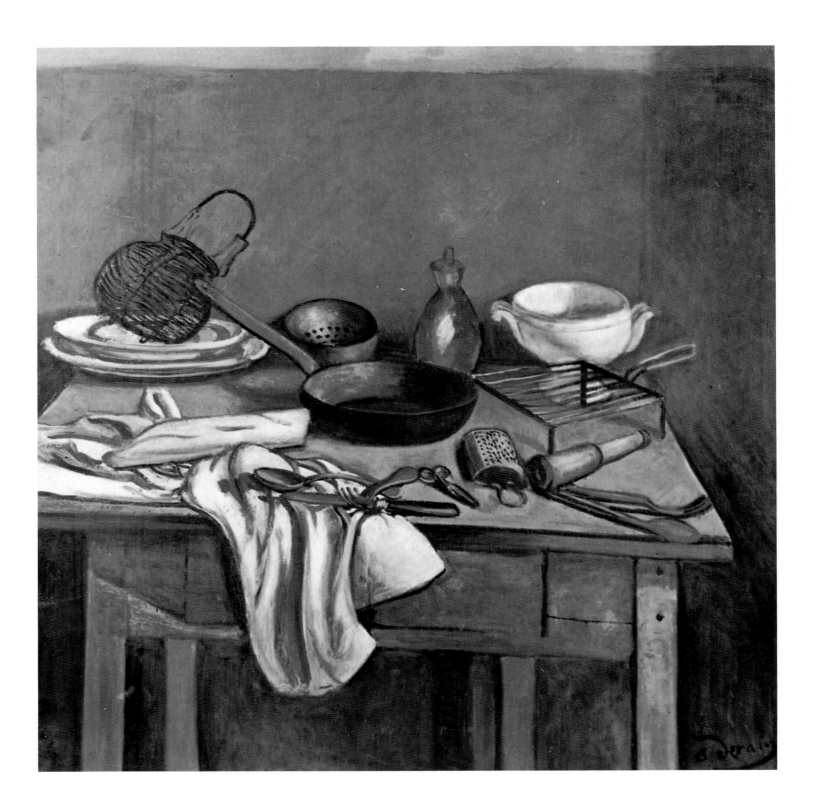

'Art', said Derain, 'is always the same.' Between 1919 and 1921 he wrote a treatise on painting which he called 'De Picturae Rerum' in imitation of Lucretius. The treatise did not go beyond the notational stage and was never published. It takes up nearly one hundred pages in three of the manuscripts in the Bibliothèque Littéraire Jacques Doucet: MS 6912, which may date from about 1919, as part of it is quoted in André Breton's *Les Pas Perdus*, a collection of that poet's essays of the preceding few years, published in 1924; MS 6887, which dates from 1921 or after, as Derain copied into it a long passage from an article by Edouard Monod Hertzen which appeared in the journal *L'Amour de l'art* in June 1921; and MS 6889, which continues the arguments and shares the terminology of both of the above. The notes are aphoristic and disconnected, and there are several inconsistencies, some of which Derain tries to resolve, some of which he ignores. A picture emerges from them, however, of Derain's philosophy and his attitude to painting.

Derain's view of the world was 'realist' in the Platonic sense of the word, that is, a world created by and from the universal spirit, as described in Plato's *Timaeus*. Art is like the universal spirit in that it is a fatality – it 'must be as it is' – it is an unchanging 'real'. And because it shares this quality with the spirit, art can and does manifest the spirit. The seeming differences between the art of various periods are only apparent differences carried by these manifestations: 'All that can happen is that an actor creates a new intonation of tears, of love, of fear, in playing an arduous part like that of Phèdre ... so that each period has its own intonation for these sentiments, a tone that characterizes it' (Doucet MS 6887, f. 14r).

The concerns of the painter are not with the accidental details of these manifestations, the intonations, but with the spirit itself. This requires knowledge of the 'real', the development of the intelligence of the soul, which is akin to magic. It requires the freeing of intuition by initiation. Painting uses the 'fatal' language of the spirit: rhythm, perception by numbers, geometry – the 'natural pathos' of infinity. Rhythm is the essence of the artist's work, as it is the coupling of number with material, the same coupling which created the world. This rhythm is achieved by careful management of the fundamental realities of the world, as Derain explains in the section of the treatise called 'Respect aux Angles': 'Any plastic statement which does not respect angles is destined to destruction. Angles are the fate of form. They are movement towards the sublime life or towards death, that is to say towards another life, another rhythm. It is through them that an object is related to others or to the universe. It is almost impossible to change the relations of angles in a drawing' (Doucet MS 6912, f. 6r).

40. *La table de cuisine*, c. 1922, Musée de l'Orangerie, Paris, Collection Jean Walther and Paul Guillaume.

The painter is induced to paint by light, which he recognizes as of the spirit: 'Consciousness of the virtues of light urges man to bring alive in it the forms of his thought' (Doucet MS 6889, f. 14r). Light is not only his inspiration but the heart of a painter's means: 'A picture is constructed by its light and it doesn't matter what kind of light; the illumination of forms is as good as the lighting of substances or even the light of a represented atmosphere ... Light ... is a constructional means that makes the dimensions of opposing surfaces precise and orients the rhythm of their relationship ... It is the field of drawing' (Doucet MS 6887, f. 42v, 43v) (fig. 41). Drawing is itself rhythm, which is the creative principle of the universal spirit: 'Drawing is a spiritual rhythm which goes incessantly from the container to the contained and from the contained to the container. It is the rhythm of limitation and the way of integrating entities. Light is therefore the sign of the sum which, once arrived at, allows the rediscovery of the elements which don't count in appearance but which are, nevertheless, bound up with the spirit' (Doucet MS 6887, f. 43v).

Derain confronts the 'grand mystère', the Symbolist concept which overshadowed his intellectual youth, with a Platonic model in which he can know and act, in which he can become an initiate into the inner secrets of the world. Derain's metaphysics are firmly rooted in the practice of his art, particularly drawing. Painting, however, is profoundly tied to the natural world. Its materials are minerals and vegetable substances; its principles of composition are the same rhythms which have ordered the world; its origins are in magic incantations which summon up in memory the experience of the world. Because of its microcosmic quality, painting is a kind of divination and 'the expression of divine grandeur through the opening of an angle of view, the complete evolution of the visual angle or macrocosm' (Doucet MS 6887, f. 31r).

41. *Rythme des Rectangles*, c. 1921, Private collection.

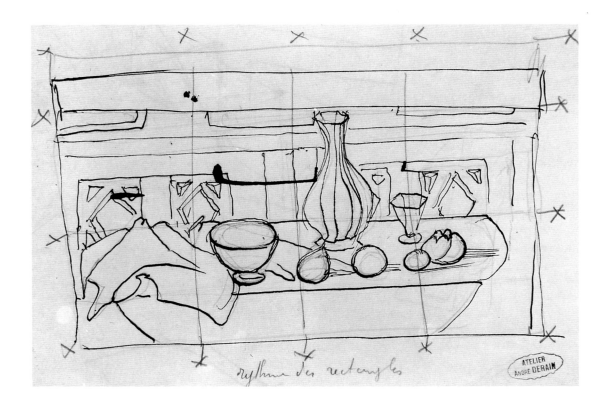

Derain's philosophy is that of the age before the Enlightenment. Some of his arguments are those of Paracelsus, and others reveal his deep involvement in alchemy. Derain's respect for tradition is connected with his concept of the origins of painting, with its relationship to the world soul and to universal knowledge. The question of imitation does not exist. Faced with millennia of art, which of its manifestations can be said to represent the 'real form' of anything? The current problem of tradition, for Derain, involved, rather, the way museum paintings were seen, which was too often akin to the way one reads a book everyone else has read, in order not to seem illiterate. The painter, however, must of 'necessity' go to the museums and receive the real emanation from the masterpieces. All culture comes from that necessity which is 'the passion to understand the truths which constitute the eternal obsession of the human mind' (Doucet MS 6887, f. 32v).

Nothing, however, is to be explained, that is, to be expressed by a direct equivalent: 'il n'y a rien d'exprimable par le direct'. A painting such as *Arlequin et Pierrot* (fig. 66), for instance, is a subtly nuanced field of references. It does not parade its ulterior subject or a precise model in past painting, but it alludes to traditions rich in meaning. What is transmitted is concordant with the subject of all painting, according to Derain's treatise – the pathetic, the reciprocal relation between life and death, the incessant death and rebirth of all things, the '*ego sum resurrectione et vita*'.

Derain's still-life painting provided the richest field for uniting his metaphysics and his practice as a painter. Here, more than in any other genre of painting, Derain took his models consistently from the seventeenth and early eighteenth centuries, when the fall of light itself was significant of life and death, when all still life was at some level *vanitas* painting, and when the portrayal of an inanimate object posed questions of time, existence, and fate. In the period 1920–4 Derain painted still lifes which were recognizably in the manner of Spanish and Italian still life or in the manner of Chardin (cat. 22). André Salmon called them 'healthy, like bits of the Last Supper' (Salmon, 1923, p. 14). *La table de cuisine* (Musée de l'Orangerie, Paris) is equal to the earlier masterpieces of the tradition which it continues (fig. 40). It is also a *tour de force* of that 'expressive power' of angles of which he wrote. The angular disposition of the elements fans out from the complex knot of intersection formed in the centre foreground by the knife, fork, spoon, and folds of the napkin. The management of this part of the composition had already been considered in much simpler still-life paintings such as *Nature morte* (cat. 21) and the still life included in Derain's self-portrait of this period (cat. 46).

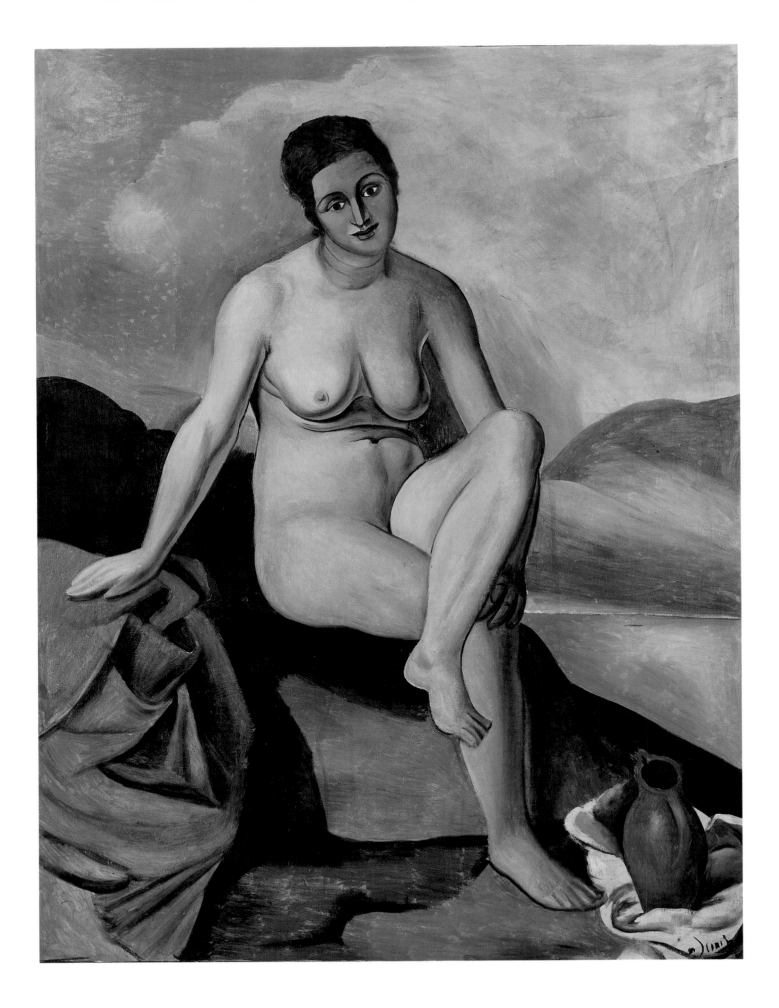

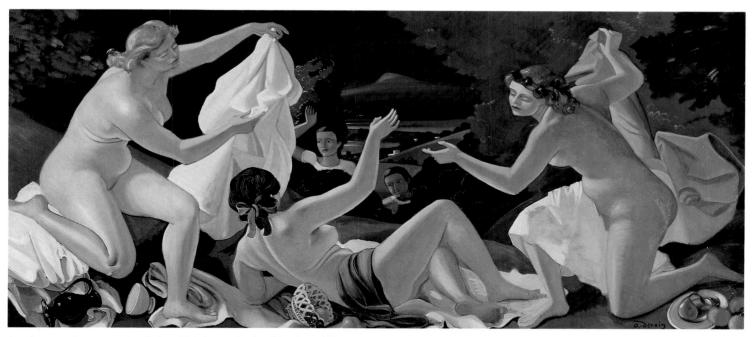

43. *La surprise*, 1938, Art Salon Takahata, Osaka City (cat. 17).

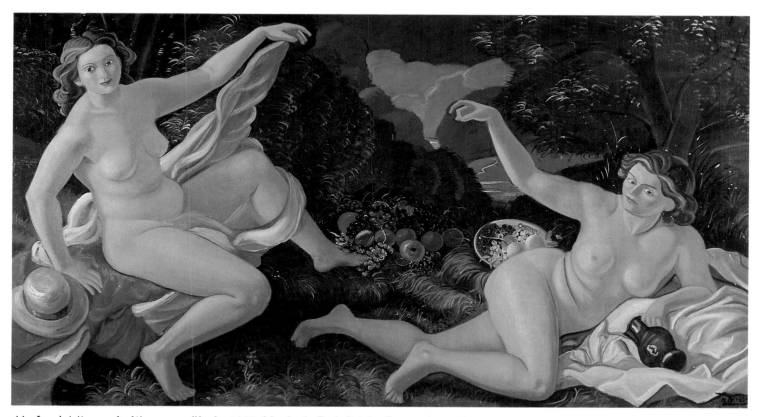

44. *La clairière, ou le déjeuner sur l'herbe*, 1938, Musée du Petit Palais, Geneva (cat. 16).

42. (opposite) *Nu à la cruche*, c. 1921–23, Musée de l'Orangerie, Paris, Collection Jean Walther and Paul Guillaume (cat. 6).

THE 'BANDE À DERAIN'

The audience for Derain's views on painting in the 1920s was the circle with which he met daily in the cafés of Boulevard Saint Germain. The 'bande à Derain' included more poets than painters. Derain was also a close friend of the printer/publisher Bernouard and may have given some financial support to the publication of the works of young poets such as Georges Gabory. Derain illustrated two of Gabory's books in 1920, *La Cassette de plomb* (cat. 117), published by Bernouard, and *Le Nez de Cléopâtre* (fig. 45), published by Galerie Simon. At the same time Francis Carco, André Billy, Vincent Muselli, and André Salmon were all friends of Derain. Salmon was the most prolific writer on Derain's work, and Derain illustrated Muselli's work in the late 1920s (cat. 119 and fig. 46).

The young poets who would form the Surrealist group were also friends of Derain. Breton's first book, *Mont de Pieté,* was published in 1924 with illustrations by Derain. One of the poems in this collection is entitled 'André Derain' and is a homage to the painter's pre-war works, including the *Portrait of Iturrino,* which Breton eventually bought. In 1924 in *Les pas perdus* André Breton reported Derain's views on painting and his metaphysics, declaring 'a view of this order turns the universe upside down'. He presented Derain's meditations on the mystery of life – 'The life of a tree is a mystery that no painter has succeeded in breaking through' – and his attachment to the pre-Enlightenment concept of inherent signs, which is the basis of all arts of divination.

Derain was a subscriber to Breton's journal *La Littérature* and then to *La Révolution Surréaliste.* When the Surrealist painters had their first exhibition in 1925, it was in the Galerie Pierre Loeb which was directly under Derain's studio at 13 Rue Bonaparte. Derain seems to have retained friendly relations with the Surrealists throughout the 1920s, as Desnos wrote a long dedication to him as late as 1930 in which he addressed Derain as one initiate of the arcane arts to another, and in 1934 he illustrated *Héliogabale* (cat. 120), a work by Breton's early collaborator, Antonin Artaud.

At the same time Derain frequently saw Cocteau's circle, and the musicians known as 'Les Six' were his friends, particularly Georges Auric, whose ballet *La Concurrence* Derain designed in 1932. Derain collected antique musical instruments and restored more than one organ. He developed an experimental notation for organ music and eventually interested Auric in this project. Robert Rey described Derain's studio in 1925 as an *antre*, an alchemist's cave, in which a pet owl flew about the strange flotsam among the canvases and paints. It was a continuation of the life in the Rue Tourlaque in Montmartre, of which, since the war, the younger painters and poets had an historical sense. Derain and Salmon became the focus of this interest. Apollinaire had died in November 1918; Max Jacob was occasionally in Paris, but had adopted a semi-monastic life; Picasso was rarely seen at the café tables, as his wife preferred a

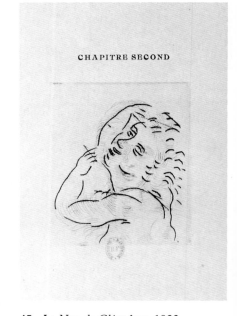

45. *Le Nez de Cléopâtre*, 1922, La Bibliothèque Nationale, Paris (cat. 118).

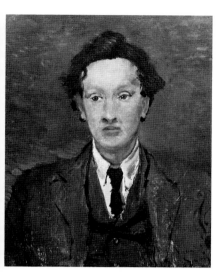

46. *Portrait of Vincent Muselli*, 1925, Private collection (cat. 50).

different style of life. Into Derain's studio every day, however, came Georges Braque, and always with the same greeting, '*Quoi de neuf?*' The Braques and the Derains often spent their weekends together, Braque and Derain sometimes going out onto the Seine in a ramshackle boat which Derain had bought from his dentist.

Derain saw his dealer Paul Guillaume frequently, but he seems rarely to have kept company with collectors, except for John Quinn, whose secretary Jeanne Robert Foster sat for two portraits in 1923. An anglophile, although he spoke virtually no English, Derain kept in touch with London through his friend Clive Bell who was frequently in Paris. Derain had a wide circle of friends among artists. Some, like his neighbour in the Rue Bonaparte, Dunoyer de Segonzac, he had known before the war. Mondzain became a close friend after the war, joining Derain on his landscape painting trips in 1920 and 1921.

Having long been a friend of Kisling and, before his death, Modigliani, and their dealer Zborowsky, Derain was also involved with the Montparnasse artists. His friendship with Florent Fels kept him in touch with the artists whom Fels supported in his journal *L'Art vivant*, and among this group, particularly in the mid-1920s, Derain was much imitated. Derain had a reputation as a bon vivant and a connoisseur not only of the *grands crus* but also of the 'little' wines of the villages, an interest which he seems to have combined with his landscape painting.

His circle overlapped considerably with that of Galtier-Boissière, the editor of the journal *Crapouillot*, which included not only Carco, Bernouard, and Mac Orlan but Dunoyer de Segonzac, Villeboeuf, Dignimont, and Bompard. He was devoted to Galtier-Boissière's rowdy dinners, famed for their consumption of wine, and the noise of Dignimont's accordion and Bompard's trumpet. Two of Galtier-Boissière's protégés, regular illustrators of *Crapouillot*, were Jean Oberlé and Paul Devaux. They became Derain's guard of honour in Montparnasse and at the Deux Magots in the late 1920s.

In 1924 Derain bought a house in the little town of Chailly-en-Bière, a short walk from Fontainebleau and the Barbizon Forest. Both Millet and Rousseau are buried in this small town, and both they and Camille Corot had painted many landscapes there. It is likely that the house was suggested to him by Dunoyer de Segonzac whose own estate was not far from that area. Derain's father-in-law had recently died, and Alice's sister Suzanne Géry and her five-year-old daughter Geneviève (see cat. 53 and 54) had come to live with the Derains. The apartment in Rue Bonaparte was too small and unsuitable for the child, so Suzanne and Geneviève lived at Chailly-en-Bière. Being so close to Paris, it was a convenient spot for landscape painting, and on one of the main routes to the south, it was often used as an overnight port of call.

In 1929 he acquired another property a little further away, the Château Parouzeau near Donnemarie-en-Montois. This was an eighteenth-century estate with a large park and good shooting and fishing, formal lawns and, eventually, a fine rose garden, the work of Alice Derain. In 1928 Derain moved his Paris studio and residence from the Rue Bonaparte to a quieter quarter which was, nevertheless, an area that housed many painters. He and Braque built houses facing each other at 5 and 6 Rue du Douanier near the Parc de Montsouris. Suzanne Géry and Geneviève then came to live in Paris with André and Alice (fig. 1), although Derain kept the house at Chailly-en-Bière for landscape painting and for the regular use of his close friends. In 1929 the painter Jean Oberlé was paralysed with polio, and Derain established him at Chailly-en-Bière with Devaux to look after him. He visited them frequently on his way to Parouzeau, often bringing them a carload of friends from Paris. Since the war, Derain had been an enthusiast for fast cars, and now he owned a large Renault and a racing Bugatti in which to roar from Paris to his country homes in record time.

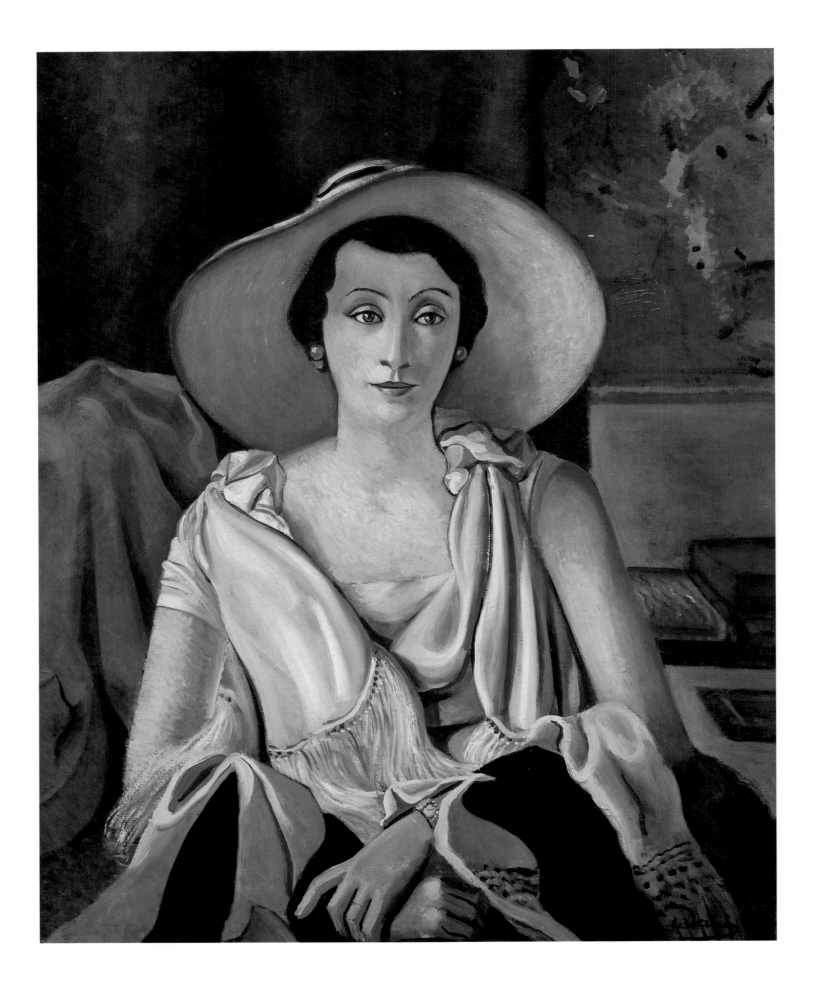

THE PAINTINGS OF THE LATE 1920s

Derain's harlequins of the early 1920s were replaced by genre figures (*see* cat. 51 and 52) and by studies of ballet dancers in the late 1920s. Sobriety made way for sensuality in the still-life paintings as early as 1925, and Derain's dark canvases glisten with his fascination with the fall of light. The light still-life paintings have both the clarity of composition and the rich colour of early sixteenth-century Italian painting. The paint is liquid, the drawing rhythmic and flowing without being artificially attenuated.

The landscapes of the later 1920s are deceptively simple. The space is coherent, without straining to impose a structure on the composition. The light, the atmosphere, is recognizable without any attendance to the rigour of a momentary vision. The forms swell and establish themselves in rhythmic progression. It is painting of delight without puerility, of sensuality without sentiment.

Derain's portraits also reflected this sensuality. The *Portrait of Madame Guillaume* (fig. 47) of about 1928 is one of the finest portraits of the period. Draped and posed as a Roman patrician in the manner of Ingres' portraits, Madame Guillaume is far from the severe classical matron in Derain's *Portrait of Mlle Lacaze* a few years earlier (*Les Arts à Paris,* no. 6, 1920, frontispiece). The pose is erect but slopes slightly off the vertical axis. The silhouette is drawn in a sharp angular fashion but against this plays the rhythmic flow of the drapery, the grand sweeping curve of the hat, and the smaller curves of the lips, eyes, and fashionably arched eyebrows. The columns of the neck and arms are all softened by the handling of the paint which defines the flesh. Similarly the sharp angles which divide the background and define the space in which Madame Guillaume sits are softened by the dark undulations of the velvet curtain and the frothy study for *Arlequin et Pierrot.*

In the late 1920s Derain's painting was widely considered to be of the highest achievement. The dealer René Gimpel, for instance, used it as a touchstone with which to correct his protégé Mintchine: 'I placed two of his canvases ... near my lovely Derain, a beautiful sunlit pathway in the Midi, and showed him that he hadn't yet acquired fluidity, that his shadows still lack transparency ...' (Gimpel, 1963, p. 380). This celebration by the 'connoisseurs' was inevitably accompanied by a critical backlash: 'The moment isn't far off when Derain will join Bonnat in the provincial museums ... Really, Louis Vauxcelles is the bravest among us. After the hymns of praise sung in front of André Derain's canvases, what a joy to hear an objective judgement of works which owe their fortune to nothing but an artificial accumulation of legends and mysteries' wrote Georges Charensol in *L'Art vivant* in 1929.

It had become rare to see a major Derain; they went quickly into private

47. *Portrait of Madame Guillaume,* c. 1928, Musée de l'Orangerie, Paris, Collection Jean Walther and Paul Guillaume.

collections. In June 1929, however, Paul Guillaume put his own collection on show in the Galerie Bernheim Jeune. The exhibition opened with an address by Albert Sarraut, the Minister for the Colonies, who four years later became the Président du Conseil. The most influential of all Paul Guillaume's ministerial and diplomatic friends and clients, Sarraut not only had Derain's paintings in his own collection but knew the painter as an expert collector of African and Far Eastern art. This exposure of some of Derain's finest pictures of the preceding decade sparked off an increase in critical commentary on Derain which Guillaume seems to have sustained by increasing the number of Derain canvases on display in his gallery in 1929 and 1930. In January 1929 in *Les Arts à Paris* he had announced a Derain album, then in preparation, which would include about 400 fine photographic reproductions of Derain's works. It was perhaps a victim of the stock-market crash, and the remnants of this project are now in a private collection in Paris. A much more modest album was produced in that year, not by Guillaume but by the *Librairie de France* as one of the series *Les Albums d'art Druet*.

There were major Derain exhibitions abroad at this time. Alfred Flechtheim, in 1929, held large Derain shows in both his Berlin and his Düsseldorf galleries. In Scandinavia, a major exhibition of modern French painting which travelled between March and June 1931 to Stockholm, Oslo, Göteborg, and Copenhagen included forty-two works by Derain. In London, where in 1928 Paul Guillaume had set up a branch gallery and Knoedler had already had a one-man show, the Lefevre Gallery held an exhibition in 1931. The most important exhibitions at the turn of the decade, however, were in America. In 1928, Derain's *Still Life with Dead Game* (fig. 54) won the Carnegie Prize and entered the Museum of Art in Pittsburgh. In 1929 the Phillips Collection in Washington acquired an important recent painting, *Mano the Dancer*. In April 1931 the Knoedler Gallery, New York, held a major exhibition which included important works from before the First World War, as well as paintings from the 1920s. A large part of this exhibition was seen again in December of that year, joined by works from public and private American collections, in the Derain exhibition held in the Cincinnati Art Museum. Also in 1931 the Marie Harriman Gallery in New York held the first of four important exhibitions of Derain's most recent work.

In Paris the journal *Les Chroniques du jour* published, in January 1931, (no. 8, n.s., pp. 3–14) an *enquête*, 'André Derain, Pour ou Contre'. Only about half of the writings were 'responses', and among these was an attack upon Jean Cocteau which, as Cocteau subtly indicates, had nothing to to with Derain. The rest were quotations from texts which would already have been well known to the readers. On the *contre* side, these went back to Raynal's attack of 1921. On the *pour* side to Elie Faure and André Salmon. The editor reiterated the critical balance of the beginning of the 1920s by adding Pierre Courthion to one side and Waldemar Georges to the other. For the rest, the *enquête* was simply laudatory and not serious enough to please Derain's dealer, who in the next issue of *Les Arts à Paris* published a far more extensive series of quotations (*Les Arts à Paris*, no. 18, July 1931, pp. 12–27).

There is no sign that any of these opinions was of the slightest consequence to Derain. In the late 1920s his foremost concern was with his drawing. Derain's drawings had been published early in the 1920s by Paul Westheim, Elie Faure, Robert Rey, and others and continued to appear in reproduction not only in articles about Derain but also in the growing number of studies in modern journals which concerned the history of drawing from the Renaissance. They were justly celebrated and sold as works in their own right. Derain drew also for lithographs, most notably the suite *Metamorphoses*

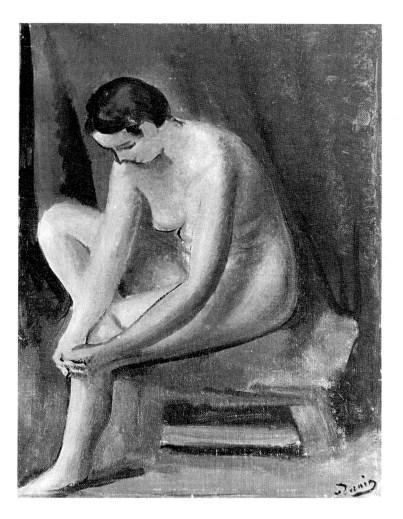

48. *Nude*, undated, National Museum of Art, Bucharest, K.H. Zambaccian Collection.

in 1927 published by *Les quatres chemins* and a suite of nudes published in the same year by H. M. Petiet (cat. 62). Derain frequently drew the landscape, but most of his drawings were of the model posed in the studio. There are several small paintings of posed models (cat. 11) which are studies, like the drawings. Derain's drawings were an essential preparation, not only for the fine paintings of nudes through the 1920s (fig. 48), but also for the large compositions of the 1930s.

Gimpel records in his diary a visit to Derain's studio in September 1928: 'Derain explained to us that, if he has so few pictures, it's because he has painted only one all winter; he has only sketched. He brought in three full boxes; always the same woman ... Why all these sketches of the model, five or six months of work ... four or five hundred studies? "To find a certain position", Derain told us, "and I haven't found it".' (Gimpel, 1963, p. 347).

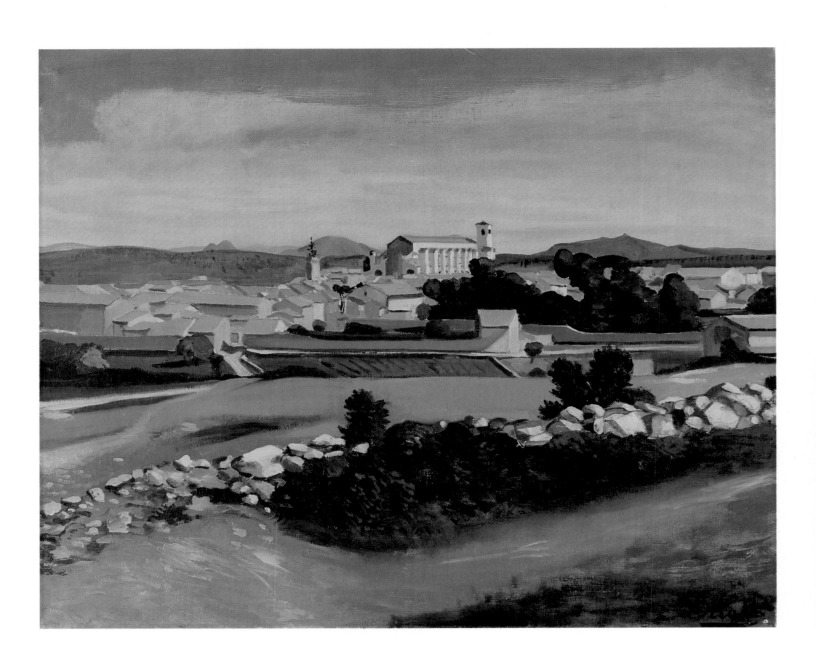

If Derain spent the winter drawing he spent the summer painting the landscape. Around 1930 Derain's landscapes became still more classically inspired, with the influence of Poussin as important as that of Corot. Among the large-scale photographs still left from Derain's studio, the greatest number are of paintings by Poussin, including details of landscape. There are also reproductions of Claude. These may well reflect the tendency which culminated in the series of views at Saint Maximin in the summer of 1931 (fig. 49). Derain wandered far in his Bugatti, and not all of his landscape motifs of the time are as easy to identify, but there is a renewed interest in the 'antique' south which corresponds to the changes in his reading and his collecting in the 1930s.

By 1930 Derain had formed a large collection of paintings, sculpture, other objects of art, and curiosities which he housed in his two country homes, as well as in Paris (fig. 52). When he died in 1954, there were three sales at auction to break up his collection and another sale of his rare books. In the early 1930s he began to sell some of his African sculptures and to acquire Renaissance and antique bronzes. This was a refinement – he kept the best African pieces – but also a sign that after the crash he could not go on buying without selling. He bought a large number of archaic terracottas from the Mediterranean and bronzes from China and the Near East.

He acquired paintings, among them three small Renoirs which he had taken from Jean Renoir in 1923 in payment for a portrait of his wife Catherine Hessling. He owned five Corot oils, including a *Portrait of Madame Puyparlier* which he seems to have acquired in the early 1920s. The other Corots are landscapes, and one at least was not in Derain's collection until after 1929, as it belonged to Pierre Rosenberg at that date. His collection contained a small Cézanne painting and several drawings, and he also owned drawings by Ingres and Seurat, as well as by his contemporaries.

Among his old master paintings was an early copy of Hieronymus Bosch's *Garden of Delights,* a fitting piece for a collector with Derain's reputation for arcane knowledge and, according to Jean Oberlé, already in Derain's collection in the 1920s. Most significant for his own painting, however, were the works in his collection by two great still-life painters, the early seventeenth-century Flemish painter Clara Peeters (fig. 50) and the late sixteenth-century Dutch painter Joachim Beuckelaer. The choice of these two pictures, the most distinguished in his collection, is telling of Derain's intentions in his own still-life painting. The Peeters canvas is a characteristic *mono-chrome banketje,* a particular type of Dutch still life in which the palette is reduced almost to black and white. The subject of this subtle genre of still life is the metaphysics of light. No other type of painting was so direct an exponent of the metaphysics of the

49. *Vue de Saint Maximin,* 1930, Musée National d'Art Moderne, Centre Georges Pompidou, Paris (cat. 37).

turn of the sixteenth and seventeenth centuries, and Derain took up the tradition in his 'black' still lifes of the mid-1930s (*see* cat. 30).

Joachim Beuckelaer represents a different tradition in which rough, almost brutal kitchen or market scenes, with their several obtrusive still lifes, are replete with symbols often derived from the emblem books of the sixteenth century. Continuing the tradition of his uncle and mentor Pieter Aertsen, whose *Fish Market,* for example, unites the cut and bleeding fish in the foreground with the Flagellation of Christ in the background, Beuckelaer's paintings often refer to sacrifice. It is a tradition which confronts *vénérie* in all its meanings and treats human carnality in an essentially Christian manner as a demand for sacrifice. The blood sacrifice of Derain's *Nature morte au lièvre* is informed by this tradition (fig. 51). The prominent display not only of the body of the creature but, separately, of the offal and the blood gives the still life a sacrificial nature, and the presence of the bread and wine on the same table increases its connection with the eucharist.

Many of Derain's interests as a collector, particularly as a collector of archaic terracottas, are reflected in his notes and poems. In the 1930s Derain had a wide interest in myths, legends, and rituals which centred on the essential identity of the great mythic cycles. He studied the similarities among religions, both etymological, as in the list he made of Ram ... Ramses, Abram, Hiram ... etc., and doctrinal, as in his study of the Osiris – Bacchus – Christ resurrection myths which includes Arthur and Charlemagne. Myths of the Mediterranean world, extending to India as it did under Alexander, were written out at length. Judaism was of particular interest to him. Jewish spirituality was for Derain an integral part of the classical world and a kind of Orphism, which knew the voluptuousness of forbidden words and was essentially a cult of Dionysus, whose name must not be spoken.

Neither Derain's interest in nor his attitude toward these things was unusual. The popular abridgements and several translations of J. G. Frazer's *Golden Bough* through the 1920s was only one of many spurs to the fashion for ancient cults and the tourism of archeology. In the 1930s, journals as different as the Surrealist *Minotaure* and the modish *Voyage en Grèce* (cat. 121), to both of which Derain contributed a cover drawing, fed their readers' fascination with myth and ritual. Derain was known to be learned in these things because his interest was one which had been sustained since the Montmartre days with Jacob and Apollinaire. His association of Judah and Bacchus, for example, was something to which Apollinaire had alluded as early as 1908 in 'Onirocritique'.

Derain's classical and archaic interests were bound up with the several projects of theatre décor and book illustration which he undertook in the 1930s. The notes he made on dances in the classical world, particularly erotic dances associated with fertility rituals, were for *Les Fastes,* one of the two ballets he originated and designed for Edward James' short-lived company, *Les Ballets 1933. Les Fastes* takes place at the feast of the Lupercal, and its sets, costumes, and masks were inspired by Etruscan and Greek works of art. The genie mask and Derain's drawing for the Lupercalian priest in *Les Fastes* are similar to the illustrations to *Le Satyricon,* which he made in 1933–4 (fig. 55), and the costumes of the matrons in the ballet influenced Derain's illustrations for Oscar Wilde's *Salome* in 1938. This overlapping of inspiration and design is characteristic of Derain in the 1930s. He was greatly interested in the theatre and in fine books, and his notes show the beginnings of projects which did not come to fruition. He had, for instance, another ballet to offer set on the docks of ancient Alexandria, which was never produced and which still lies among his papers.

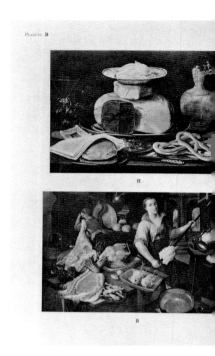

50. Page from catalogue of sale of Derain's collection, after his death, on 9 October 1955 at the Hôtel Drouot, Paris, showing paintings by Clara Peeters (top) and Joachim Beuckelaer.

51. *Nature morte au lièvre*, 1938–40, Musée National d'Art Moderne, Centre Georges Pompidou, Paris.

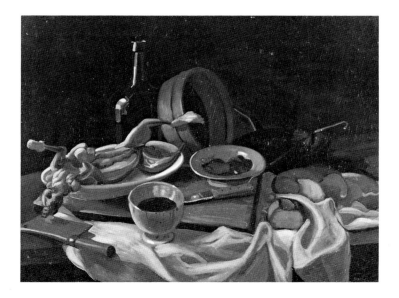

52. Sculpture from Derain's own collection, sold at the Hôtel Drouot, Paris, 9 October 1955.

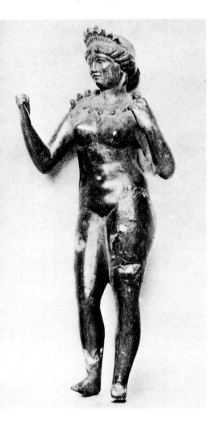

Rather than a return to Renaissance painting or antique statuary, the classicism of the 1930s was overwhelmingly a literary classicism, associated with the illustration of classical texts. Derain illustrated Petronius' *Satyricon*, Ovid's *Héroïdes* (fig. 56) and later the *Anacreonic Odes*. Braque illustrated Hesiod's *Theogeny*, Picasso Ovid's *Metamorphoses*, and Dunoyer de Segonzac the four books of Virgil's *Georgics*, to name only a few of the great projects of which Derain would have been well aware. On the whole Derain's classical interests seem to have had little direct influence on his paintings, save a few major works such as the Bacchic *L'Age d'or* (cat. 4) and *Le retour d'Ulysse* (cat. 2). One might argue, however, that Derain's classicism appears in his paintings at a more subtle level. In the later 1930s an increasing number of Derain's landscapes are green, leafy *sous bois*, and like those of Corot, increasingly peopled by dancing maenads. These works lead directly to the small Bacchanals which seem to have been done in the 1940s. According to his notes, Derain certainly intended to undertake paintings on classical themes. Among lists of titles and themes which Derain made are recognizable works such as 'les prétendants', which might be his *Le retour d'Ulysse*, and themes upon which there are surviving works such as '*la bacchanale*' (Doucet MS 6891, f. 3r). For others no painting survives. It seems, for example, that he was planning a series on the loves of Jupiter. The large paintings of nudes from the mid and later 1930s may have been started with this in mind, and the supine and abandoned postures in works such as *Nu blond couché* (cat. 14) and *Nu au chat* (cat. 15) may actually reflect poses in sixteenth- or early seventeenth-century paintings on this or a similar theme.

Many of Derain's pictures in this period, as with those of the 1920s, can be associated with either Courbet or Renoir. The association is by no means a simple one; Derain was well aware of the long history of each pose and the balance of every composition in these nineteenth-century paintings. If the two large paintings which were shown in Marie Harriman's gallery in 1938, *La surprise* (fig. 43) and *La clairière ou le déjeuner sur l'herbe* (fig. 44), were influenced by Renoir's *Baignade* in Philadelphia, they were equally influenced by the Ecole de Fontainebleau painting on which Renoir's work was based. Derain's *La surprise* shares with Renoir a Mannerist tradition of 'Diana surprised' and plays subtly with the rearrangement of the poses given by that tradition. It is the carefully deliberated painting of a connoisseur. It is in this that

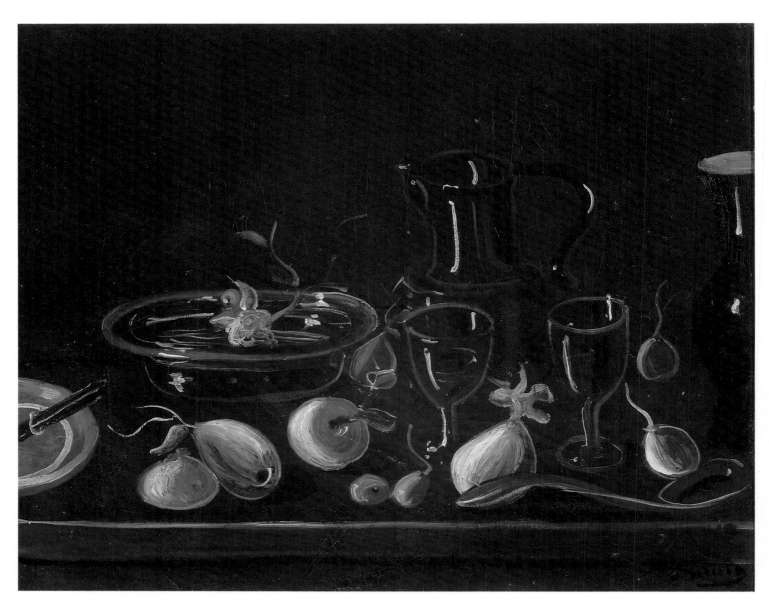

53. *Still Life With Fruit*, 1938, Stanford University Museum of Art.

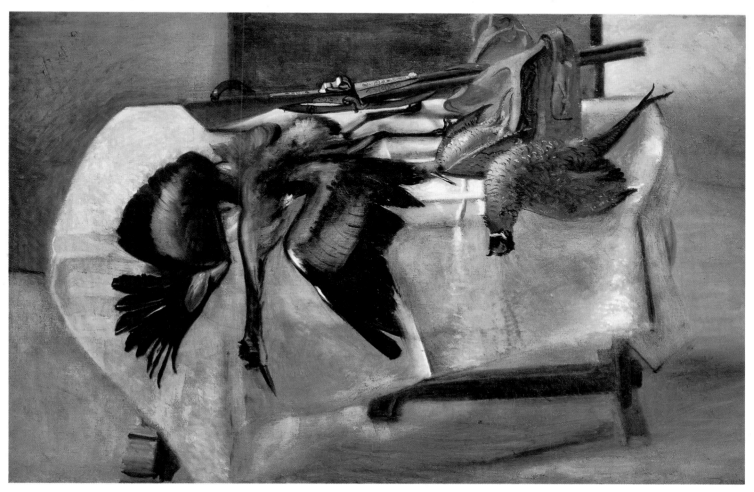

54. *Still Life with Dead Game*, 1928, Museum of Art, Carnegie Institute, Pittsburgh (cat. 24).

Derain is a member of the 'Ecole Française', where the French school is not an ideal of measure and order but a long series of subtly linked models in painting. In 1943 he wrote: 'Nothing belongs to us absolutely, neither our sensations, nor any of the data we get from nature. What then is to be obtained from a self-styled originality? It is an idea which is completely foreign to art up to the eighteenth century.' (Derain, 1943).

Derain's attitude to the union of art and tradition mirrors the contemporary attitude to myths as a language of universals: 'It is the mission of art to equalize time. And the notions of universals and of identity must be respected, so that the expression can be understood by everyone ...' There is a teleological parallel: 'Art is still and always will be the memory of generations.' Art functions in a similar way to myth – 'Art is a scale of perpetual revelations ...' – and begins with initiation – 'The museum is the initiation of the spirit' (Derain, 1943). These statements, published in the Collection Comoedia–Galerie Charpentier pamphlet of 1943, are comprehensible in the light of the traditionist paintings of the mid and late 1930s.

The statements actually published in the mid-1930s, however, reveal a side to Derain's deliberations which seems to contradict the key place of the museum. In 1935, the Communist journal *Commune* published an *enquête* asking 'Where is painting going?' René Crevel who edited the article was a Surrealist poet who much admired Derain. His introduction lauded Derain's populist ideas on art and included an interview with Derain in which he said: 'It is not for the artist to educate the people but for the people to educate the artist. It is the people who create words and give them flesh, while the poet finds them a rhythm. I have learned a lot from watching a sailor repaint his boat. The great danger for art is an excess of culture. The true artist is an uncultured man.' Derain's words are sincere. The interest in graffiti which he expresses in his interview with Crevel, for example, is supported by his records of the inscriptions made by passing soldiers on the walls of the church at Saint Maximin among his notes. His collection included ships in bottles and other objects of popular and folk arts, and he was largely sympathetic with the position which Crevel took in his *enquête*. The 'culture' to which Derain objected was the bourgeois cult of an exclusive 'canon', a canon too narrow for the needs of the artist, and this included the limiting regulations of the 'cabals' of the avant-garde. This objection coincided with Crevel's two main targets: on the one hand, the abstract painters, and on the other, the xenophobic, anti-Semitic movement which was growing rapidly in the mid-1930s. Derain was a bastion against both. His painting respected the need for 'the subject', around which socialist critics built their defence of a new realism based on the traditions of Goya and Manet. In Derain's 'pour que l'expression puisse être comprise par tous' – 'so that expression can be understood by everyone' – was the basis of their argument and in works such as *La tasse à thé* (Musée National d'Art Moderne, Paris) was a sympathetic link to the new realism. In addition Derain was a painter eminent among Jewish artists and had been a steady influence in Montparnasse for over twenty years. Derain was soon to disappoint the active Communists, however, with his bourgeois sense of the place of art and artists in the political world, refusing in 1936 to attend the conference '*La querelle du réalisme*' on the basis that lectures were not only boring but damaging to an artist.

Two young artists of this period whose admiration for Derain continued undiminished until his death were Balthus and Giacometti. Balthus was virtually a disciple of Derain, in that no other painter had as clear an influence upon his mature work, which was itself 'peinture des musées'. Giacometti was most interested in the metaphysics implied in Derain's still-life painting, in the 'power' of an object as a link between the material and the spiritual, a link made by the association of line and light,

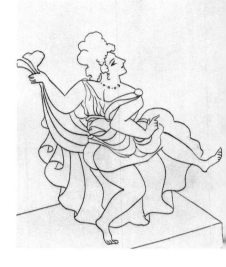

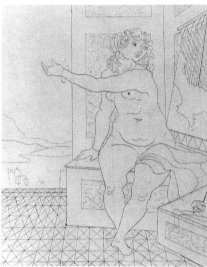

56. *Les Héroïdes*, 1938, La Bibliothèque Nationale, Paris (cat. 123).

55. (top) *Satyricon*, Musée d'Art Moderne de la Ville de Paris (cat. 122).

as in *Still Life With Fruit* (fig. 53; Stanford University Museum of Art). In an article in the Galerie Maeght journal *Derrière le miroir,* Giacometti describes his attraction to Derain beginning from the moment when he first saw a painting of three pears on a black background in a moment of sudden understanding.

The years 1935 to 1940 form a period in Derain's career which is distinguished by a large number of major still-life paintings. Some of these are influenced by the still-life paintings in his own collection, but others seem to have been inspired by the sixteenth- and seventeenth-century Italian paintings which were shown in the great exhibition at the Petit Palais in 1935 and the several gallery exhibitions which accompanied it. The greatest of Derain's still-life paintings of the period were taken to America by Pierre Matisse, where they were exhibited with many other important recent Derain paintings in 1941 to raise money for the Allied War Effort.

In 1935 Derain sold all of his property, the house he had built with Braque near the Parc de Montsouris, the house at Chailly-en-Bière, and the Château Parouzeau. He bought a large house, La Roseraie, with a pavilion and several small outbuildings at Chambourcy, less than an hour's drive from Paris. He moved to this house with Alice, her sister Suzanne, and niece Geneviève. At the top of this house was a very large, well-lit room which became his studio. At the same time he began to share the spacious studio of his friend, Léopold-Lévy, in the Rue d'Assas near the Jardin de Luxembourg. Soon afterwards Léopold-Lévy took a post in Istanbul, and although he left all his works there in storage until he returned, Derain had the studio to himself. He may have begun several of the large late works simultaneously in 1935, some in the Rue d'Assas, some in the studio at Chambourcy, as he spoke of the move in terms of the opportunity to work on large paintings. He often entertained at Chambourcy at weekends, not only old friends such as Reverdy, Braque, and Oberlé but younger men such as Balthus and Giacometti, and there is still a small copy after Masaccio by Balthus in Derain's studio. His old friend Paul Poiret lived in the area, and increasingly enfeebled with Parkinson's disease, he was frequently a guest at Chambourcy.

In 1934 Derain had sustained a terrible loss in the sudden death of his dealer Paul Guillaume. He now dealt with several galleries both in Paris and abroad. One of Guillaume's last achievements had been a major Derain exhibition in the Durand-Ruel Gallery in New York in 1933, and Marie Harriman and other New York dealers kept up a lively demand for his paintings in America. Derain's paintings were sent abroad to exhibitions repeatedly in the 1930s; he represented France in the Venice Biennales, and in 1937, during the Universal Exhibition, Derain was one of the artists to have a separate room in the Petit Palais devoted to his work. In the mid-1930s the French state and the city of Paris both acquired works by Derain.

Both of his studios were filled with canvases and drawings from the model, as well as with prints and book illustrations. In the late 1930s the lithographer Mourlot had asked Derain for a great number of large prints to be divided into three series, nudes, landscapes, and theatre décor, and at the same time Skira had commissioned him to produce 150 woodblock prints to illustrate Rabelais' *Pantagruel* (cat. 124). When war was declared, Derain was hard pressed to protect his work and his collection, as well as his family. In 1939 he arranged for his sister-in-law and his niece to move to his wife's cousin's house at Castillon en Cousserau in the Pyrenees, accompanied by his old friend, André Utter. Derain also moved most of his collection to this house, where it survived the war. Derain and Alice returned to Paris and did not leave until the general exodus in 1940, when they went to the Free Zone. Derain was sixty years old, Alice was fifty-six, and they had many friends in Paris who needed their help.

57. Derain in his studio with his papers, early 1940s, Private collection.

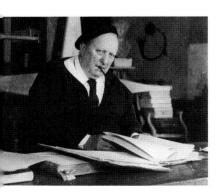

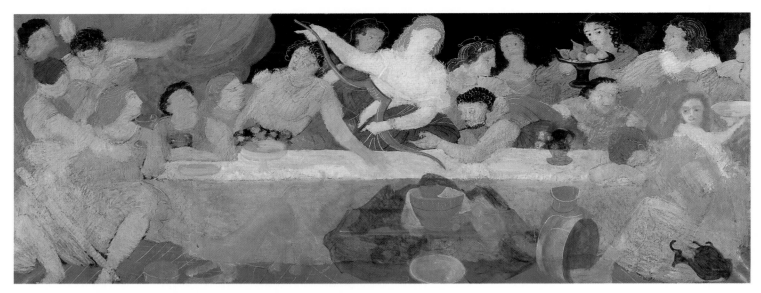

58. *Le retour d'Ulysse*, after 1935, Musée National d'Art Moderne, Centre Georges Pompidou, Paris (cat. 2).

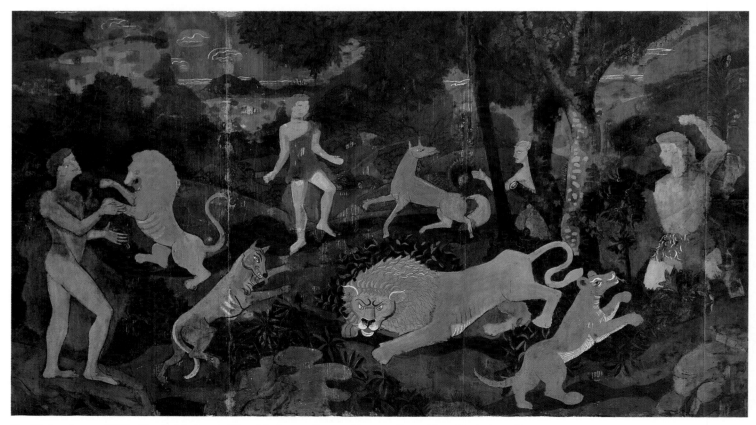

59. *L'Age d'or*, c. 1939, Musée National d'Art Moderne, Centre Georges Pompidou, Paris (cat. 4).

60. (opposite) *La chasse au cerf*, c. 1935, Musée d'Art Moderne de la Ville de Troyes, Donation Denise and Pierre Lévy (cat. 3).

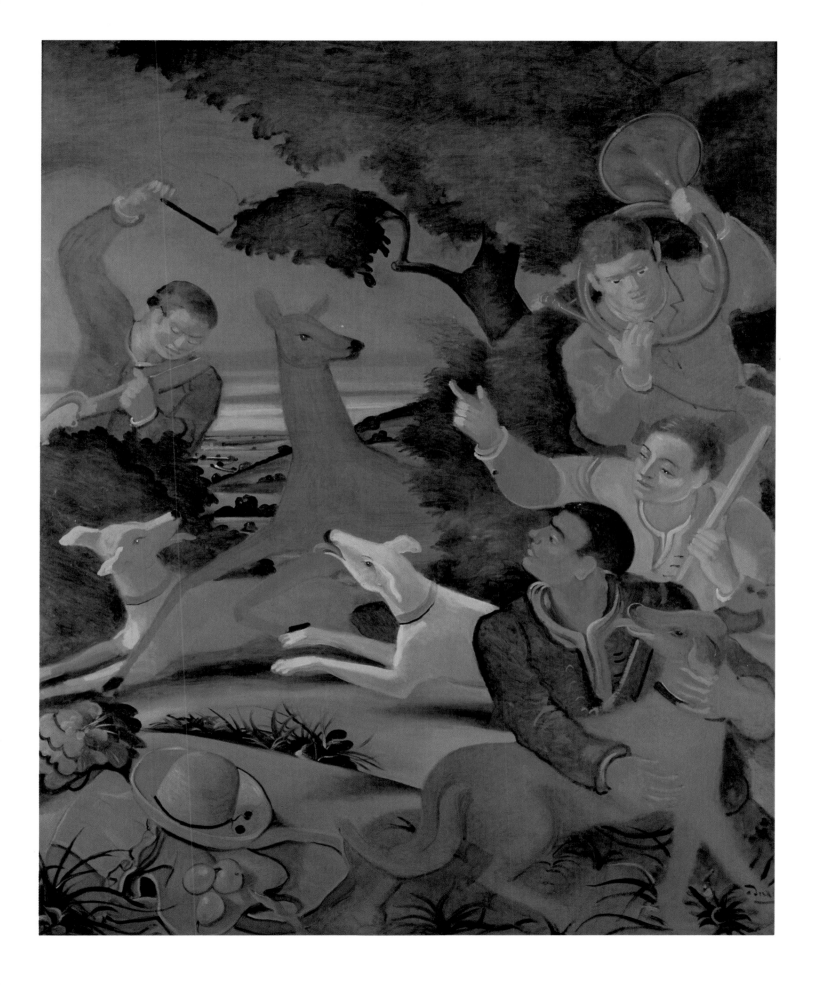

THE SECOND WORLD WAR

At the end of October 1940 Derain returned to Chambourcy to find his house in a shambles and occupied by German soldiers. The villagers told him that the Germans were going to shoot him, that they had said he was a Jew, and that they had found obscene drawings in his house representing Hitler. The local baker gave Derain lodgings in his house. By November, seventy soldiers were billeted in Derain's house, and troops were to move in and out of it throughout the war, doing untold damage and destroying a great deal of his work. Derain, who had always been a cinema addict, had made several short films, some with Georges Braque, and all of these were destroyed. At the beginning, the Germans left him two rooms, one in which to put his valuables and one in which to work. The woodblocks, tools, and paper of his half-finished *Pantagruel* were in the library, one of the rooms which he was allowed, but it was impossible to work there, and he left to stay with friends in Paris. A month later, he heard that the Germans had gone. He and Alice attempted to return to their house but were brutally evicted by machine-gunners and had no other choice now but to live in the studio rooms in the Rue d'Assas where there were no facilities. Eventually, a friend found them an apartment which they rented from a Jewish woman who had escaped to the Free Zone.

Around 20 December 1940 Derain was called in for interrogation by the Gestapo. He was asked first if he was Jewish and secondly if he was the one who wanted to accuse the German Army of theft and vandalism in his house. He answered that he could make no precise accusations, as several different detachments of the German Armed Forces had occupied his house in the last six months and that it was widely known that he was not a Jew. A few days later a German came to his studio in Rue d'Assas, asking to see his paintings. After complimenting him a great deal, the German officer said pointedly, 'We've taken your house, would you like it back?' Derain answered that it was a great nuisance that his current work was in the library, but no, he did not want to ask for it back. The German then told him that there was an artists' trip to Germany being planned for the end of May 1941, a tour of studios, museums, and art centres. Derain told him that he never travelled and that his work did not allow him to leave the studio. The German responded ironically that a trip to Germany would do him good, that it would help him relax. He heard no more of the trip until September 1941 when suddenly there arrived at his studio a woman he had employed as a model twenty years before. She had become the wife of Arno Breker, a sculptor who in the late 1920s had been a follower of Despiau and who was now a high-ranking favourite of the Nazis. She told him about the trip to Germany and that he was on the list.

A month later there were other sudden visits, and finally by mid-October the same Gestapo officer came every day both to the flat and to the studio to let Derain know how closely he was being watched. One day he simply told Derain to pack his bag. The German took his luggage and came back for him four days later. In the intervening days, when Derain knew he had no recourse but to go and hope he would come back, he moved the work of his friend Léopold-Lévy, as he suspected that while he was away the Germans would enter his studio and destroy it. He also contacted his friend Constant-Lebreton who was an organizer of the appeals to the Germans for the release of French prisoners of war. Derain took with him on the trip four typewritten copies of two lists, one of the members of the Société des Indépendants who were imprisoned in Germany and the other of the youngest students at the Ecole des Beaux Arts who had been captured. The idea was to give the lists to artists in Germany and ask them to see to the welfare of their fellow artists – nothing more, nothing less. Even this, however, was quixotic in the circumstances. To the Germans, Derain's only function was to smile for the newsreel cameras under the eye of the ever-present Gestapo officers. The journey was hard, cold, and annoying, with a great deal of time spent waiting in hotel rooms. There is no doubt that the danger he was in traumatized Derain. When he returned, he attempted to dispel the trauma with his café-table humour. He quickly received a warning from the Gestapo, however, to stem his boyish jokes about the testicles on Breker's gigantic sculptures.

Derain managed to work during the war despite the privations, interruptions, and shortages of material. He finished his Rabelais illustrations. Skira published *Pantagruel* in Switzerland in 1943 and, as a series of modern colour woodcut prints, it has yet to be equalled. He also continued his large paintings, such as *La grande bacchanale noire* (fig. 67). In 1943, when food was short in Paris and there were frequent rumours of bomb attacks, he and Alice stayed for a while in Donnemarie en Montois, near the Château Parouzeau where they still had friends. Here Derain painted the landscape and made several drawings.

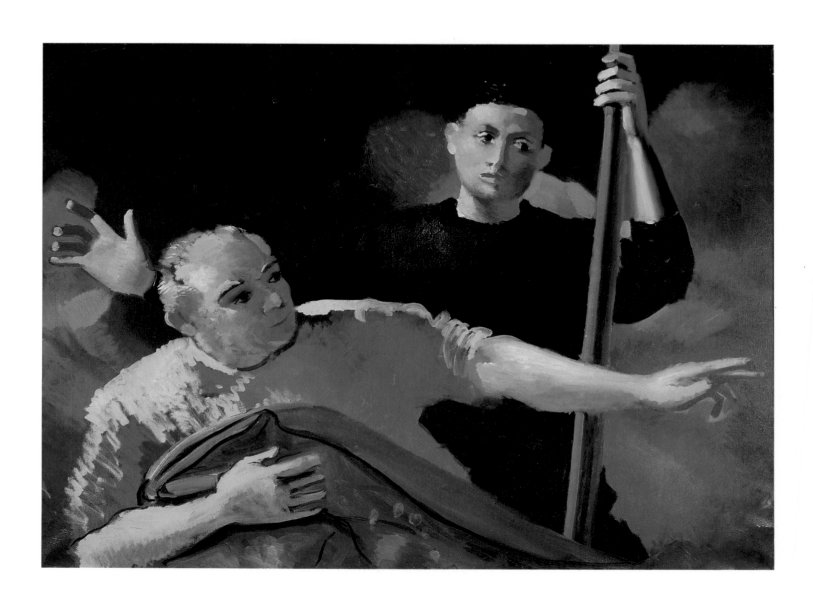

It was not until the end of 1944, however, that Derain regained the house at Chambourcy, and even then the troubles of war were not over. On the basis of the trip to Germany, he was accused of collaboration. Malicious rumours soon grew of portrait commissions from German officers and exhibitions and sales of paintings in Germany, all of which were entirely unfounded and quickly dismissed by the 'Purification' committee which considered Derain's case. Derain did not put a single painting into German hands. To the young socialist artists who had been his admirers before the war and to Derain's Jewish friends of many years, any suggestion of sympathy with the Germans was ridiculous. Braque publicly upbraided the scandalmongers. The committee, however, demanded a formal explanation of the trip to Germany. Derain was incensed. Everyone knew the circumstances in which he had been taken to Germany, and the Committée d'Epuration was not legally instituted but simply an *ad hoc* vigilante group, formed at the liberation before the restoration of the judiciary of the Republic. He refused to respond to the call from the committee or to answer any of his detractors. When the Cour de Justice of the restored Republic did not condemn the activities of the Committée d'Epuration, Derain condemned the government. Although he shrugged off any suggestion that he was embittered by the insults after the war, he refused henceforth to have any dealings with the French government. Not only would he not give or sell his work to the nation or cooperate in exhibitions, but he would have no dealings with a government official. When the renowned art historian, Jean Adhémar, wanted to write a monograph on Derain, he was turned away because he was a curator of Prints and Drawings in the Bibliothèque Nationale. When a government minister attempted to buy a picture in a commercial gallery for his private collection, Derain had it removed from the exhibition, with the explanation that it already belonged to another collector, and gave it to Pierre Lévy. Lévy, who was a friend as well as a collector, had special sway with Derain, and in 1954 the painter allowed him to lend *Nature morte sur fond noir* (cat. 30) to the Venice Biennale.

Derain led a quieter life than he had done before the war. He gave up the studio in the Rue d'Assas in 1947 and retired to Chambourcy. Raymonde Knaubliche, his friend and the model for several paintings of the 1930s, had borne him a son in 1941, named André after his father but always known as 'Bobi'. Raymonde and Bobi lived at Chambourcy with André and Alice Derain, and Suzanne and Geneviève and her family lived in the pavilion across the courtyard. Old friends were again frequent guests at La Rosarie, and the Derains often met the Braques in Dieppe and travelled to their house in Varangeville.

61. *Two Men*, c. 1935, Santa Barbara Museum of Art, Wright Ludington Collection.

Some distance from the house, standing in its own fields, was the largest of the outhouses which just before the war Derain had converted into a studio for sculpture. In 1938 lightning had struck one of the trees in the garden, and when it was uprooted, it had revealed a deposit of fine red clay. From this time Derain did a great deal of clay modelling, returning to it after the war. When the red clay was exhausted, the whole family prospected for more. Derain continued to use clays which he had discovered. Among his notes is a list of good clay deposits at his landscape painting sites and along the road to Poissy. The characteristics of each type of clay are described. There are simple coded recipes for their mixture with kaolin and other clays and notes of the results of his firing experiments (Doucet MS 6898). Many of his terracottas are glazed in one or two colours, and there is such a subtle variety in the colour and quality of the clay that he probably envisaged this as the finished work. In order that a substantial part of this work would survive, however, the Swiss publisher Pierre Cailler had seventy-four pieces cast in bronze in 1961. Many of the pieces were very delicate, little more than baked mud, and the few of them that were left, Cailler wisely left aside. Several of these terracottas are now in public collections in France and Switzerland. Most of the sculptures are small plaques with figures or faces on them, but there are many larger works, including several masks or slightly conical heads. They are influenced by archaic terracottas and metalwork from the Mediterranean and Near East and by the art of ancient Gaul. Many are influenced by the same nineteenth-century book of Gallic coins that Derain used as the basis of his illustrations to Antonin Artaud's *Héliogabale* in 1934. It is likely that Derain's plaques with Gallic heads were inspired by Picasso's plaster reliefs of heads, photographed by Brassai and reproduced in *Minotaure* in 1933. Giacometti had certainly been impressed by these works of Picasso's and may well have fixed Derain's attention on them. The major influence on Derain's sculpture was his own collection, including the bronzes of Luristan which he and Braque began collecting in the early 1930s.

Around 1950 Derain began another series of sculptures, not modelled in clay but cut and formed directly in sheet metal. He had worked directly with metal in the First World War when he made masks from shellcases, and these very late sculptures have something in common with those wartime experiments. Precedents for this work exist in the sculpture of Julio González and Pablo Gargallo, although a comparison of Derain's playful pieces with the work of González is as distant as that between Derain's pedestrian poetry and the verses of his friend Pierre Reverdy. It is worth noting, however, that González is the sculptor most important to Giacometti's development. Again the material itself seems to have excited Derain to produce sculpture. When the guttering and cladding were being removed from the roof of the big house at Chambourcy during general repairs, Derain watched the workmen carrying sheets and rolls of lead and other metals past his studio window. He asked for the metal to be put in the front courtyard, and he chose the better half of it for sculpture. These works are still at Chambourcy and have rarely been exhibited. Some of them are whimsical pieces such as a delicate figure made of bits of metal which has been invested with a real set of heavy keys to make it into a Saint Peter. Others are large faces or figures with 'hair' of cut and rolled metal, most of which are unfinished. When he died, Derain left a considerable body of sculpture, impressive in its imaginative conception and material facility.

Between 1947 and 1953 Derain designed the sets and costumes for four ballets and decorated several fine books. He painted constantly (fig. 64), producing many small landscapes with and without figures and occasional larger pictures, such as the late *Still*

Life in the Maeght collection (cat. 32) or the *Portrait of Denise and Claire Lévy* now in the Musée d'Art Moderne de la Ville de Troyes. He drew regularly from the model, and his late drawings are strong, deft, and full of his undiminished fascination with his art. His health had begun to fail by 1953, and he passed that winter with severe bronchitis. Weakened by this illness, he had a tendency to sudden spells of feebleness. One day in August 1954 his car gave him some trouble not far from his house, and as he went to lift the bonnet, he staggered into the path of an oncoming car. He died nearly three weeks later in a hospital in Garches as a result of this accident.

Until her death Madame Derain preserved her husband's studio just as it was when he left it for the last time and then left its preservation in the charge of her niece.

The concept of a National School, an Ecole Française, which the critics of the 1920s and 1930s had painstakingly created, indirectly led to the eclipse of Derain's reputation after the Second World War. The devastation of war and the degradation of France in the occupation had changed the values and aspirations of painters and collectors. In every country which had been occupied, as well as in Germany and Italy, there grew up a new primitivism in painting, both material and thematic, which turned away from the rich and complex figurative painting of the 1930s towards an aesthetic of childlike purity and romantic individuality or an ideal abstract art. Derain remained a highly respected painter until his death, but he was conscious of the denouement of his generation. He accepted it not only with stoical grace and good humour but with a good deal of sympathy and understanding. The notorious irritability at the end of Derain's life was directed towards men like Raymond Nacenta, of the Galerie Charpentier, whose exhibitions, mixing the masters of past centuries with modern masters such as Derain, he thought misconceived and damaging. Derain saw these exhibitions as a cultification of *traditionisme* where he, and others, had seen it as a great cosmopolitanism, a universalism in which the touchstones of human achievement and of culture in the deepest sense were available to all through the museums. It was to Derain the basis of constant renewal in the arts.

Happily, over the last twenty years a growing number of painters have come to view the works of the 1920s and 1930s in Derain's own terms. It is to a great extent their demands which lead to exhibitions such as this at the Museum of Modern Art, Oxford, a situation which would have pleased the master from Chatou.

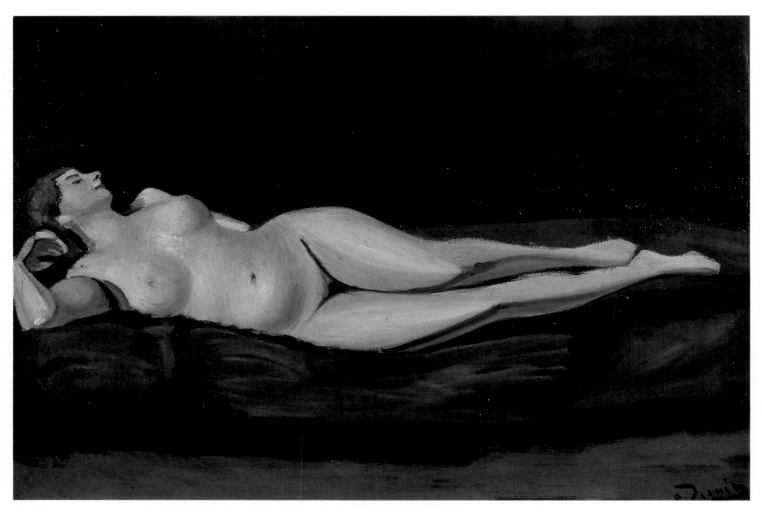

62. *Nu au canapé vert*, 1935–36, Musée d'Art Moderne de la Ville de Paris (cat. 13).

63. (opposite) *Nu à la pomme*, c. 1941, Ryoko Company Ltd, Tokyo, Japan (cat. 18).

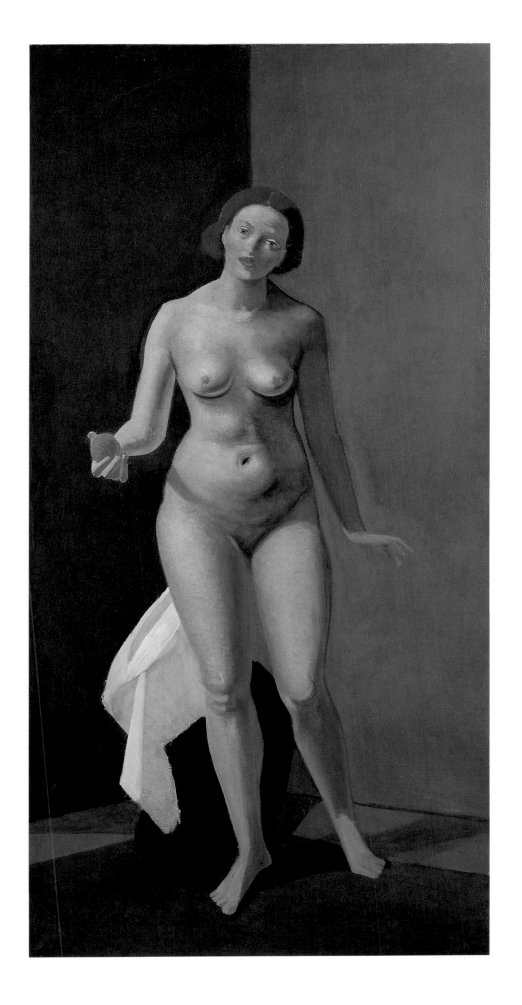

SELECTED ONE-MAN EXHIBITIONS

1916   Paris, Galerie Paul Guillaume, October (catalogue includes a preface by Guillaume Apollinaire and poems by Apollinaire, Divoire, Reverdy, Cendrars, and Jacob)

1917   New York, Modern Gallery, November

1922   Berlin, Flechtheim Gallery, October

1922   Munich, Thannhauser Gallery, December 1922–January 1923

1922   New York, Brummer Gallery (catalogue preface by J. Brummer)

1922   Stockholm, Svensk-Franska Konstgalleriet, September

1927   Düsseldorf, Flechtheim Gallery

1928   London, Lefevre Gallery (preface by Etienne Bignou), March

1929   Berlin, Flechtheim Gallery, November

1929   Düsseldorf, Flechtheim Gallery, November

1930   Cincinnati, Cincinnati Art Museum, 'An Exhibition of Paintings by André Derain', December 1930–January 1931

1930   New York, Knoedler Gallery, 'Works by Derain' (preface by Etienne Bignou, as in 1928 Lefevre Gallery), April

1931   London, Lefevre Gallery, 'New Paintings by Derain'

1931   New York, Marie Harriman Gallery, 'Nine New Landscapes by A. Derain', March

1933   London, Arthur Tooth and Sons, 'An Exhibition of Recent Paintings by André Derain', November–December

1933   New York, Durand-Ruel Galleries, (catalogue preface by Waldemar Georges), February–March

1933   Paris, Galerie aux Quatres Chemins, May

1934   New York, Marie Harriman Gallery, 'Watercolours and Drawings by Derain', March–April

1935   Basle, Kunsthalle, June

1935   Berne, Kunsthalle, July–August

1935   London, Thos. Agnew and Sons, 'New Pictures by Derain'

1935   Paris, Galerie Renou et Colle, May

1935   Stockholm, Svensk-Franska Konstgalleriet, February

1936a New York, Marie Harriman Gallery, 'Lithographs and Etchings by André Derain', January

1936b New York, Brummer Gallery (catalogue preface includes texts by Apollinaire, Clive Bell, Jean Cassou, and T. W. Earp), November 1936–January 1937

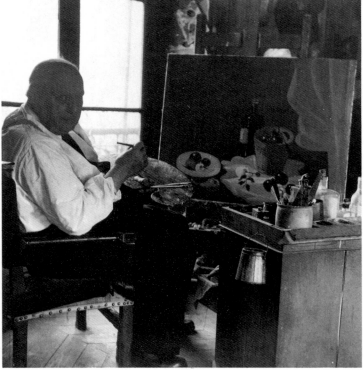

64. Derain seated in his studio, 1952, Private collection.

1937   London, Reid and Lefevre Gallery

1938   New York, Marie Harriman Gallery, 'Two New Derains', November–December

1939   New York, Lilienfeld Galleries, February–March

1939   New York, French Art Galleries, 'Derain Drawings', April–May

1940   New York, Pierre Matisse Gallery, 'Derain Paintings From 1938 and After', April–May

1944   New York, Pierre Matisse Gallery, January

1947   Chicago, The Arts Club of Chicago, January

1949   Paris, Galerie de Berri, 'Hommage à Derain', March

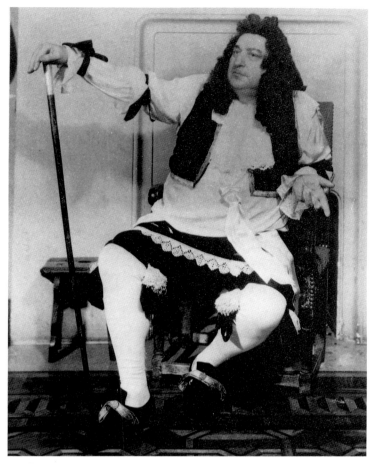

65. Derain in fancy dress as Louis XIV, 1925, Private collection.

1954   Paris, Musée National d'Art Moderne (catalogue preface by J. Cassou), December 1954–January 1955

1955   Geneva, Galerie Motte, October–November

1955   Lausanne, Galerie Paul Vallotton, September–October (catalogue preface by V. Photiades)

1955a   Paris, Bibliothèque Nationale (catalogue preface by Julien Cain, 'Derain Peintre-Graveur' by Jean Vallery-Radot, Catalogue by Jean Adhémar)

1955b   Paris, Galerie Charpentier, 'Cinquante tableaux importants d'André Derain', May–September

1955c   Paris, Galerie Jeanne Castel, July (catalogue preface by Georges Hilaire)

1955d   Paris, Salon d'Automne (catalogue preface by André Dunoyer de Segonzac)

1955   São Paolo, Museu d'Arte Moderne, Second Biennale (Derain retrospective)

1957   London, Wildenstein Gallery (catalogue and preface by Denys Sutton), April–May

1957   Paris, Galerie Maeght, 'Dessins de Derain' (catalogue preface includes a text by Alberto Giacometti), March

1958   Asnières, Salon d'Asnières, 'Hommage à Derain' (texts by André Salmon and Florent Fels)

1958   Paris, Galerie Maeght

1959   Geneva, Musée de l'Athénée, July–October (text by Apollinaire)

1959   New York, Charles E. Slatkin Gallery, 'Sculptures by André Derain', October–November

1961   Houston, Houston Museum of Fine Art, 'Derain Before 1915', November–January

1962   Paris, Galerie Bellechasse, 'André Derain Sculpteur', June–October

1963   New York, Museum of Modern Art, 'André Derain in the Museum Collection', June–September

1964   Marseilles, Musée Cantini (catalogue preface by Frank Elgar), June–September

1964   New York, Hirschl and Adler Galleries (catalogue preface by Jean Bouret), October–November

1967   Edinburgh, Royal Scottish Academy, August–September (catalogue preface by J. Leymarie, texts by Apollinaire, Breton, and Giacometti)

1967   London, Royal Academy, October–November (as above)

1971   Paris, Galerie Knoedler, June–July

1973   Cologne, Baukunst (Drawings exhibition), November–February

1974   Albi, Musée Toulouse-Lautrec, 'Derain connu et inconnu' (catalogue preface by Claude Roger-Marx and Gaston Diehl), June–September

1975   Lausanne, Galerie Paul Vallotton, June–September

1976   Paris, Galerie Schmit (catalogue preface by J. Bouret), May–June

1976   Rome, Villa Medici (catalogue preface by J. Leymarie), November 1976–January 1977

1977   Paris, Grand Palais (as above), February–April

1980   Paris, Musée d'Art Moderne de la Ville de Paris, 'Hommage à André Derain', December 1980–March 1981

1981   Marcq-en-Baroeul, Septention Fondation Anne et Albert Prouvost, October–January 1982

1981   Tokyo, Osaka, Kyoto, Takashimaya Art Gallery, (catalogue preface by Denys Sutton), April–June

1981   Nagoya, Nagoya City Museum (as above), June–July

1982   Regina, Norman Mackenzie Art Gallery, University of Regina, 'André Derain in North American Collections' (catalogue and introductory essays by Michael Parke-Taylor), October–December

1983   Berkeley, University Art Museum, University of California at Berkeley (as above), January–March

1984   Melun (Seine et Marne), Musée de Melun (catalogue and preface by Annie-Claire Lussiez)

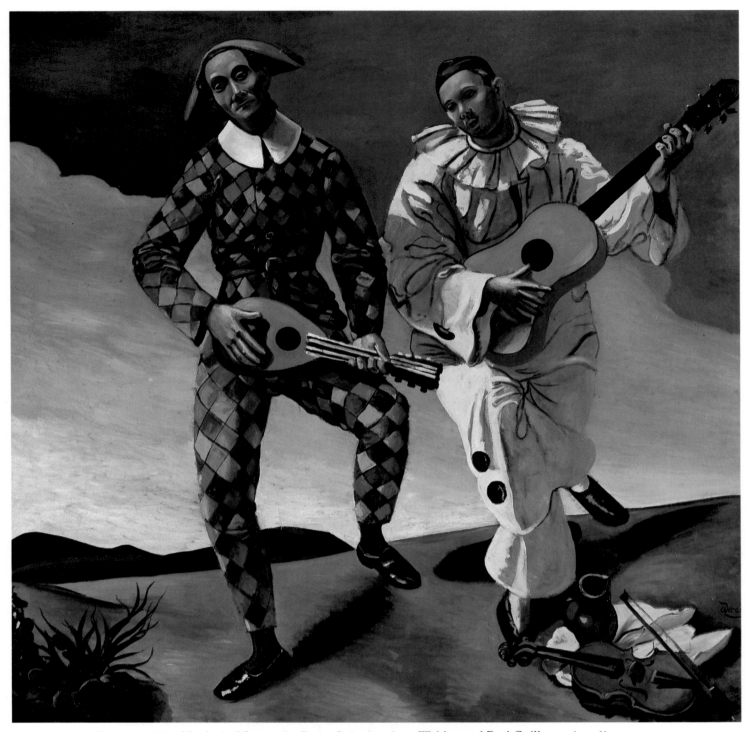

66. *Arlequin et Pierrot*, c. 1924, Musée de l'Orangerie, Paris, Collection Jean Walther and Paul Guillaume (cat. 1).

PAINTINGS

LARGE WORKS

1 *Arlequin et Pierrot c.*1924
oil on canvas 175 × 175 cm
Musée de l'Orangerie, Collection
Jean Walther et Paul Guillaume
(fig. 66)
Exhibitions: 1929, Paris,
Galerie Bernheim Jeune, 'La
Collection Particulière de M.
Paul Guillaume'; 1935,
Paris, *Les Expositions des
Beaux Arts et de la Gazette
des Beaux Arts*, 'Les Etapes
de l'Art Contemporain'
(49); 1954, Paris (51); 1966,
Paris, Musée de l'Orangerie,
'Collection Jean Walther –
Paul Guillaume' (69); 1972,
Paris, Galerie René Drouet,
'André Derain' (57); 1976,
Rome (36); 1980, Paris,
Musée National de l'Art
Moderne, 'Les Realismes'

This work is thought to have
been commissioned by Paul
Guillaume, and it never left his
private collection. It can be seen
hanging in the dealer's
apartment in the photographs
published in *Cahiers d'art* in
1927. It appears also to be the
painting behind Madame
Guillaume in the great society
portrait which Derain painted
of her in the 1920s (fig. 47), a
portrait which Derain seems at
least to have started, therefore,
in the Rue Bonaparte before his
move to Rue du Douanier in
mid-1928.

In the early 1920s *commedia
dell'arte* figures appeared in the
work of many of Derain's

contemporaries. The *commedia
dell'arte* is a pathetic theatre
where the plots often hinge on
death or transformation, and the
complex relations of alchemy
are wound into the characters
and their gestures. Harlequin as
Don Mercurio, the very spirit of
alchemical change in multi-
faceted dress, appeared in
Picasso's and Juan Gris's Cubist
paintings before and
throughout the First World
War. In the 1920s the sinister
Harlequins were joined in Juan
Gris's work by mystical
Pierrots, whose Cubist
translucency referred to
Pierrot's alchemical relation to
the moon. Both Gris and
Picasso related their *commedia
dell'arte* figures to paintings by
Raphael, Bellini, and other
Renaissance masters by alluding
to Renaissance composition,
poses, and palette. It is within
this context that Derain's
Arlequin et Pierrot was painted.

There is no doubt of the
pathetic intent of this painting.
The two figures, although they
dance, look down with the sad
regard associated with paintings
of the Lamentation or the
Entombment. The painting has
often been compared to the
works of Watteau in its sad
silent reverie, but there is little
in the style of the work to
associate it directly with
Watteau, despite the fact that
Derain had made a copy after
one of Watteau's *commedia
dell'arte* paintings. The earthy
palette, the strong light, bare
landscape, and simple
composition are closer to

seventeenth-century Spanish
painting than to any French
school, and this is an influence
which can be seen in Derain's
still lifes of the period.

The most direct influence
upon Derain's treatment of the
subject, however, comes from
the early seventeenth-century
commedia dell'arte drawings and
prints by Jacques Callot,
Jacques Bellange and Johannes
de Gheyn II, an influence which
is reflected in the post-war
Harlequinade drawings of both
Derain and Picasso. The sharp
drawing and the pose of the
figures, the bare landscape, and
the individual club-shaped
shadows between the feet all
point to a source in the works of
Bellange or de Gheyn. Both of
these painters express the
nature of human life and the
inexorable dance towards death
in a far more direct manner than
Watteau. A small painting by
Derain, an oil sketch for
Arlequin et Pierrot, now in a
private collection in Britain, was
reproduced in the Paul
Guillaume Gallery journal *Les
arts à Paris* in May 1928
(vol. 15, p. 31). In this sketch the
figures overlap, and this tighter
composition is very close to a
particular drawing by de
Gheyn, one of the seventeenth-
century images published in
1924 by the historian of the
commedia dell'arte, P.-L.
Duchârtre, an author whose
works are still among the
remnants of Derain's library at
Chambourcy.

The 'Zanni' in de Gheyn's
drawing hold a grill and bellows

as though they were musical
instruments. This was the
farcical 'accompaniment' to the
silent mime which opened the
play and was meant to make
their silence a comic sign of the
impotence of the two 'Zanni'
performing. Derain's 'Zanni'
hold instruments which are
equally silent, as they have no
strings, and even the violin in
the foreground still life is
without strings. A stringed
instrument, usually a lute or a
violin, is the first image in the
most important of all emblem
books, that of Alciati, and there
it is a symbol of silence. Alciati's
verse explains that a fool will be
indistinguishable from a
learned man as long as he
refrains from playing, and the
appended text links this to
Plato's saying that one knows
the quality of a man by his
speech, as one knows an
earthenware pot by its ring
when you hit it. The still life in
the foreground brings the two
parts of the emblem together.
Even the landscape of the
Arlequin et Pierrot may be
intended to reinforce the image
of silence and not only because
it is barren, with no listening
ear. Derain, in his extensive
manuscript notes on the culture
of Europe, declares that the
races which live on the dry, hot,
intensely lit, and shadowless
plains of the south would never
have achieved language if they
had not mixed with races of the
mountainous and stormy areas
(Doucet MS 6889, f. 38r).

Derain was always conscious
of the difference between his

own art and that of the poets who were his closest friends, and this may explain his meditation on silence in this painting. All of the musicians in Derain's paintings in the 1920s, the Harlequins and the 'gypsy' figures which follow them, hold stringless and silent instruments. The speechless impotence of the *Arlequin et Pierrot*, however, may be an extension of the dance-of-death imagery into an image of death as the failure to live, to live fully and well. This consideration takes on some importance when the painting is seen as a portrait, and indeed Pierrot seems to be a portrait of Paul Guillaume (*see* fig. 36).

It is well known that in the early 1920s Derain and Picasso both employed a Spanish painter, Jacinto Salvado, to model for them dressed as Harlequin. Derain's *Arlequin à la guitare* in the Orangerie collection, his *Arlequin à la mandoline* in the Statensmuseum in Copenhagen, and his half-length *Arlequin* in the National Gallery in Washington all have the features of Salvado. It is likely that, as Georges Charensol remembered, Salvado also posed for the figures in *Arlequin et Pierrot* (Charensol, 1955, p. 15). Neither the tight-skinned, bony face of Harlequin nor the spherical head and puffy, round face of Pierrot, however, correspond to the features of the Spanish model.

2 *Le retour d'Ulysse* after 1935
oil on canvas 151 × 393 cm
Musée National d'Art
    Moderne, Paris (AM 1982–
    252) (fig. 58)
Provenance: donation of
    Madame Alice Derain
Exhibitions: 1955b, Paris
    (25); 1974, Albi (25)
Bibliography: Parke-Taylor,

Regina exh.cat. 1982, p. 26, with a photograph of Derain in front of this work in his studio at Chambourcy.

Surrounded by the decadent, feasting pretenders to her husband's position and palace, Penelope brandishes Ulysses' bow, dares each of them to string it and shoot straight through iron targets to win her hand or, if defeated in this test, to leave the palace.

This work was left in the studio at Chambourcy during the Occupation, and when Derain's house was taken as a billet, the painting was badly damaged. There are several bullet holes in the work which have been skilfully restored, the whole painting having also been cleaned and relined after the war. The muted tone is due to Derain's painting over a dark matt ground, the 'sunken' colour bringing to mind wall painting. Over the paint Derain has drawn lightly with an oil crayon, defining the image and allowing forms to emerge distinctly from the dark background, or from areas of blocked-in colour. This alludes to 'Pompeian' style in the same manner as Derain's contemporary illustrations to *Salome*. Although the paint seems fresh and thin, there are areas which have been considerably repainted, in particular the bottom centre where the loose still life of vessels and drapery only just conceals the goat which preceded it. The goat would have located the scene more precisely in Homer's poem as the moment at which a goat was brought in amongst the pretenders as a sacrifice to Apollo, the archer god, before their contest should begin. The cat with a dish at Antinous' feet is not from the Homeric text but is a symbol from sixteenth-

century emblem books of the combination of lust and greed which corrupts marriage, a fitting attribute to Antinous, the boldest of Penelope's suitors.

It is likely that Derain had in mind the greatest of the decorations for the Royal Palace at Fontainebleau, the series of paintings, *Les Travaux d'Ulysse* (1541 to 1570) by Primaticcio and Niccolò dell'Abbate which survive only in painted copies and engravings. The series of prints by Theodore van Thulden, with moralizing captions in French, is a source of mannerist style not only for *Le retour d'Ulysse* but also for the illustrations to *Les Héroïdes* (fig. 56) and for drawings of the same period, such as the blue ink sketch of *Diane* (cat. 104). The expressively gesturing figures, the lyrical drawing, and the *allégresse* of *Le retour d'Ulysse* all indicate the attraction of the Ecole de Fontainebleau. The composition of the work, however, is confined and balanced, a rigorously controlled series of responding angles across a horizontal, and is inspired not by the Ecole de Fontainebleau but by Giovanni Bassano's *Last Supper* (Galleria Borghese, Rome) a painting much admired in France in the mid-1930s when it was argued to be a source for the Le Nain brothers.

Derain intended his canvas to be seen initially as a Last Supper and, only as we approach the canvas, to have it revealed that the subject of his painting is a sacred Homeric moment rather than a biblical one. Penelope glows in a lighter tone than the other figures because this is the moment at which she is inhabited by the genius of Ulysses' patron, the goddess Minerva. Derain had been resanctifying the seemingly profane by

appropriating sacred forms since his illustrations to Max Jacob's poetry in 1912. In the 1930s this process was related to his interest in the re-integration of classical and Judeo-Christian mythology, a central element in the Humanism of the day which is amply indicated in Derain's notes. *Le retour d'Ulysse* should be compared with the illustrations for *Les Héroïdes* (of which one is Penelope at her loom). In 1947 the publisher Skira, who had recently published Derain's illustrations to Rabelais' *Pantagruel* (cat. 124), announced a forthcoming *livre d'artiste* of the *Odyssey*, to be decorated by Derain in a new technique of print-making (presumably silk screen prints), but the project did not come to fruition. The drawing *Le banquet* (cat. 107) is a study for this painting.

3 *La chasse au cerf c.*1935
oil on canvas 199 × 160 cm
Musée d'Art Moderne de la
    Ville de Troyes, Donation
    Denise et Pierre Lévy (fig. 60)
Provenance: Theo Schemp
    collection (1938); Art
    Institute of Chicago
    (Winterbotham Collection),
    de-accessioned 1957; Ian
    Woodner collection
Exhibitions: 1939, Pittsburgh,
    Carnegie Institute, '1939
    Carnegie Institute
    International
    Exhibition'; 1971, Paris
    (15); 1976, Paris (43); 1977,
    Troyes, Hôtel de Ville,
    'Donation Pierre Lévy' (30
    bis)

The source of this work is in eighteenth-century French hunting pictures. The overall composition is based upon Desportes' *Self-Portrait as a Hunter* in the Louvre (*see also* cat. 55), and the central element of the stag worried by the hounds is taken from Jean Baptiste Oudry's great *Stag*

Hunt in the Royal Castle, Stockholm. Derain's interest in such painting is evident as early as 1915 in the large painting *The Artist's Dog* (fig. 33), now in the Musée d'Art Moderne de la Ville de Troyes, a heroic canine portrait like Desportes's paintings of the king's hunting dogs (*see* fig. 87). The decorative stylization of the dog in the work of 1915 is comparable to that of the deer and the dogs in *La chasse au cerf*, as is the landscape, particularly that in the farthest plane. Another likely source for *La chasse au cerf* is Gainsborough's large 'fancy picture', *Two Shepherd Boys with Dogs Fighting* (Kenwood House, London), which Derain may have seen on one of his several trips to England or may have known from the Henry Birche mezzotint or from photographs.

Although the work is of a specific eighteenth-century type, the clarity of the drawing and the stark contrasts in the lighting of the scene reveal Derain's current interest in Italian painting of the early seventeenth century. *Two Men* (fig. 61), a late Renaissance painting now in the Wright Ludington collection in Santa Barbara, is related to both *La chasse au cerf* and to the figures in *Le retour d'Ulysse* (fig. 58) and confirms Derain's interest in the paintings of late Renaissance and baroque masters.

La chasse au cerf is also the culmination of a particular quality in Derain's work which was first announced by Jacques-Emile Blanche in 1919 in his analysis of modern French painting in the *Revue de France*. Blanche held that Derain would develop into a great 'décorateur', by which he did not mean simply a painter of decorations but one who would attempt complex and striking compositions on a large scale; these would be so well drawn and composed that they could easily be read over a great distance and would be dominating works like those of the Baroque age.

It is likely that Derain made several drawings for this composition, and the series of tumbling spheres through the heads of the figures on the right and the hat in the still life call to mind the drawing in Derain's *Crucifixion* etching (cat. 78). There is a drawing for this painting in the Musée d'Art Moderne de la Ville de Troyes, a sanguine of the whole composition with slight differences in the disposition of the figures and in the still life. There is also a sketch for this painting in a private collection in London (cat. 85). A tapestry was eventually made of *La chasse au cerf* at Aubusson.

4 *L'Age d'or (Paradis terrestre, la chasse)* c.1939
oil on canvas 274 × 479 cm
Musée Nationale d'Art Moderne, Paris (fig. 59)
Provenance: Madame Alice Derain (donated to the nation 1962)
Bibliography: Dorival, B., 'L'Age d'or de Derain', *Revue du Louvre*, 3, 1964

The current title of Derain's very large painting was suggested by Professor Bernard Dorival who pointed out that the subject was undoubtedly classical. To Dorival there seemed no animosity between the beasts and men, and he suggested that it is a painting of the Golden Age. The Golden Age had been a favourite theme of mural painting in France since the 1880s, and the size of Derain's work, as well as the 'sunken' tonality of the painting, suggest wall painting.

The Golden Age was often combined with Orphic or Dionysian themes in wall paintings, such as Maurice Denis' decorative panel *Bacchanale* made for the 'Tigre Royal' in Geneva, exhibited in the Salon d'Automne of 1920. In this painting a tiger rises on his hind legs and walks towards a maenad in a manner similar to the behaviour of Derain's heraldic animals.

In both composition and detail, however, Derain's painting is more closely comparable to works by Raoul Dufy on the theme, which that painter treated several times between 1911 and 1939, of *Orpheus Charming the Beasts*. Since his woodcut illustrations to Apollinaire's 'Cortège d'Orphée' in 1911, Dufy had repeatedly portrayed a figure of Orpheus, derived from classical images of Apollo, among beasts stylized in the manner of heraldic devices and late medieval tapestry decoration. The young man facing us, the central figure of Derain's composition, is similar to Dufy's figures of Orpheus and might also be compared to the archaic classical style in favour among the sculptors in Paris in the late 1920s, such as that of Pablo Gargallo's *Flute Player* of 1927 (coll. Madame Gargallo). The angles of Derain's composition are arranged around this figure; he marks the centre and the superior point of a pentangle. Derain had already used this device in his drawing of Dionysus for *Le Voyage en Grèce* (cat. 121). The pentangle is in itself a symbol of the Astral Dionysus and may well indicate that the young man is the god of Orphic religion. Comparison of this work with Derain's much smaller Bacchic work *La danse* (fig. 4) supports this identification.

There are two great moments 'of beasts and men' in the legend of Dionysus; one is that portrayed in Derain's *Le Voyage en Grèce* drawing, Dionysus attacked by sailors and protected by wild beasts. The other is that recounted dramatically by Euripides in the *Bacchae*, in which Dionysus' followers miraculously saw the unbelievers as wild beasts rather than men and joyfully set upon them, thinking that they were tearing apart lions, bears, and ravening wolves in the presence of their god. This last may be the theme of Derain's painting.

Derain had long had an interest in Dionysus/Bacchus as the centre of cycles of transformation myths and death and resurrection myths. In his manuscript notes are studies of the Osiris/Bacchus/Christ figure as the sacrificial god and of eucharistic ritual in its various forms. He identifies Dionysus with Ram and establishes him as the centre of all the pre-classical and classical divinity myths from Egypt and India through to France. As in *Le retour d'Ulysse* this painting may have a theme sacred to a religion older than Christianity.

Apart from his ballet drop curtains, there is no work of a comparable size in Derain's oeuvre, and it may have been made either to decorate his own house at Chambourcy or as a study for tapestry. It was sent to the Lambesc factories for tapestry in 1939, where the work was halted due to the war, and was finally woven at the Gobelin factories in 1965. The Gobelin tapestry is in a private collection in Paris. There are several sketches for heraldic beasts among Derain's drawings, and there is one sheet of drawings which includes a study for either the *Le Voyage en Grèce* illustration or for *L'Age d'or* itself. On this same page is an

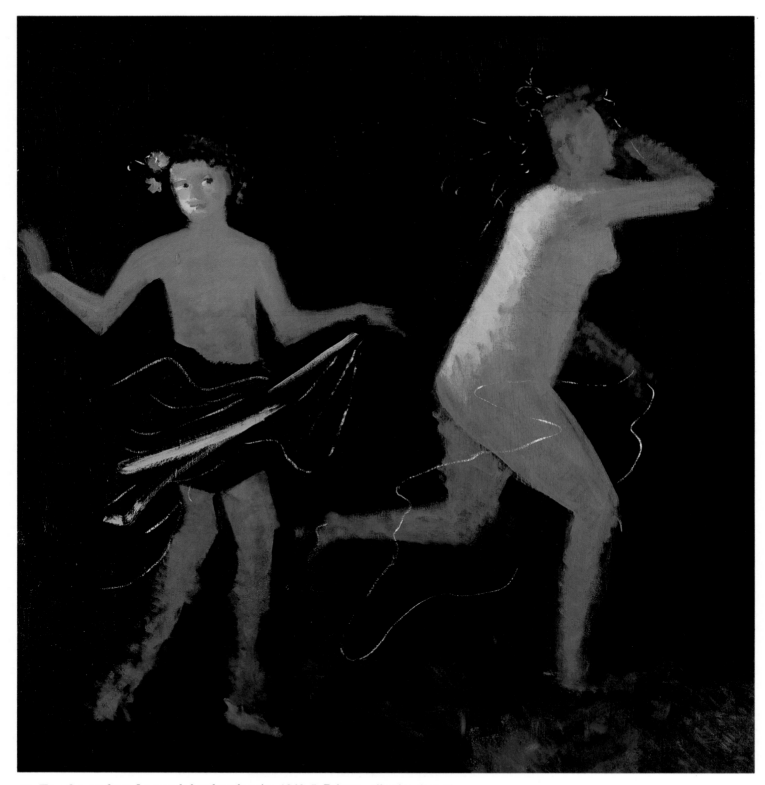

67. Two figures from *La grande bacchanale noire*, 1940–5, Private collection (cat. 5).

ink sketch of a figure after a medieval source which might be compared with the figure of Dionysus in the painting. The landscape compares with that of *La chasse au cerf* (fig. 60) but also looks ahead to the decorative landscapes of Derain's very late work after the Second World War.

5 Two figures from *La grande bacchanale noire* 1940–5
oil on canvas (dim. unknown)
Private Collection, London
(fig. 67)

This painting once formed part of a very large composition which we know from photographs in the possession of Derain's family and in the collection of the American painter Leland Bell (fig. 68). Another part of the original work, including several of the figures on the right-hand side, is now in a private collection in Japan. The history of the dismantling of Derain's picture is obscure, but it seems to have been done under Madame Derain's instructions after Derain's death, and it is unlikely, therefore, that it was intended by the artist. Photographs of different stages of the painting indicate a change in the composition, with the addition of two more life-size figures to the group on the right, making of this group a large and stable mass in contrast to the two 'free' figures on the left exhibited here.

The bravado of Derain's large picture is supported by his long experience of studio poses, realized through hundreds of drawings in the 1920s and 1930s. The figures reflect the range of Derain's life drawing, from the fluid movement of the nudes in this painting to the awkward poses of the figures in the right-hand foreground of the larger work in which Derain

stresses the pull of gravity on the heavy forms emerging from the darkness of the canvas.

The Caravaggist modelling of large nude figures in light tones against a dark background associates this painting closely with the *Deux femmes nues et nature norte* which Pierre Lévy bought just after the war, and it is likely that they are close in date. The dark background of the Lévy painting, however, is only a deeply shadowed area between the models and still life while the background of *La grande bacchanale noire* forms an extensive dark surface, on which the figures are drawn. This drawing in light on a dark ground associates *La grande bacchanale noire* with the dark still-life painting of the period and the metaphysics of light which the painter elaborated in his notes on painting (*see* cat. 30). As well as the followers of Caravaggio, Derain may have had in mind certain works of the Bassanos, who painted not only on dark backgrounds but sometimes on slate.

Before the Second World War Derain's 'bacchanale' themes were in imitation of Corot (*see* cat. 40) and an extension of his current landscape painting. After the war, however, Derain painted several small pictures of summarily drawn, dancing and gesticulating figures picked out in light tones on a dark surface which are influenced by seventeenth-century Neapolitan painting rather than by Corot. Among these studies, two which are now in the Musée d'Art Moderne de la Ville de Troyes are related to *La grande bacchanale noire*. *Les bacchantes* (fig. 69), a picture of a dark wooded glade crowded with several leaping nude figures, may directly precede *La grande bacchanale noire*, in which similar poses are assumed by the

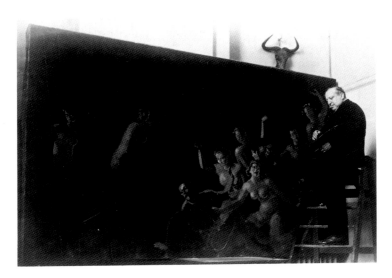

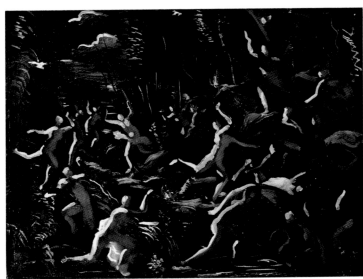

69. *Les bacchantes*, 1950, Musée d'Art Moderne de la Ville de Troyes, donation Denise et Pierre Lévy.

68. (top) Derain with *La grande bacchanale noire*, Private collection.

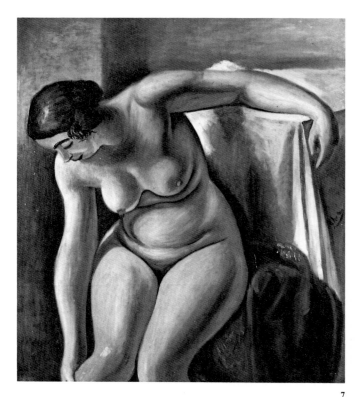

7

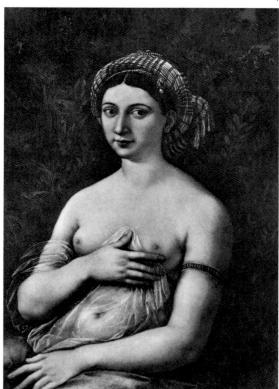

70. *Portrait of a Nude Woman* or *La Fornarina*, by Raphael, 1518, National Gallery, Palazzo Barberini, Rome.

figures. In the quick compositional sketch, *Embarquement pour Cythère*, the structure of *La grande bacchanale noire* is already clear, with the weight of the composition on the right hand side.

NUDES

6 *Nu à la cruche c.*1921–3
oil on canvas 170 × 131 cm
Paris, Musée de l'Orangerie,
    Collection Jean Walther et
    Paul Guillaume (fig. 42)
Exhibitions: 1954, Paris; 1966,
    Paris, Musée de l'Orangerie,
    'Collection Walther
    Guillaume'
Bibliography: Hoog, M., *Les
    Grandes Baigneuses de
    Picasso*, Musée de
    l'Orangerie, Paris, 1988

Nu à la cruche belongs to a particular type of nude painting done directly after the First World War. Michel Hoog refers to the monumentality in the treatment of the bather theme, which is common to this work and to works by Picasso, such as *Nu assis s'essuyant le pied*. The work by Picasso is derived, Hoog argues, from a classical Roman bronze in the Louvre, *Le Tireur d'Epine*, and from Renoir's *Eurydice*, a late seated bather in Picasso's own collection. The Renoir was inspired by Marco Dente's famous print after a lost Raphael, *Venus Wounded by a Rose's Thorn*, and this print seems also to have been the 'classical' inspiration for Derain's *Nu à la cruche*, despite the changes in the pose.

The treatment of the anatomy of the model and the heavy outline and systematic rounding of the limbs and torso are all comparable to the print.

The date of this painting is difficult to determine. A related

painting, with a very similar treatment and landscape background, was reproduced in 1925 in an article by Robert Rey, which credited it to the collection of Paul Guillaume (Rey, 1925). Drawings similar to both of these bather pictures were published in 1923 by Elie Faure, who dated them to 1920 and 1921 (Faure, 1923). Paul Guillaume had nudes by Derain in his gallery at least as early as February 1922 when Kahnweiler wrote to Derain: 'I saw your nude in the Faubourg St Honoré, at least as much as I could see it in a dark room, stunned by a bare light bulb, and I like it very much. Kindly keep it for me' (Leiris archive). Seemingly an unsuccessful request as there are no nudes among the twenty-five paintings acquired by Kahnweiler in that year.

In a preparatory etching for this painting (cat. 61) only the bather has been etched, and the landscape and jug have been added in pencil to the only remaining proof. There is also a sanguine drawing for the jug in the Kunstmuseum in Berne.

7 *Nu féminin c.*1923
oil on canvas 75 × 65 cm
signed nearly half-way up the
    right side
Musée d'Art Moderne de la
    Ville de Troyes, donation
    Denise et Pierre Lévy
Provenance: Galerie Paul
    Guillaume, Paris

In the winter months in Paris, Derain posed the model in the studio for drawing and painting nearly every day. It is difficult to date *Nu féminin* precisely, but a comparison of this picture with drawings such as those published by Elie Faure in 1923, dated 1920 and 1921 respectively, suggests a date in the early 1920s (Faure, 1923, pl. 45, 50). In the early 1920s Derain produced many paintings of nudes. These were very much in demand, as can be seen from Kahnweiler's unpublished letter to him of May 1922: 'Here is what I need, as well: nudes. They've got them everywhere – lots of them at Bernheim Jeune – except with us. Anyway, I hope you'll be able to give me some this autumn.'

Nu féminin is an example of all that the critics lauded in Derain's nudes at this time. The sober studio setting and the rhythmic swelling of the forms of the model were seen as an earthy engagement with the real, material world equal to the work of Courbet. There is also, however, a pronounced linear rhythm in this work, in the undulating silhouette of the model's right arm, the arabesque of shadow which flows across the hip and torso, and the long gentle arc of the left arm which makes the work suave and seductive. The pose, displaying the curvaceousness of the model against the hard angles of the table and studio wall, owes more to Degas than to either 'Académie' tradition or Courbet.

8 *Nu devant un rideau vert*
  *c.*1923
oil on canvas 92 × 73 cm
Musée National d'Art
  Moderne, Paris (fig. 71)
Provenance: Madame Paul
  Guillaume, 1936
Exhibitions: 1933, New York
  (17); 1955, São Paolo; 1956,
  Cavaillon, Salle des Fêtes de
  l'Hôtel de Ville; 1969–70,
  Montreal, Musée des Beaux
  Arts; 1970, Quebec City,
  Musée de Quebec; 1970–1
  Paris, Grand Palais,
  'Hommage à Christian et
  Yvonne Zervos'; 1974, Albi
  (17); 1976, Rome; 1977, Paris
  (37); 1978–9, Paris, Musée
  Jacquemart André, 'La
  Ruche et Montparnasse';

1980, Tokyo and Kyoto,
National Galleries of Japan,
'Centre Georges Pompidou,
L'art du vingtième siècle'

Here Derain paints the nude model as though she were sitting for a portrait, and *Nu devant un rideau vert* could be compared with portraits of the time, such as that of *Madame Derain* (cat. 49), as well as nude studies of the period such as the *Nu au chat* (cat. 15). The conflation of these two particular genres of painting, in its individualization rather than idealization of the model, is a tradition associated with 'realism', and it occurs frequently in the nineteenth century. It begins, however, in the Renaissance, with Raphael's portrait of *La Fornarina* (National Gallery, Rome) (fig. 70), and its popularity in the nineteenth century is due in part to Ingres' drawings and studies for *La Fornarina and Raphael* (e.g. Musée du Louvre, Paris). Derain used this tradition more than once, and, characteristically, his work reflects an interest in its history.

It is likely that a picture by Camille Corot, *Jeune femme assise, la poitrine découverte* (Private Collection, Paris) was a direct inspiration for *Nu devant un rideau vert*. In the 1920s Corot's picture was in the collection of Paul Rosenberg, from whom Derain bought a Corot landscape, and its influence can be seen in Derain's painting at a later date. The quiet reserve of Corot's picture is apparent in Derain's nude, and there are particular debts to Corot in the pose, the drawing, and the dark shadows beneath the chin and breasts. The smooth and systematic modelling of the warm, dark skin against the rich green and brown of the background seems to reflect Derain's admiration

not only for Corot but for Raphael's *La Fornarina* itself. Derain's model, however, is entirely nude, posed in the studio with a minimum of external details, and to that extent consistent with a great number of drawings and smaller studies among his works of the period.

The special quality of this picture lies in the finesse in modelling the head, the smooth 'classic' beauty of the torso, and the fine balance in the pose. The model leans slightly forward at the hips, and this potential instability is corrected by the counterpoise of the head and the supportive triangulation of the arms. To some extent Derain owes this quality to the example of the sculptor Charles Despiau. The subtle relationship between movement and stability is a characteristic of the work of Despiau, who modelled the head of Madame Derain at about the time *Nu devant un rideau vert* was painted.

9 *Le dos c.*1923
oil on canvas 63 × 54 cm
Musée d'Art Moderne de la
  Ville de Paris (fig. 38)
Provenance: bequeathed by Dr
  Girardin
Exhibitions: 1974, Turkey and
  Czechoslovakia 'Art
  français'; 1980, Tampere
  (Finland), Sara Hilden Art
  Museum, 'André Lhote and
  la Finlande'

Derain frequently posed the model so he could draw her from the back. Although there are relatively few finished paintings of such poses, there are a large number of drawings and lithographs. In *Le dos* Derain uses a broken, flickering brushstroke to model the broad planes and to build the mass of the shoulders and columnar neck. His concern with modelling in this painting reflects a similar concern in

many of the drawings. Among these drawings are some which can be readily identified as well-known poses. A drawing of 1920, for instance, is based on Ingres' *Bather*, and another of the same year is based on one of the figures in Delacroix's *Death of Sardanapalus* (Louvre, Paris), both works which had also been used as models by Renoir.

As in this painting, several of Derain's drawings focus on the nape of the model's neck. Among the drawings which Elie Faure published is one of 1919 in which the model pulls her long hair to one side just to reveal the nape (Faure, 1923). The drawings closest to *Le dos*, however, are those which Derain did of his wife in the early 1920s, showing the graceful curve of her shoulders, with a gentle rise toward her neck and the mass of her chignon. *Le dos* might also be compared with a similar painting, *La blonde*, in the Musée National d'Art Moderne.

10 *Jeune fille c.*1925
oil on canvas 91.4 × 73.7 cm
Detroit Institute of Arts (fig. 72)
Provenance: Galerie
  Paul Guillaume, Paris;
  Galerie Georges Bernheim,
  Paris
Exhibitions: 1939, Pittsburgh,
  Carnegie Institute, '1939
  Carnegie Institute
  International Exhibition';
  1970, Detroit Institute of
  Arts, 'Museum Director's
  Choice'; 1982, Regina; 1983,
  Berkeley (31)
Bibliography: W. R.
  Valentiner, 'André Derain',
  *Bulletin of the Detroit Institute
  of Arts*, vol. X, no. 2, 1928–9,
  repr. p. 25

The position of the head, the angular pose, and the long loose limbs of the model in this painting indicate the debt

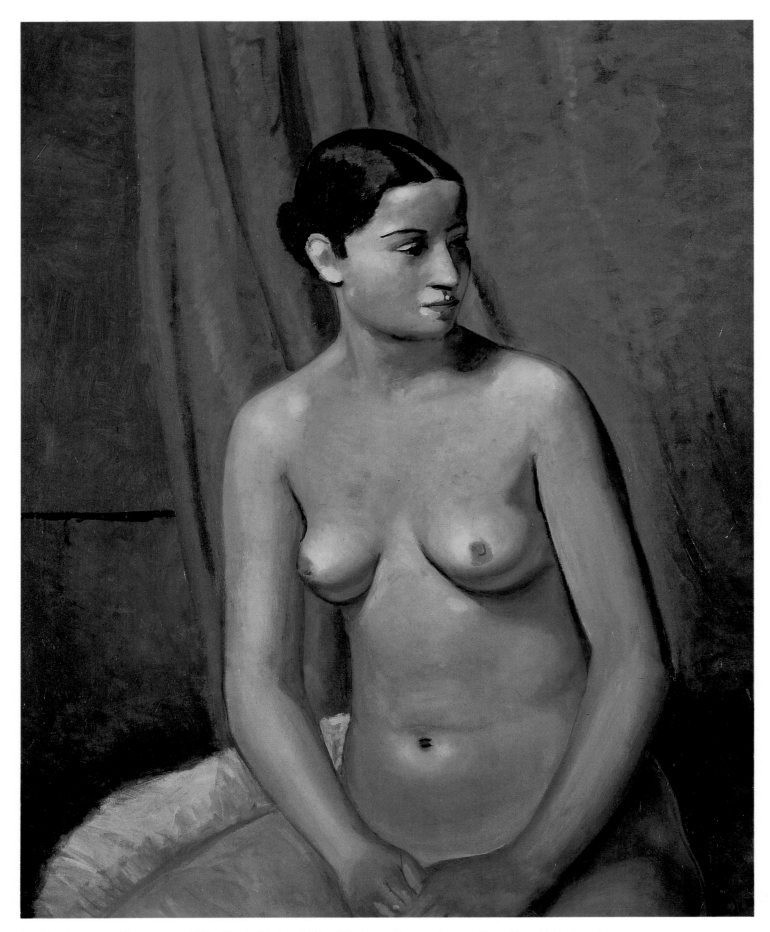

71. *Nu devant un rideau vert*, c. 1923, Musée National d'Art Moderne, Centre Georges Pompidou, Paris (cat. 8).

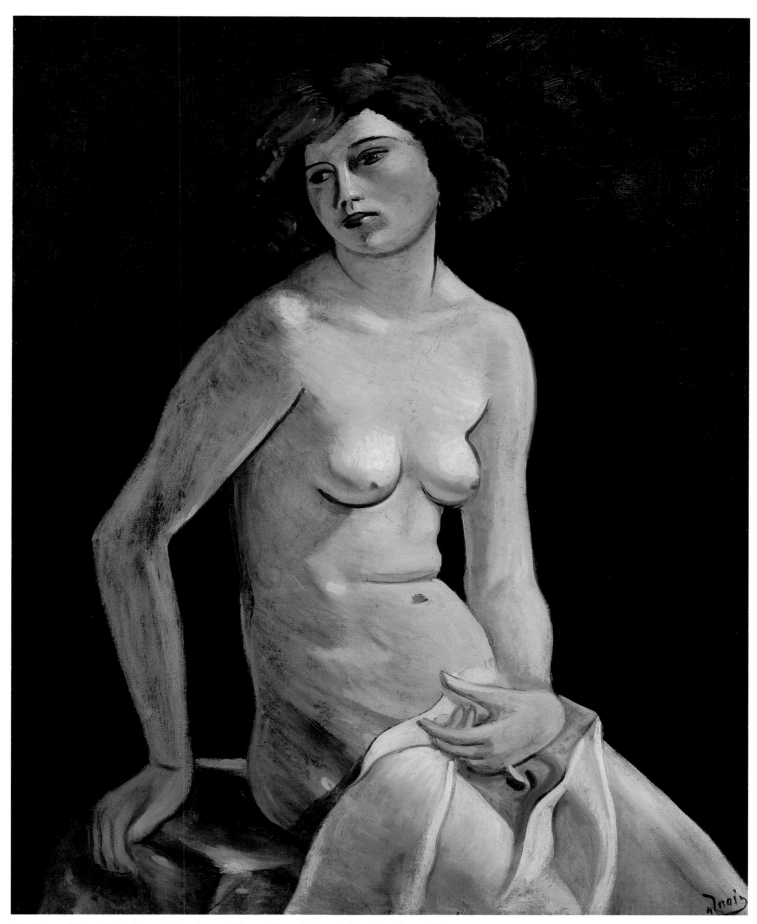

72. *Jeune fille*, c. 1925, Detroit Institute of Arts, City of Detroit Purchase (cat. 10).

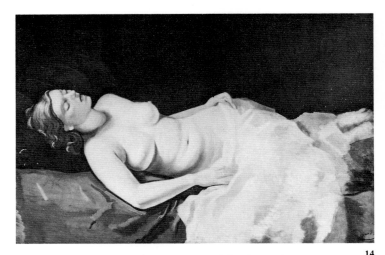

14

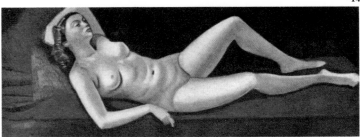

12

Derain's 'classicism' owes to the fifteenth century. The spare but exact anatomy and the equivocation between grace and awkwardness is reminiscent of the style of Signorelli. The early 1920s in Paris saw a general revival of interest in fifteenth-century masters, such as Pollaiuolo, Mantegna, and Signorelli. Critics writing in Florent Fels' journal, *L'Art vivant*, established a direct relation between these masters and the 'constructive' classicists of the early 1920s such as Derain. Derain's interest in the fifteenth century, however, spanned his whole career, and according to his reminiscences, it was his prime interest in the Louvre at the turn of the century (Derain, 1942).

11 *Le modèle posant* before 1928
oil on canvas 83 × 73 cm
Musée d'Art Moderne de la
    Ville de Troyes, donation
    Denise et Pierre Lévy
Provenance: Galerie
    Charpentier, Paris
Exhibitions: 1956, Paris,
    Galerie Charpentier (193)

This picture seems to have been painted in Rue Bonaparte which Derain left for a studio in Rue du Douanier in 1928. The Rue Bonaparte studio had a sloping window providing fairly poor, directional light, although Derain seems to have made good use of it in such pictures as this. The painting is strongly reminiscent of Corot's paintings of women seated in his studio, such as *L'Atelier* (formerly in the Esnault-Pelterie collection, Paris).
This work well illustrates what Derain called the 'rhythm of angles' upon which a painting should be built. The sharp angles in the pose of the slim model answer the angles created by the canvases leaning against each other under the window.

Although the setting seems simple and accidental, everything has been carefully arranged.
Works comparable to *Le modèle posant* were sold into the English gallery system from the time of Guillaume's collaboration with the Brandon Davies Gallery in 1928–9 and eventually inspired the painters of the Euston Road School.

12 *Grand nu allongé c.*1935
oil on canvas 72 × 185 cm
Collection André Derain fils
Exhibitions: 1955b,
    Paris 1959, Geneva (40)

13 *Nu au canapé vert* 1935–6
oil on canvas 38 × 55 cm
Musée d'Art Moderne de la
    Ville de Paris (fig. 62)
Provenance: Amos Collection
Exhibitions: 1984, Melun (17)

14 *Nu blond couché* 1936
oil on canvas 97 × 146 cm
Musée du Petit Palais, Geneva
Provenance: Germaine
    Lecomte collection
Exhibitions: 1955b, Paris
    (33); 1981, Tokyo, Nagoya
    (47)

Nu blond couché was inspired by Courbet's paintings of similar sleeping nudes with their hips and legs swathed in drapery, and particularly by Courbet's *Femme nue endormie* of 1866, which in the 1920s belonged to Paul Rosenberg. Details such as the loose hair and slightly parted lips also associate this work with the Courbet. An earlier Courbet, *La blonde endormie* of 1849, which is also similar to Derain's work, was in the collection of Henri Matisse by the time of the great Courbet exhibition at the Grand Palais in 1929. The colour and finish of *Nu blond couché*, however, refer directly to the Flemish Baroque, a reference which is consistent with the nineteenth-century sources of this painting.

Nu blond couché is one of a series of studies Derain did of the model lying on a green couch. This series began sometime before 1931 with *Nu au canapé* (Musée de l'Orangerie), in which the influence of Courbet is not as striking as that of Renoir's late paintings. The model for both *Nu au canapé* and *Nu blond couché* was Raymonde Knaubliche, the mother of Derain's son André.

15 *Nu au chat* c.1936–8
oil on canvas 108 × 150 cm
Hokkaido Museum of Art, Sapporo, Japan
Provenance: Michel Kellermann, Paris
Exhibitions: 1955b, Paris (37); 1957, London (65); 1974, Albi (22); 1976, Paris (53)

This painting is closely related to *Grand nu allongé* (cat. 12) and *Nu au canapé vert* (cat. 13). Against the horizontal and vertical grid implied by the couch in each of these works Derain sets up a rhythmic sequence of opposing diagonals. In *Nu au chat* this is developed around one long diagonal line which extents from the upper left to the lower right corner of the picture, effectively dividing the work into two equilateral triangles. Against this forceful compositional line, the horizontal created by the head and extended left arm stabilizes the grid. Across this grid are counterpoised the lesser diagonals created by the left leg and right arm. This bold construction elucidates Derain's insistence that painting is a 'matter of angles'.

The square table at the right introduces both the double horizontal and the opposed

diagonal that echoes powerfully throughout the composition. The shape of the spherical vase on a round dish is echoed in the sphere of the head resting in the dish of the accentuated collar-bone, the globular breasts above the concavity of the diaphragm, and the round rise of the stomach over the cradling concavity above the pubis. The translucency of the vase and dish connects materially with the translucency of the flesh, and Derain underscored this by extending the vase's translucency into transparent drapery wrapping the flesh of the arm. Similarly, the red, white, and green of the bouquet are a code for the palette of the whole work: the red flowers extend into the hair where the most intense red highlights are to be found; the green leaves lose themselves against the green couch; and the white flowers extend into the white of the drapery.

The rhythm of form, accentuated palette, and linear extension of the model's pose retain the whole of the composition in the front plane despite the dark background, the incidental shadows, and the strong modelling of the nude. *Nu au chat* is a fine example of the constructive function of light which Derain details in his manuscript notes on painting. Here, to use Derain's terminology, 'lumière', that is, diffuse ambient light, is virtually suppressed in favour of 'éclairage', the specific lighting of surfaces. This concentration upon lighted surfaces gives a heightened appearance to the model, pushing 'appearance' to a sense of 'apparition', or as Giacometti described it 'the marvellous appearance of things' (*see* cat. 26). In this sense *Nu au chat* and *Grand nu allongé* are works which are entirely consistent

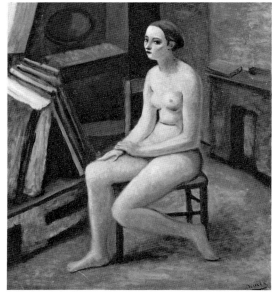

11

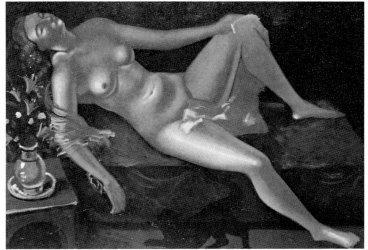

15

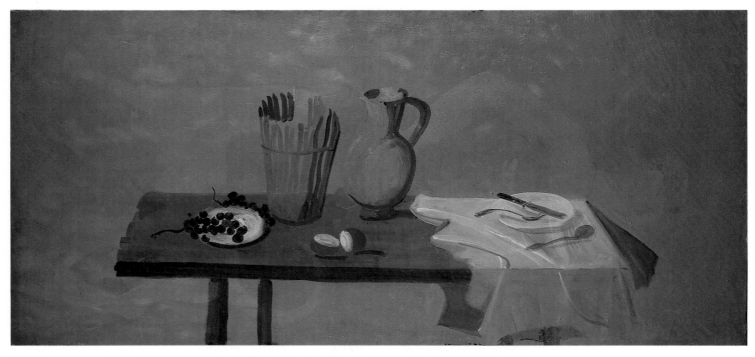

73. *Nature morte à la corbeille d'osier*, after 1953, Collection Galerie Adrien Maeght, Paris (cat. 32).

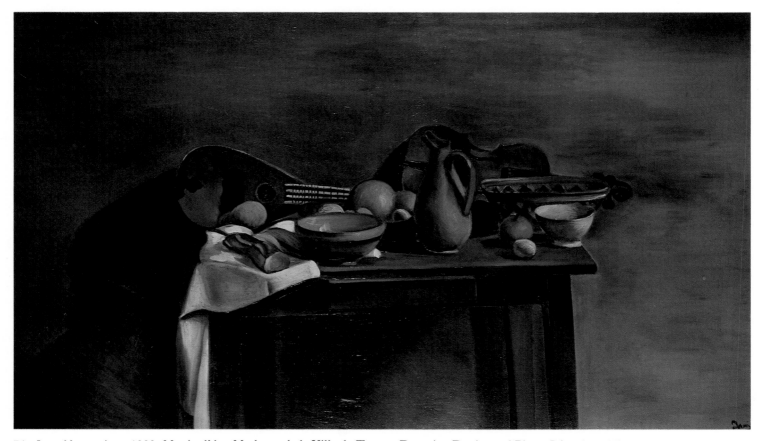

74. *La table garnie*, c. 1922, Musée d'Art Moderne de la Ville de Troyes, Donation Denise and Pierre Lévy (cat. 22).

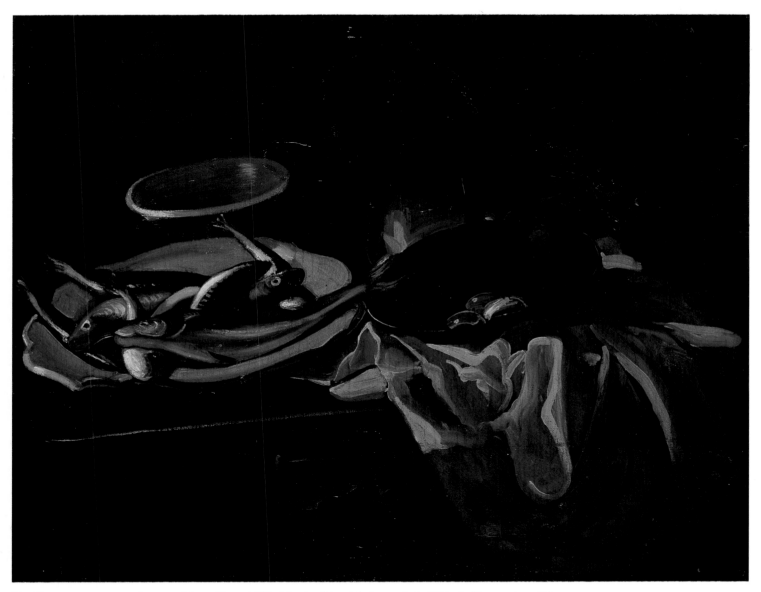

75. *Nature morte aux poissons et à la poêle*, c. 1938, Musée d'Art Moderne de la Ville de Troyes (cat. 27).

with Derain's still-life painting of the time. Similarly, in terms of angular composition, simplification of systematically modelled forms, and choice of palette, they are in keeping with the major compositions of the mid and late 1930s such as *La chasse au cerf* and *The Painter and his Family*.

Despite the idiosyncratic developments in Derain's painting, the source of these three nudes (cat. 12, 13, 15) can still be traced to Courbet. *Grand nu allongé* results from the conflation of two of Courbet's poses, *Femme nue couchée* (Private Collection, Paris) of 1862 and *Femme couchée; le repos* (Private Collection, London) of 1858. *Femme nue couchée*, a classical 'Ariadne' pose for the nude, was in the Baron Hatvany collection in Paris during this period and was illustrated in Léger's book on Courbet in 1929. This work may have been the direct inspiration for *Nu au canapé vert*, although the pose is too generalized to be certain. Derain made an etching of Courbet's *Femme couchée; le repos* (cat. 60), probably not from the painting itself, at that time in the Ernest Cognac collection, but from the reproduction in Pierre Courthion's book on Courbet (Courthion, 1931). The etching was done directly, so the print reverses the pose to the direction in which we find it in *Grand nu allongé* and *Nu au chat*. In *Nu au chat* the position of the model's right shoulder results from Derain's subsequent removal of drapery from the shoulder of Courbet's model. Derain's capriciousness with the model's anatomy accommodated certain elements of the pose of Courbet's notorious *La femme au perroquet* (Metropolitan Museum of Art, New York). The result of this

manipulation of the area around the model's shoulders is that in both *Nu au chat* and *Grand nu allongé* the column of the neck fits firmly and deeply into the torso of the model. This is true of Derain's etching, as well, and is a characteristic of Courbet's paintings of the nude.

16 *La clairière ou le déjeuner sur l'herbe* 1938
oil on canvas 138 × 250 cm
Musée du Petit Palais, Geneva (fig. 44)
Provenance: Marie Harriman collection
Exhibitions: 1938, New York; 1947, Chicago (7); 1981, Tokyo, Nagoya (52)

17 *La surprise* 1938
oil on canvas 140 × 306 cm
Art Salon Takahata, Osaka (fig. 43)
Provenance: Désiré Kellerman collection; Marie Harriman Gallery, New York; Averell Harriman collection, New York; American Friends of Israel Museum; Waddington Gallery, London
Exhibitions: 1938, New York; 1947, Chicago (9); 1963, New York, Metropolitan Museum of Art, 'Paintings from Private Collections' (34)

La clairière and *La surprise* represent the culmination of Derain's concerns in the carefully composed and strongly lit nudes of the mid-1930s. Posed in landscapes rather than studio interiors, Derain's two large pictures recall Renoir's famous *Bathers* of 1887 (Philadelphia Museum of Art), a painting which was for a long time in the collection of Jacques-Emile Blanche. This work was always very well known, and prints and drawings connected with it were published in the 1930s. A lithograph of a

variation of the Philadelphia *Bathers* was published, for instance, in 1930 as the frontispiece to Adolphe Basler and Charles Kunstler's book *Le dessin et la gravure moderne en France* in which drawings and prints by Derain were also reproduced. In addition, Derain had one of Renoir's preparatory drawings for the *Bathers* in his own collection. The poses, the crisp drawing, and the systematic but reduced modelling are all similar to Renoir's picture. When Renoir's picture was first shown, he titled it *Baignade: Essai pour une decoration*, and Derain's paintings are equally 'decorative', frieze-like arrangements of figures against a landscape background.

Like Renoir's figures, Derain's nudes are influenced by sixteenth-century Italian pictures. When *La clairière* and *La surprise* were first exhibited in New York in 1938, in an exhibition which Marie Harriman had mounted specifically to introduce these two great paintings, the reviewer for *Art News* wrote: 'The resemblance of the new panels is clearly to the great painters of the high Renaissance. Indeed, in poetic feeling for beauty and colour, and in their pictorial brilliance of nudes in a romantic landscape, they seem to stem from the bright, joyous painting of the Venetians'; even more striking, however, than Derain's admiration for Italian painting is his observation of Poussin's powerful geometrical compositions, carried along counterpoised limbs.

The composition in Derain's two pictures is a continuation of his programme of composing paintings structured by opposing diagonals. The composition of *La clairière* is a direct extension of that in *Nu au*

chat (cat. 15), and as in the earlier picture, the figures occupy the space almost to the top of the canvas. The increase in still-life elements and the introduction of landscape enriches the composition. The canvas is divided vertically into a greater and lesser triangle, and over these the two nudes extend their limbs to describe a rectangle which tilts gently into space. The composition of *La surprise* is more complex. Organized in chains of opposing diagonals in several registers, from the carefully poised still-life elements in the foreground to the raised hands of the figures, it has the rhythmic, repetitive quality of Poussin's *Triumph of Pan*.

The decorative flamboyance of these paintings resembles that of *La chasse au cerf* (cat. 3) with which many details of landscape and still life are shared. The figures themselves, and particularly the male figures in *La surprise*, are also like those in Derain's hunting picture. The landscape in *L'Age d'or* (cat. 4) also bears a close resemblance to that in *La surprise*, and it is likely that all of these pictures were in the studio together, or are at least very near in date.

At the same time there are similarities between these works and the dark paintings which were not exhibited until after the war. The combination of two figures and a still life in *La clairière* is undoubtedly related to *Deux femmes nues et nature morte* (cat. 19), and the still life is of the same Neapolitan type. The theme of sudden discovery in *La surprise*, the classical surprise of Diana or of nymphs in a sacred grove, is close to that of the small dark *Bacchanales* from after the Second World War and to *La grande bacchanale noire* (cat. 5) painted during the war.

The larger gesturing nude figures in *La surprise* are also like those in *La grande bacchanale noire*.

Both *La clairière* and *La surprise* were carefully planned in a series of preparatory drawings and exhibit none of the loose pentimenti of closely contemporary works such as *Le retour d'Ulysse* (cat. 2). Several sanguines which were studies for these panels hung in a separate room in the Marie Harriman Gallery when these works were first shown. 'These', wrote the *Art News* critic, 'serve to indicate how Derain renders contour and modelling' (Horne, 1938). From this description one might deduce that at least some of them were studies of the posed nude, rather than compositional sketches such as cat. 105.

18 *Nu à la pomme* c.1941
oil on canvas 195 × 96.5 cm
Ryoko Co. Ltd., Japan (fig. 63)
Provenance: Galerie Schmit, Paris
Exhibitions: 1955b, Paris (43); 1976, Paris (59)

Nu à la pomme is not a simple extension of Derain's paintings of a model in the studio but an idealization of a pose originating in classical sculpture. The source of this painting, however, is as much in the Renaissance and in Derain's own day as it is in the antique. The pose is derived from paintings after classical statuary such as Raphael's *Three Graces* in the Musée Condé in Chantilly, but the athletic tension and the strong modelling associate Derain's work more closely with Renaissance engravers such as Giorgio Ghisi and Marcantonio Raimondi than with Raphael himself.

Despite its relation to paintings or prints, there is no doubt that this near life-size

figure, strongly modelled and enriched, is inspired by sculpture, Derain may have been impressed by Charles Despiau's near life-size and life-size figures of the very late 1930s such as *Assia* of 1937 which he may have seen in Paris by 1938 in either plaster or bronze.

There are drawings by Derain in a private collection in Paris which are close in pose and manner to this work and an etching of a figure enriched in the corner of a room in a manner similar to *Nu à la pomme* in the Bibliothèque Nationale (1955a, Paris, exh.cat., 63).

19 *Deux femmes nues et nature morte* before 1945
oil on canvas 112 × 104 cm
Musée d'Art Moderne de la Ville de Troyes, Donation Denise et Pierre Lévy
Provenance: bought from the artist, 1945
Exhibitions: 1952, Paris, Musée des Arts Décoratifs, 'Cinquante ans de peinture française dans les collections particulières' (46); 1953, Paris, Galerie Charpentier, 'Figures nues de l'Ecole française depuis l'Ecole de Fontainebleau' (55); 1954, Venice, Biennale; Rome, Villa Medici; Paris, Grand Palais (6); 1955b, Paris (34); 1959, Geneva (39); 1967, Edinburgh, London (83); 1971, Paris (12); 1976, Troyes, Hôtel de Ville, 'A la découverte de la Collection Pierre Lévy'; 1978, Paris, Musée de l'Orangerie, 'Donation Pierre Lévy' (44)

In the catalogue of the exhibition at the Musée de l'Orangerie, Michel Hoog points out the influence on this work of the important exhibition of Italian art which was held in the Petit Palais in 1935 (Paris, 1978, exh. cat., p. 70). Hoog identifies two works, Caravaggio's *Bacchus*

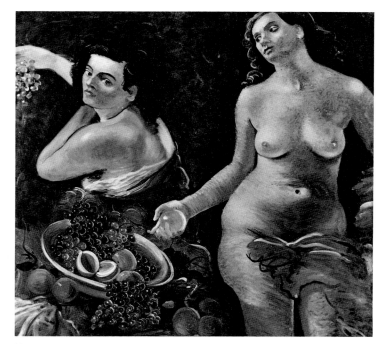

19

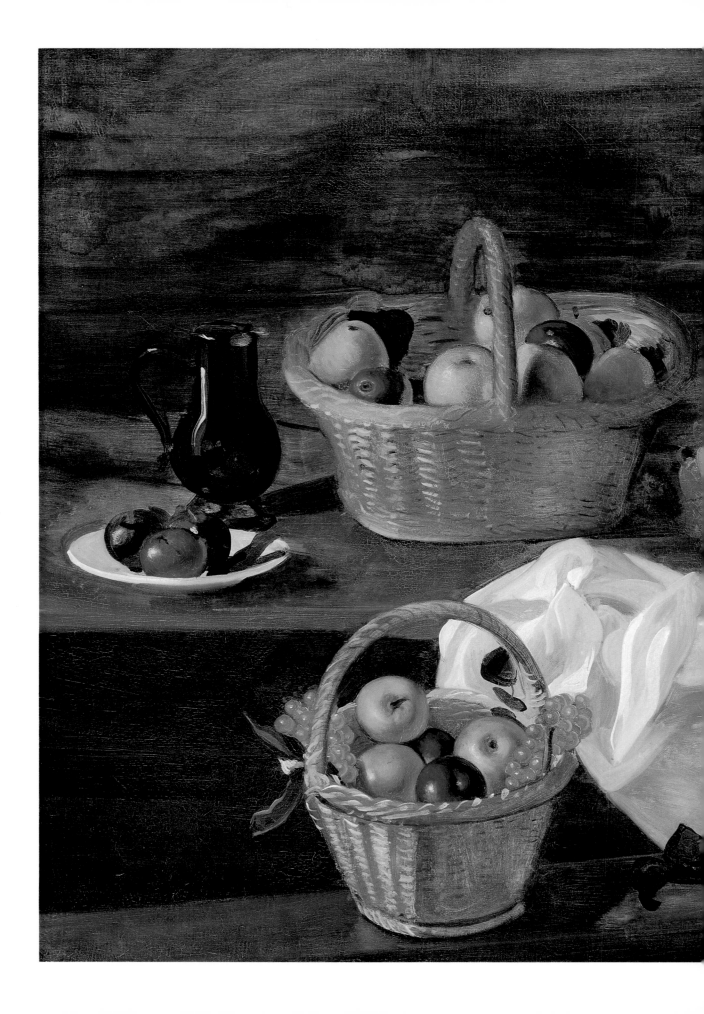

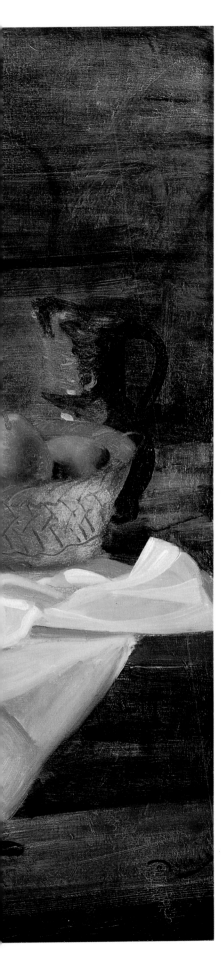

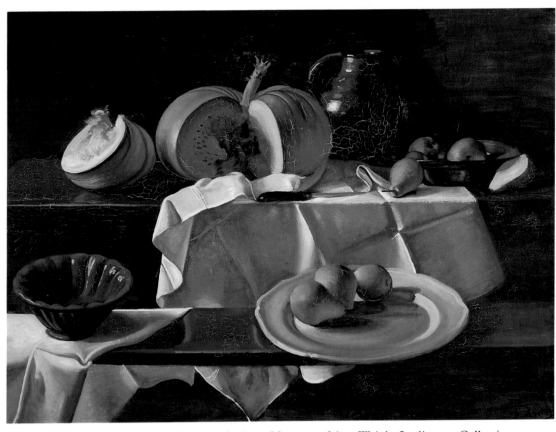

77. *Still Life With Pumpkin*, 1938, Santa Barbara Museum of Art, Wright Ludington Collection.

76. (opposite) *Les trois panniers*, c. 1939, Cincinnati Art Museum, Gift of John Warrington (cat. 28).

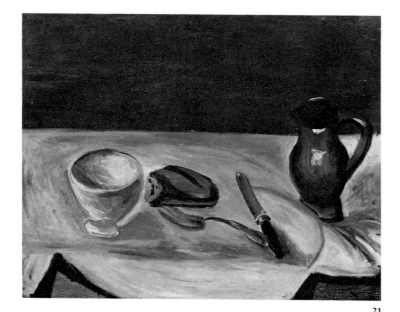

21

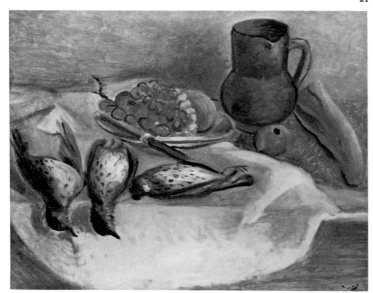

23

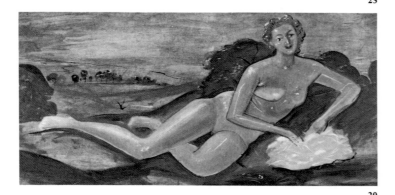

20

(Petit Palais, 'L'Art italien', cat. 84) and Annibale Carracci's *Satyr and Bacchante* (Petit Palais cat. 90) as the most likely sources for *Deux femmes nues et nature morte*. The Italianate nature of this painting is comparable with *La grande bacchanale noire* (cat. 5).

As with many of Derain's late paintings, the immediate sources for the figures in this picture can be found among his drawings and earlier works. There are several drawings which relate closely to the blond figure holding an apple, and Derain's etching *Venus marine* (cat. 73) is a related work. The dark-haired figure turning away and looking over her shoulder is very close to a painting, *La danseuse, Ruth*, which was published in 1931 in *Les chroniques du jour* (No. 8, n.s.) as an illustration to the *enquête*, 'Pour ou Contre Derain'. Drawings executed around 1930 (Private Collection, Paris) which may be related to this picture might also have served for the *Deux femmes nues et nature morte*. The smaller work, *Table de fruits avec deux femmes*, in the Musée d'Art Moderne de la Ville de Troyes, is also related to this painting.

20 *Diane* after 1945
oil on canvas 196 × 96 cm
Collection André Derain fils
Provenance: Alice Derain
Exhibitions: 1959, Geneva (55)

This work is inspired by the Ecole de Fontainebleau and may have been made as a part of a decorative programme at the same time as *La chasse* (cat. 43).

STILL LIFE

21 *Nature morte* c.1922
oil on canvas 65 × 81 cm
Private Collection, Paris
Provenance: Jacques Doucet collection, Paris
Exhibitions: 1976, Paris (29)

Among the ambitious still-life pictures, such as *La gibecière* (Musée de l'Orangerie), *Nature morte* (Hermitage, Leningrad), and *Nature morte au crâne* (Pushkin Museum of Fine Arts, Moscow), which Derain painted before the First World War, there were many sober and simple works, far less grand in design. It is to these that Derain returned after the war and particularly to the tenebrist paintings surrounding *Nature morte au crâne*, representing a few objects, pots or cards, painted in browns and greys with a sweeping active brushstroke.

This work establishes at the beginning of the 1920s a particular type of still life which would be continued in Derain's later work. In a limited palette Derain builds up the still life over layers of red-brown and black or grey underpainting. This comes from a seventeenth-century tradition of tenebrist painting to which the major works of 1921 to 1924, such as *Table chargée* and *Table de cuisine*, as well as many later works, adhere. This much simpler painting retains the opposing curves and other elements of pre-war 'Cézannisme' which were subdued in the more complex still-life paintings of the period. It is, however, close to the still-life element in Derain's self-portrait of about the same date (cat. 46).

22 *La table garnie* c.1922
oil on canvas 97 × 132 cm
Musée d'Art Moderne de la Ville de Troyes, donation Denise et Pierre Lévy (fig. 74)
Provenance: Vienna Municipal Museum (1924); Galerie Simon (1925); Mrs R. A. Workman Etienne Bignou, Paris; Mrs S. Kaye Reid and Lefevre Gallery, London; Sotheby's, 1963

Exhibitions: 1922, Berlin; 1927, Düsseldorf; 1930, New York (5); 1930, Paris, Galerie Georges Petit, 'Cent ans de peinture française' (5); 1930, Cincinnati (39); 1932, London, Lefevre Gallery, 'L'Ecole de Paris' (4); 1932, Amsterdam, Stedelijk Museum, 'Tentoonstelling van Fransche Schilderkunst' (60); 1933, Amsterdam, Jacques Goustikker Gallery, 'Het Stilleven' (80); 1936b, New York (41); 1936, Detroit, Institute of Arts; 1936, Montreal, Musée des Beaux Arts, 'The School of Paris' (4); 1943, London, Lefevre Gallery, 'Picasso and his Contemporaries' (6); 1954, Rotterdam, Museum Boymans-van Beuningen, 'Four Centuries of Still Life in France' (139); 1954, Paris (40); 1957, London (40); 1959, Worcester, Mass., Art Museum, 'The Dial' (27); 1967, Edinburgh, London (69); 1971, Paris (9); 1974, Paris, Musée Jacquemart André, 'Poiret le Magnifique' (310); 1974, Saarbrücken, Moderne Galerie, 'Les années folles en France 1920–1930' (12); 1976, Rome (29); 1977, Paris (33); 1977, Berlin, Nationale Galerie, 'Tendenzen der Zwanzigsten Jahre' (438)

This, perhaps the best known of Derain's still-life paintings, was one of the most celebrated works of the period after the First World War. It went almost immediately to Germany, and in the course of the 1920s was written about by important critics such as Paul Westheim and Carl Einstein, as well as by André Salmon and Elie Faure. Thus, it might be said to have been at least as influential on the German realism of the period as

on that in France.

The composition, tightly bound in the curves of a continuous silhouette extended by the shadow on the wall, is unusual among Derain's works. The only directly comparable work is a smaller still life of the same period, also known as *La table garnie*, which is now in a private collection in Stockholm (*see* Paris, 1976, exh. cat., 28).

The isolation of the laden table against the expanse of the wall creates a certain distance, a quiet alienation, like that of *Arlequin et Pierrot*. These two important pictures of the early 1920s are, in fact, representative of the mystical sobriety and melancholy that characterize much post-war painting. The palette, relatively high finish, and tight surface of *La table garnie* is also comparable with Derain's painting of 1924 (cat. 1).

23 *Nature morte aux grives*
c.1925
oil on canvas 46 × 54.8 cm
Private Collection
Exhibitions: 1987, New York, Grace Borgenicht Gallery

In its subject, composition, and handling, this picture is related to Derain's Carnegie prize winning still life of 1928 (cat. 24). Derain painted several still-life paintings in the mid-1920s which combine simple rustic motifs and an earthy or red-brown palette with lyrical drawing and sensuous, foamy brushwork. In its brushwork and in the quiet, unprepossessing treatment of its subject, this painting might be compared with the Chardinesque still life of about the same time, *Nature morte aux raisins* in the Galerie Schmit, Paris. At the same time that fluid drawing by which a single brushstroke turns the curve of the jug or the wing of the thrush and by which the

stem of the grapes extends to join the rhythm of the drapery folds makes this work comparable to the most alluring of Derain's still lifes of the 1920s, such as *Nature morte au melon* in the Orangerie collection.

When this work was exhibited in the Grace Borgenicht Gallery in 1987, it was accompanied by two smaller works of the same period, *Poires* and *Nature morte au pain*, which indicate the process by which Derain arrived at compositions such as *Nature morte aux grives*. Such small individual studies of still-life elements appear among Derain's works in the great periods of his still-life painting, in the mid-1920s as well as in 1912–13 and in the late 1930s.

24 *Still Life with Dead Game*
1928
oil on canvas 132 × 196 cm
Museum of Art, Carnegie Institute, Pittsburgh (fig. 54)
Provenance: Carnegie Prize, 1928
Exhibitions: 1930, Cincinnati (37); 1937, Paris, Petit Palais, 'Les maîtres d'art indépendants' (23)

Derain's painting of a dead heron and pheasant, spread on a table with gamebag and gun, is his most direct homage to Jean Baptiste Oudry, the greatest of eighteenth-century painters of *nature morte de la chasse*. The grandeur of the composition, the sweep of the heron's wings, the lush soft brushwork, and areas of precise surface drawing in liquid dark paint give Derain's prize-winning still life a similarity to Oudry's works of the 1720s and 1730s which goes beyond the general nature of the subject.

Shooting and fishing were activities that Derain enjoyed throughout his life (Oberlé, 1956). Derain's purchase of the

Château Parouzeau in 1929 seems to have been connected with this outdoor life. It was a taste which Derain shared with his friend in the Rue Bonaparte, Dunoyer de Segonzac, with whom he also shared his admiration for Courbet. The presence of occasional shooting still lifes among Derain's works may be related to this admiration. He had perhaps seen, fairly recently, Courbet's *The Girl with Seagulls, Trouville*, a painting less than half the size of Derain's but with an impressive display of shimmering plumage on the outstretched wings of dead birds. This painting was in the possession of Paris dealers at the time, appearing in an exhibition at the Galerie de la Renaissance in 1928, and it may even have been offered for sale to Derain or to Dunoyer de Segonzac, who was the owner of one of Courbet's well-known *Trout* pictures.

The linear quality of Derain's work, however, distances *Still Life with Dead Game* from the work of Courbet. The heraldic silhouette of the heron's neck and wings is answered in the sweeping folds of the table-cloth behind. The rhythmic progression of these folds entails slight shifts of plane, and combined with the general spatial ambiguity of both the upturned table and its setting, the picture as a whole is influenced by the Cubist subtleties of Georges Braque's works. It is not surprising that, at a time when their close friendship led them to establish their studios in the same street, one painter should have influenced the other. The current of ideas between Derain and Braque was, in fact, continuous. It is evident particularly in still life, the subject of nearly all of Braque's

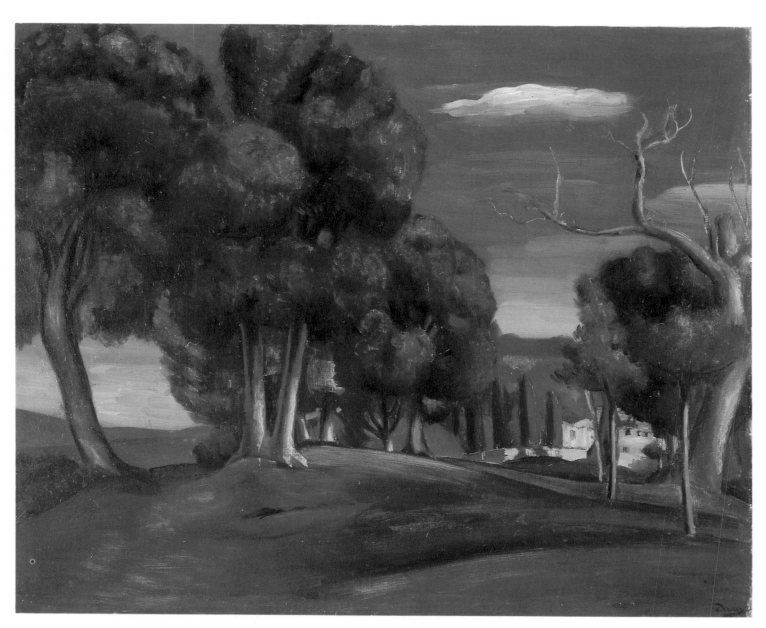

78. *Castelgandalfo*, 1921, Kunstmuseum, Berne (cat. 33).

work. As well as an exchange of influence between the two friends, there was also a common understanding of sources which should not be understated. For example, the simple division of a flat background into three by the inclusion of a shaded plane in the centre is Braque's device in many of his *Guéridon* paintings of 1927–8, and Derain's use of this in *Still Life with Dead Game* depends on Braque's example. A great still life by Jean Baptiste Oudry, however, such as *Still Life with Dead Wolf* (Wallace Collection, London), uses just this device. Moreover, Oudry combines it with a grand stone scroll rising in the background and another appearing under the table, bringing the same rhythmic order to a spatially complex composition as that provided in Braque's still lifes by very similar means. Georges Braque was just as aware of the tradition in which he was a master as was his friend André Derain.

25 *Nature morte aux poires*
before 1936
oil on canvas 24 × 41 cm
Musée d'Art Moderne de la Ville de Paris
Provenance: presented by André Derain, 1936

26 *Nature morte aux poires*
1938–9
oil on canvas 44 × 58 cm
Musée d'Art Moderne de la Ville de Paris
Provenance: Henry Thomas collection

'... ever since that day, or I might even say the moment of that day in 1936, when a chance sight of one of Derain's canvases in a gallery – three pears on a table silhouetted against a vast black background – arrested my attention and impressed me in a completely new way

(it is there that for the first time I really penetrated beyond the immediate appearance of one of Derain's paintings), ever since that moment all Derain's canvases without exception, the best of them as well as the less good, have impressed me and compelled me to look at them for a long time and search for what lay behind them ...' (Giacometti, 1957)

Alberto Giacometti, writing in the Galerie Maeght publication, *Derrière le miroir*, three years after Derain's death, identifies in his phrase 'beyond the immediate appearance' the metaphysical intentions of Derain's dark still-life paintings of the 1930s. To Giacometti, whose own work after the war was integrated into the existentialist and phenomenological philosophies of the day, Derain's concept of appearance as a crossing point of 'powers' revealed by light, first formulated in 1921 in his treatise on painting, was of lasting interest. The young sculptor was a friend of Derain and understood the term 'virtu', as the painter had intended it when he spoke of the virtue of an object, in the full, classical sense of the power to sustain existence against the immensity of non-existence. As all knowledge and the subjective sense of one's own existence depends, in the terms of the French phenomenologists of the period, on the recognition of these other existences, to locate them precisely in space became the main task of Giacometti's work. Derain's rendering of this concept in painting is the traditional one of a point of light upon a pervasive dark ground in the manner of Clara Peeters. Giacometti's understanding of the theme of Derain's dark stilllife paintings meant that

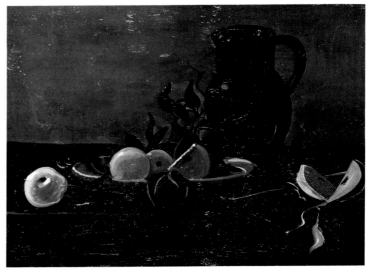

26

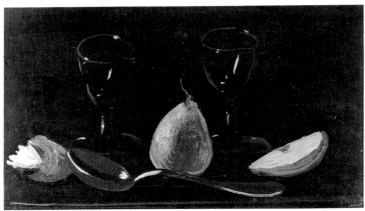

25

through them Derain forged a link between the great age of existential metaphysics, the seventeenth century, and the age of the last great metaphysicians, the existentialists themselves.

These small works are the basis for his larger *Nature morte sur fond noir* paintings of the late 1930s, and their simplicity and starkly reduced palette bring a sobriety to Derain's work which contrasts with the extravagance of the nudes he was painting at this time.

27 *Nature morte aux poissons et à la poêle c.*1938
oil on canvas 86 × 108 cm
Musée d'Art Moderne de la Ville de Troyes, donation Denise et Pierre Lévy (fig. 75)
Provenance: Pierre Lévy
Exhibitions: 1940, New York (3); 1950, Paris, Galerie Charpentier 'Autour de 1900' (40); 1954, Venice, Biennale (4); 1959, Geneva (45); 1964, Marseilles (56); 1965, Paris, Galerie Knoedler, 'Quarante

tableaux d'une collection privée (10); 1967, Edinburgh, London (85); 1971, Paris (17); 1974, Albi (30); 1976, Rome, Villa Medici, and 1977, Paris, Grand Palais (47)

Derain painted several 'rustic' still-life subjects in the early and mid-1920s, of which *La table de cuisine* (Musée de l'Orangerie) is the most outstanding. *Nature morte aux poissons et à la poêle*, however, differs from these earlier works. It is a particularly Spanish type of still life, best known through Velázquez's paintings, which does not seem to have been among Derain's concerns in the early 1920s. There is a still life in the Art Gallery of Ontario, which is very similar to this painting and was perhaps painted at the same time. In the Musée d'Art Moderne de la Ville de Troyes, there is also a smaller painting, *Nature morte*, which is a study for *Nature morte aux poissons et à la poêle*. Although the composition is otherwise exactly that of the larger painting, this work includes a black jug which does not appear here but which can be seen in the same position in the related still life in Ontario.

The extended, horizontal composition of this painting is constructed around the elongated S-shaped double curve created by the sinuous line of the fish, which draws the plate and frying pan together. This rhythmic, linear attitude to composition associates *Nature morte aux poissons et à la poêle* with the still lifes Derain painted just before the war, such as that in the Pierre Matisse Collection (Regina, 1982, exh.cat., 45), in which elements of Spanish and Netherlandish still lifes are treated in the abstract, idiosyncratic, and Cubist-

inspired manner which after the war strongly influenced the second School of Paris. Such comparisons highlight the narrowness of the margin between *traditioniste* and avant-garde painting in Paris just before the Second World War.

28 *Les trois paniers c.*1939
oil on canvas 137.2 × 137.7 cm
The Cincinnati Art Museum, gift of John Warrington in memory of his mother, Elsie Holmes Warrington, 1941 (fig. 76)
Provenance: Pierre Matisse Gallery, New York, 1940; Mr John W. Warrington
Exhibitions: 1940, New York (1); 1947, Chicago (3); 1982, Regina; 1983, Berkeley (47)

At the beginning of 1940, Pierre Matisse held an exhibition of twelve paintings he had chosen from among Derain's most recent works. As Michael Parke-Taylor has pointed out, the four large still lifes in this exhibition were what most excited the critics (Regina, 1982, exh.cat., p. 114). *Les trois paniers*, *Nature morte aux poissons et à la poêle* (cat. 27), *Nature morte au lièvre* (fig. 51), and *La citrouille* (*Still Life with Pumpkin, c.*1938, Wright Ludington collection, Santa Barbara, Calif., fig. 77) are all pictures inspired by seventeenth-century still-life painting from the Low Countries and Spain. Together they created a *tour de force* of Derain's *traditionism* which surpassed even the arrival of *La surprise* (cat. 17) and *La clairière* (cat. 16) in Marie Harriman's gallery two years earlier.

Les trois paniers takes up the tradition of Francisco de Zurbarán and Francisco de Vargas. The choice of still-life elements, their frontal presentation on two levels, the

balance of ambient light and shade, and the character of the modelling all point to Zurbarán. It is, nevertheless, painting of its own age. The formality of the drawing, the elision of modelling for the claims of the surface, and the references to nineteenth-century French painting all adjust the Spanish model. The clarity of colour and the 'golden tone' on which the critics of the day remarked, links *Les trois paniers* with the sensuous works of the late 1920s such as *Melon et fruits* in the Musée de l'Orangerie, while the idealizing treatment of the individual fruits associates this work with the still-life elements in *The Painter and his Family* (cat. 55) and *Girl Peeling Fruit* in the Albright-Knox Art Gallery in Buffalo, N.Y.

A double-tiered composition is also used in *La citrouille*, the most complex of the four still lifes selected by Pierre Matisse and the most ambitious of all Derain's still-life paintings. It might be seen as a culmination of the work which began in the early 1920s and by the late 1930s had resulted in complex and subtle still lifes such as *Les trois paniers*.

29 *Still Life c.*1943
oil on canvas 90 × 147 cm
Tate Gallery, London
Provenance: Galerie Renou et Colle, Paris
Exhibitions: 1986, London, Stoppenbach and Delestre Gallery, 'French 19th and 20th Century Paintings' (35)

This still life was first reproduced in 1943 in *Peintres d'aujourd'hui, les maîtres* published by the journal *Comoedia* in co-operation with Galerie Charpentier.

The elements of the still life are those close at hand in Derain's studio at a time when the majority of his works were on paper. The rolls of heavy

paper, the rule, compasses, and ribboned 'carnet des dessins' belong to his work on the woodcuts for Rabelais' *Pantagruel* (cat. 124) published in 1943 and the lithographic suites to which he had agreed with Mourlot and for which, Mourlot says, the proofs were destroyed in 1946. The photograph of Derain on p. 81 shows the context in which this still life was painted.

This was not the first time that Derain had painted such a subject, and this late *Still Life* might be compared with *Nature morte au carton à dessin*, 1914 (Private Collection, London; Edinburgh, 1967, exh.cat., 33). The composition of Derain's *c.*1943 *Still Life* owes something to Chardin, but the exaggerated play of curves and angles with the dazzling display of large areas of white paper opposes a strong sensuality to Chardin's eighteenth-century sensibility.

30 *Nature morte sur fond noir c.*1945
oil on canvas 97 × 130 cm
Musée d'Art Moderne de la Ville de Troyes, donation Denise et Pierre Lévy
Provenance: a gift of the artist to Pierre Lévy, 1952
Exhibitions: 1952, Paris, Musée des Arts Décoratifs, 'Cinquante ans de peinture française dans les collections particulières' (58); 1954, Venice, Biennale (1); 1954, Rome, Villa Medici 1955b, Paris (55); 1957, Paris, Galerie Charpentier, 'Cent chefs-d'oeuvre de l'art français (26); 1965, Paris, Galerie Knoedler, 'Quarante tableaux d'une collection privée' (13); 1967, Edinburgh, London, (101); 1971, Paris (24); 1976, Troyes, Hôtel de Ville, 'A la découverte de la collection de Pierre Lévy' (38); 1977, Paris

(56); 1977, Troyes, Hôtel de Ville, 'Donation Pierre Lévy' (31)

The long ligatures of drawing in white light on an infinity of black poise this work between sign and image. It is the culmination of Derain's attitude to light as 'the sign of the whole which, once arrived at, allows us to rediscover the elements which don't count in appearance but which are meanwhile bound up with the spirit' (Doucet MS 6887, f. 43v). The revelation of physical objects by light and the reciprocal relationship of light and dark imply the reciprocity between the seen and the unseen, the real material and the real immaterial world. This work is the most extreme statement of the metaphysical position which Giacometti had recognized in Derain's painting of three pears in 1936 (see cat. 26).

The inspiration for all Derain's dark still lifes lay in early seventeenth-century Dutch painting, and Derain's ability to realize his metaphysics in these works depended particularly upon the Clara Peeters in his collection. It is, nevertheless, in such works of the mid-1930s that the development towards *Nature morte sur fond noir* began. In *Nature morte aux fruits, table et fond noir* (Musée d'Art Moderne de la Ville de Troyes) Derain added a wineglass and glass compote to the simple composition of fruit, increasing the complexity of his indications of reflected and transmitted light. A composition of the late 1930s, *Still Life with Fruit* (fig. 53; Stanford Museum of Art), shows the combination of lighted surfaces, reflected highlights, and indications of translucency which make up the elements of Peeters still lifes

(fig. 50). Derain's loose drawing, however, leaves the forms open and incomplete. There is a degree of ambiguity between the polished surface of the black jug and the transparency of the glasses. The dark background emanates through the fruit, rendering it ethereal, and the spoon and even the table itself are signalled only by the thin line of light along a polished edge.

Nature morte sur fond noir completes the identification of line with light in the illuminated edge of form which is indicated in seventeenth-century metaphysical paintings. It is worth noting, however, that the first painting in which Derain took up this issue was the *Nature morte* in the Wilhelm collection in Bottmingen. In this painting of 1912 a web of highlights creates a scaffold of lighted edges which is undoubtedly a comment on the contemporary Cubist works of his friends Picasso and Braque.

Characteristically for the still lifes of this period, Derain worked out the composition of *Nature morte sur fond noir* in a smaller painting. This work is also in the Musée d'Art Moderne de la Ville de Troyes.

31 *Nature morte aux fruits et feuillage c.*1945
oil on canvas 114 × 143 cm
Musée d'Art Moderne de la Ville de Troyes, donation Denise et Pierre Lévy
Provenance: acquired by Pierre Lévy from the artist
Exhibitions: 1952, Paris, Musée des Arts Décoratifs, 'Cinquante ans de peinture française dans les collections particulières' (47); 1954, Venice, Biennale (3); 1955b, Paris (53); 1967, Edinburgh, London (97)

Around 1938 Derain began a series of ambitious still-life paintings to which he seems to

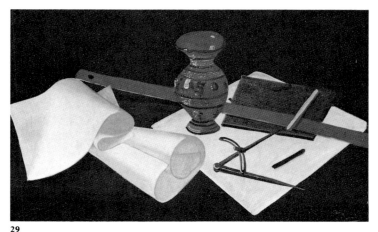

29

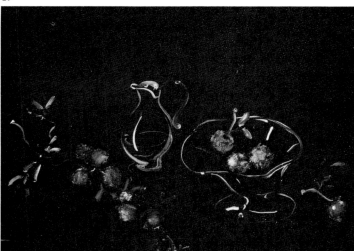

30

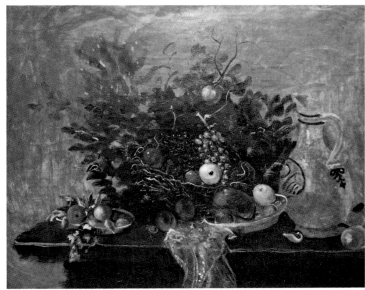

31

117

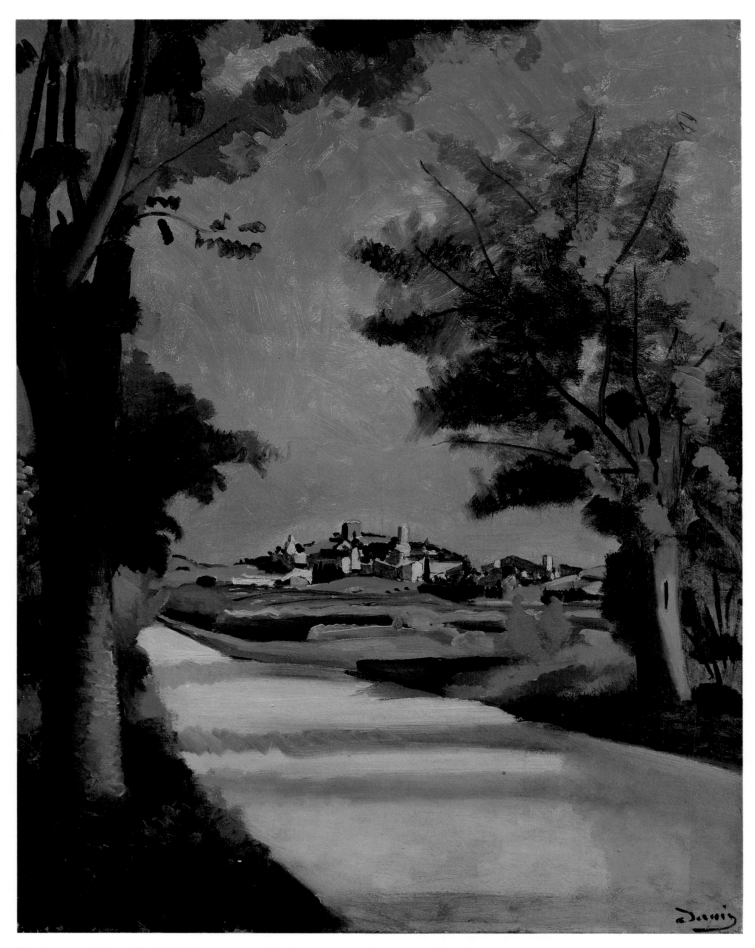

79. *La route*, 1930–1, Musée de l'Orangerie, Paris, Collection Jean Walther and Paul Guillaume (cat. 39).

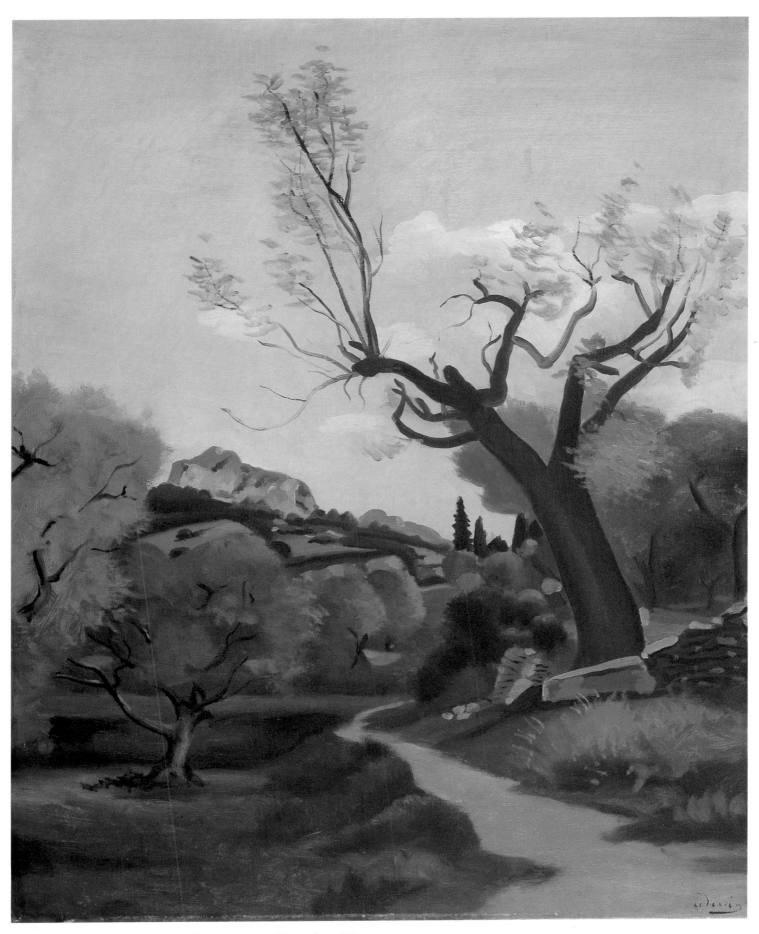

80. *La route et l'arbre*, c. 1928–30, Kunstmuseum, Berne (cat. 36).

have returned after the war. Like many of these works, *Nature morte aux fruits et feuillage* was preceded by a smaller canvas which is a compositional study. This small painting, a fresh and vigorous work, was also acquired by Pierre Lévy and is now in the Musée d'Art Moderne de la Ville de Troyes. It is similar in many respects to *Table de fruits avec deux femmes* (Musée d'Art Moderne de la Ville de Troyes), which is itself related to *Deux femmes nues et nature morte* (cat. 19) which Pierre Lévy acquired from Derain's Rue d'Assas studio in 1945. He also acquired *Nature morte aux fruits et feuillage* some years later. A comparison of the smaller studies argues for a date at the end of the war for *Nature morte aux fruits et feuillage*. The light touch, thin paint, and foamy brushwork which characterize this work appeared in Derain's work as early as, for example, the *Portrait of Louise de Vilmorin* of 1934 (Private Collection, Switzerland; Hilaire, 1959, p. 163; Tokyo, 1981, exh.cat., 45). In terms of the loose, open facture and general tonality, this painting might also be compared with *Nature morte aux poissons* (Musée d'Art Moderne de la Ville de Troyes), acquired by Lévy after 1947.

The shape and mass of Derain's composition, as well as the nature of his motif, refers to the tradition of seventeenth-century French still-life painting exemplified by the work of Louise Moillon.

32 *Nature morte à la corbeille d'osier* after 1953
oil on canvas 95 × 200 cm
Galerie Adrien Maeght, Paris (fig. 73)
Provenance: estate of the artist
Exhibitions: 1981, Tokyo, Nagoya (63); 1985,

Chambourcy, Maison André Derain, 'La célébration des fruits' (1)
Michael Parke-Taylor has pointed out that this work is painted over a picture of a woman and a dog which was visible in one of Alexander Liberman's photographs taken in Derain's studio in 1952 (Regina, 1982, exh.cat.). *Nature morte à la corbeille d'osier* is therefore one of Derain's very late works. The colour and lightness of touch in the handling is similar to that in the light still-life paintings of the late 1930s, but the spare composition and scale of the several elements in relation to the vast translucent green background is in keeping with other very late paintings such as *La chasse* (cat. 43) and *Diane* (cat. 20).

Virtually the same still life, with jug, fruit, dish and unfinished wicker basket arranged on the same trestle table, appears in a small painting, *Scène d'intérieur*, in the Musée d'Art Moderne de la Ville de Troyes. This painting has a similar palette to that in *Nature morte à la corbeille d'osier* but includes three spindly figures in nineteenth-century dress.

LANDSCAPE

33 *Castelgandalfo* 1921
oil on canvas 62.2 × 75 cm
Kunstmuseum, Berne (fig. 78)
Provenance: Private Collection, Berlin
Exhibitions: 1935 Basle (48); 1935 Berne (36)

Castelgandalfo, which Derain visited in January 1921, is on Lake Albano, along the ancient Appian Way south of Rome. Albano was a favourite site for landscape artists of all nationalities, and particularly for the French. Most notably

for Derain it was a site frequently painted by Corot. The inspiration of both Corot and Cézanne is noticeable in *Castelgandalfo*, and it might be compared with pre-war works, such as those Derain painted in 1912 of Carrières St Denis, in which buildings are viewed through a veil of trees and foliage.

A comparison might also be made between this painting and the exactly contemporary work of Maurice Vlaminck. The nature of the view, the palette, and the slight asymmetry of the buildings are all comparable to the works of Derain's old friend from Chatou who, like Derain, was greatly celebrated in the post-war period and throughout the 1920s.

34 *Forêt de pins près de Saint Cyr* 1922
oil on canvas 49.9 × 60.8 cm
Private Collection

From 1922 Derain went nearly every summer to Sanary and Les Lecques villages on the Mediterranean coast between La Ciotat and Toulon. This painting of the landscape near Saint-Cyr-sur-Mer in that region is typical of the works of the period in both its yellow palette and its spacious composition. Considering the light touch, lively handling, and almost experimental freedom of composition in this work it is difficult to associate it with Derain's brooding over the impossibility of landscape painting just a few months previously. One might better associate it with his elation over the effects of the mistral which he communicated to Kahnweiler in the autumn of 1921. During the 1920s, Derain spent at least as much time in the country as he did in Paris, and his landscapes are characterized by a freedom and variety greater than at any other

time in his life. *Forêt de pins près de Saint Cyr* is true *plein-air* painting as are many of Derain's works of the 1920s, in contrast to the carefully constructed Cézanniste landscapes of 1913 and the majestic Poussin inspired landscapes of the early 1930s.

35 *La Forêt de Fontainebleau* 1927
oil on canvas 43 × 65 cm
Musée National d'Art Moderne, Paris
Provenance: donation of the Société des Amis du Luxembourg [Friends of the Luxembourg Museum, Paris], 1929
Exhibitions: on loan to the Musée des Beaux-Arts de Dijon from 1963

Derain's house at Chailly-en-Bière, on the edge of the Forêt de Fontainebleau, provided him with access to landscape-painting sites which had been those of the Barbizon painters, of Corot and Courbet, and of earlier French schools such as the eighteenth-century decorative painters. It was likely at this time also that Derain became interested in the Ecole de Fontainebleau of the late sixteenth and early seventeenth centuries.

Derain never abandoned *plein-air* painting, and it was characteristic of him to 'prospect' for landscape motifs in the same area for several years.

36 *La route et l'arbre* c.1928–30
oil on canvas 72.9 × 59.8 cm
Kunstmuseum, Berne (fig. 80)
Provenance: Paul Bangerter collection
Exhibitions: 1935, Berne (79); 1935, Basle (79)

In the late 1920s and early 1930s Derain painted many landscapes in the area around Avignon and between Avignon and the sea. During the summer months he stayed in small hotels or rented a house in a village, just as he had done before the war. He drove along narrow country roads, either alone or with friends from Paris, looking for new motifs and stopping frequently to paint small and quickly executed sketches. Derain's friend Jean Oberlé maintains that Derain did as many as three of these sketches a day. From time to time he would also set up his easel for a much more ambitious composition such as this picture, which nevertheless retains the freshness and immediacy of the oil sketches.

The turning path, directing the view to the rocky mass in the background, is reminiscent of Corot, as is the palette and handling of this painting. The site depicted here may be the approach to the 'massif du Luberon', not far from Villeneuve-lès-Avignon.

37 *Vue de Saint Maximin* 1930
oil on canvas 60 × 73 cm
Musée National d'Art
    Moderne, Paris (fig. 49)
Provenance: Paul Guillaume
    collection Musée du
    Luxembourg
Exhibitions: 1931, New
    York; 1937, Warsaw; 1955,
    Marseilles, Musée d'Art,
    'Exposition d'art
    moderne'; 1956, Berlin,
    Kunstakademie; 1957, Paris,
    Institut National
    Pédagogique; 1960, Nice,
    Palais de la Méditerranée,
    'Peintres à Nice et sur la Côte
    d'Azur'; 1961, Paris, Musée
    Notre Dame; 1964, Nice,
    Palais de la Méditerranée, 'Le
    Midi des peintres'

Derain painted several views in this mountainous region twenty miles from Aix-en-Provence. The isolated town and its thirteenth-century basilica interested him greatly. In his notes he records the history of

the place, the legends of St Mary Magdalene's travels in the south of France and of her relics, which remained in St Maximin until this century (Doucet MS 6910, f.2r).

This picture is the most imposing of Derain's views of the basilica. It is clearly based on nineteenth-century classical views, particularly those of Ingres and Corot, and is strikingly similar to Corot's *Vue d'Avignon* of 1836. A drawing for *Vue de Saint Maximin*, now in the Lévy collection in Troyes, shows that Derain first intended to paint the basilica from just beyond the sturdy medieval town walls. Eventually, however, he drew back to include the stone rubble beside the path as a second line of retreat from the mass of the basilica, thereby bringing his composition into closer correspondence with his nineteenth-century models.

In February 1931 the Marie Harriman Gallery in New York held an exhibition of nine Derain landscape paintings from the previous summer (*see* cat. 34). Among these was a *Paysage Saint Maximin* which may have been this painting or one of the several smaller views. If it had been to America, this picture was certainly back in the Galerie Paul Guillaume in Paris by the end of 1932. It was quickly recognized as a major work in Derain's *œuvre* and of museum quality. In March 1933 the keeper of the Musée de Luxembourg wrote to the Director General of the museum that, as the Musée de Luxembourg did not own an important work by Derain and the prices of his paintings were rising very high, they risked being reproached in the near future for neglecting to buy while they could. He suggested the *Vue de Saint Maximin*, for which he had been negotiating

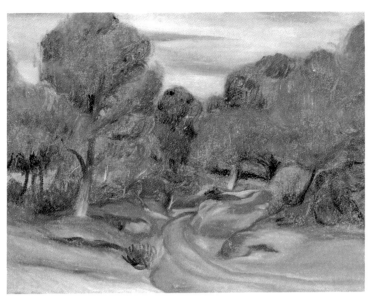

34

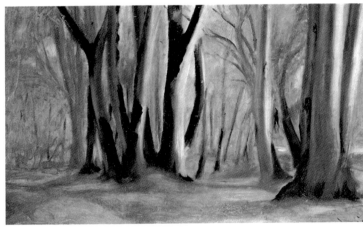

35

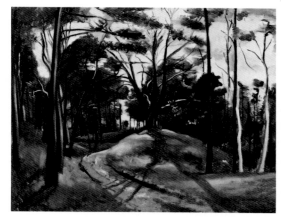

38

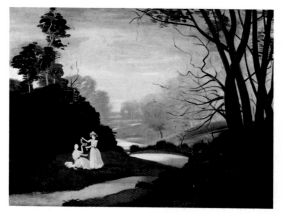

42

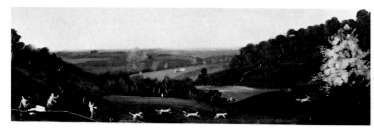

43

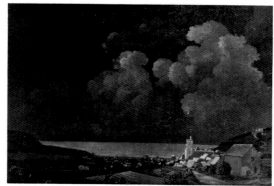

41

for some months with Paul Guillaume, and the work was subsequently acquired by the museum.

38 *Le sentier à Ollières* 1930
oil on canvas 73 × 92 cm
Private Collection, Paris
Provenance: Galerie Schmit, Paris
Exhibitions: 1976, Paris (39)

In the exhibition 'Nine New Landscapes by Derain' which was held at the Marie Harriman Gallery in New York in 1931, four of the paintings were of the landscape at Ollières. Ollières is in the rugged hills of the Vivarais, through which fast-flowing rivers such as the Ardèche descend into the Rhône. The landscape there is very different from that of Provence and Var where Derain normally painted, and yet it is not a full day's drive from Avignon.

This painting and others of the same period, particularly *La fontaine d'Ollières* (Private Collection, Paris; Sutton, 1959, p. 70; Tokyo, 1981, exh.cat., 33) are influenced by Derain's landscapes in the Fontainebleau forest of sandy or stony paths between tall trees. A precedent for *Le sentier à Ollières* can be found as early as 1912 in *Sentier dans la Forêt de Fontainebleau* in the Pushkin Museum in Moscow. The composition is also reminiscent of Derain's paintings at Chailly-en-Bière in 1926–7.

39 *La route* 1930–1
oil on canvas 65 × 50 cm
Musée de l'Orangerie, Collection Jean Walther et Paul Guillaume (fig. 79)
Provenance: Paul Guillaume, Mme J. Walther
Exhibitions: 1940, Rio de Janeiro, Museu d'Arte, 'La peinture française' (26); 1941, Los Angeles, The

Young Memorial Gallery, 'Exhibition of French Art' (53a); 1954, Paris (26); 1957, London (59); 1958, Paris (7); 1966, Paris, Musée de l'Orangerie, 'Collection Walther Guillaume' (87); 1976, Rome (44); 1977, Paris (44)

This view of the small Provençal town of Eygalières is painted from the road which leads to Saint Rémy. Derain painted Eygalières many times (*see* Musée de l'Orangerie, *Paysage du Midi* and *Arbres et village,* also Galerie Schmit, exh.cat., 1976, 44, 45) and was attracted to the combination of green farmland and rocky outcrops in this area where the 'massif du Luberon' meets the plain of Camargue. This picture is Derain's most striking study of the effect of the strong Provençal light on the landscape of the south and reflects his sustained interest in Cézanne and Corot. The composition, established by the angle cut by the road, is based on Corot's paintings at Volterra, paintings which were an important source for Cézanne. The measured approach to the rising town, subtly suggested in the series of horizontal shadows in the foreground and crop lines in the middle distance, indicates Derain's thorough understanding of the construction of Cézanne's distant views.

The frothy handling of the foliage, the liquid drawing in the trees, and the soft brushstrokes in the road create a sensuous surface which contrasts with the crystalline quality of the town and the clarity of the composition. This combination of sensuality and order is characteristic of many of Derain's works in this period, for example his *Portrait of Madame Guillaume* (fig. 47).

40 *La danse* 1933
oil on canvas 72 × 92 cm
Private Collection, Paris
Exhibitions: 1954, Paris
(84); 1976, Paris (46)

This picture is modelled on
Corot's several woodland
scenes with dancing maenads,
both the foamy glades painted in
the 1850s such as the Louvre's
*Une matinée: La danse des
nymphes* and the earlier works
such as *Silène* of 1838 (Private
Collection, USA), a painting so
similar to Derain's *La danse*
that it may have been its model.
Derain's very large decorative
piece, *L'Age d'or* (cat. 4) is
clearly linked to *La danse*. The
figure in the foreground of *La
danse,* dancing and holding a
tambourine, is similar to the
main figure in Derain's large
canvas, and the gesturing
figures appearing from behind
the trees, particularly on the
right-hand side of the
composition are also comparable
to the figures in the larger work.
The landscape of *La danse* is
related to paintings from the
mid-1930s, such as *The Spring,*
now in the J. Henry Haggerty
Collection in New Jersey, in
which the shadowy glades seem
to refer to the sacred places of a
pantheistic cult. *La danse* might
also be compared with the many
small oil studies of figures
dancing in the woods or bathing
in woodland pools, such as those
which have recently come to the
Musée des Beaux Arts in
Geneva from the Photiades
collection.
This painting, in fact, makes
reference to the rites of
Dionysius which from the
beginning of the century were of
great interest to all of Derain's
generation, steeped as they were
in Nietzsche's *Birth of Tragedy
in the Spirit of Music*. In the
1930s and 1940s Derain used
the Dionysian defence against
reason in his own ruminations.

His notes show his attention not
only to Euripides – 'those who
are wise are not wisdom itself
cry the followers of Bacchus'
(Doucet MS 6911, f. 2v) – but
also to the genesis of the cult
from ancient Panic tree worship
and the function of Dionysus as
a god of suffering.

41 *Paysage à Ault* c.1935
oil on canvas 116 × 167 cm
Private Collection, Japan
Provenance: Caroline Reboux
collection; Falk collection
Exhibitions: 1942, Paris,
Galerie Drouin, 'Rivages de
France'; 1959, Geneva (88)

Ault is on the Picard coast of
France about twenty miles
north-east of Dieppe. In the
1930s the Derains and the
Braques frequently met in
Dieppe, and Derain often
stayed in Braque's house at
Varangeville, a fishing port less
than ten miles away. Derain
made an etching of a very
similar view of Ault
(Bibliothèque Nationale, 1955,
exh.cat., 102), and when Jean
Adhémar examined the plates
remaining in Derain's studio at
his death, he recorded that this
print was etched on the same
plate as *Apollon*, a print closely
related to Derain's illustrations
to *Les Héroïdes* (cat. 123). The
seascapes in the *Les Héroïdes*
illustrations, such as *Calypso,*
and in another set of prints, *Les
Luminaires* (cat. 76), are
derived from Derain's studies at
Ault.
In this picture the great
turbulent sky over the sea at Ault
makes reference to Dutch
painting, an uncharacteristic
influence on Derain's
landscape. It is comparable to
the dramatic skies in such wartime works as *Les deux hangars*
and *La paysage triste* (both
Musée d'Art Moderne de la
Ville de Troyes), and it is likely
that this highly romantic

landscape painting of the 1940s
began with Derain's work on
the northern coasts of France in
the mid-1930s. At the same
time Derain's studies of boats at
Gravelines and Dunkirk, works
such as the *Cimetière des bateaux
à Gravelines* of 1935 in the
Musée d'Art Moderne de la
Ville de Paris, often have a subtle
melancholic quality and a
palette close to that of Georges
Braque. These are not evident
in *Paysage à Ault,* but it is an
equally emotive landscape.

42 *Paysage à deux personnages*
c.1938
oil on canvas 109 × 144 cm
Private Collection, Paris
Provenance: Marie Harriman
Gallery, New York
Exhibitions: 1938, New
York; 1980, Paris, Galerie
Schmit; 1981, Tokyo,
Nagoya (55)

In November 1938 a
photograph of this work
appeared in the New York
journal, *Art News,* with the
caption: 'Landscape: Derain's
rendering of an Eighteenth
Century Spacial Concept'. The
awkwardness of this
identification of Derain's
sources reflects the journalist's
attempt to associate this
decorative painting with
Derain's recent landscapes.
Derain's interest in the 'fancy
pictures' of Lancret, Pater and
Fragonard, however, is not
surprising in the light of his
contemporary interest in the
other 'minor genre' of the
eighteenth-century outdoors, 'la
chasse'.
Throughout the twentieth
century, long views of formal
gardens, lovers on ivy-covered
balustrades, *commedia dell'arte*
figures glimpsed in the distance
by a fountain – the
paraphernalia of the rococo –
had provided substance for the
mural decorations of wealthy

French patrons (see, for
example, Pierre Laprade's *Le
parc,* 1909, commissioned by
Xavier de Magallon). Although,
as Germain Bazin established
(Bazin, 1933), Derain's
traditionalism was far different
from that of Laprade and
Guerin, he was certainly aware
of the work of such painters.
Unlike the works of these
pasticheur decorators, however,
Derain's *Paysage à deux
personnages* shares with the
works of Lancret and
Fragonard an overriding
concern for ambient light. The
blushing luminosity of the sky is
accentuated by the shadows
in the foreground and by the
trees at the right seen *contre jour*.
The palette is carefully divided,
the masses of earth tones in the
foreground providing a foil for
the atmospheric perspective in
the farther planes.
This work might be
compared with the illustrations
to *Amie et Amille* (cat. 127).

43 *La chasse* after 1945
oil on canvas 83 × 236 cm
Collection André Derain fils
Provenance: estate of the artist
Exhibitions: 1955b, Paris
(60); 1974, Albi (36); 1976,
Paris (67); 1981, Tokyo (60)

It is very likely that this work,
which remained in Derain's
house at his death, was painted
to hang in the house at
Chambourcy and not meant for
sale. It continues the decorative
attitude to landscape painting
begun with *Paysage à deux
personnages* (cat. 42), but
referring in this case to
eighteenth-century English,
rather than French, painting.
The airy landscape and long,
frieze-like composition associate
this work with the sporting
pictures of Tillemans,
Wootton, and Seymour. Derain
made several trips to England in
the 1930s and may have known

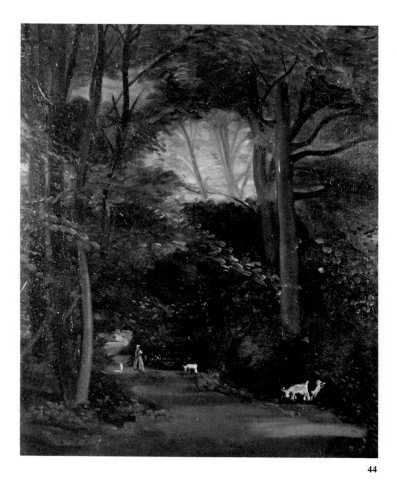

44

such works from the national collections and country houses there, as well as from dealers' exhibitions in Paris. The grand panorama implied in this work might also be compared with Derain's most ambitious late landscape, *Grand paysage classique,* now in the Hiroshima Museum in Japan.

44 *Les chèvres à Chambourcy*
c.1948–9
oil on canvas 81 × 65 cm
Musée d'Art Moderne de la
    Ville de Paris
Provenance: Germaine Henry-
    Robert Thomas collection,
    1976
Exhibitions: 1974, Paris,
    Caisse Nationale des
    Monuments Historiques et
    des Sites, 'Collection
    Germaine Henry-Robert
    Thomas' (29); 1976, Paris,
    Musée d'Art Moderne de la
    Ville de Paris, 'Donation
    Germaine Henry-Robert
    Thomas' (22); 1980, Paris,
    Musée d'Art Moderne de la
    Ville de Paris (p. 27)

In the 1940s goats roamed freely in the fields and copses at Chambourcy and often appeared in Derain's garden, where a small stream ran through a little thicket, or in the meadow near the sculpture studio. They provided Derain with a motif for works in the manner of Corot or of eighteenth-century pastoral painting. A classical and poetic theme, the association between these works and the Bacchanalian woodland scenes such as *La danse* (cat. 40) should not be overlooked, and in fact Derain's manuscript notes on Dionysius are followed by an account of another woodland god, Agni, a bearded goat or ram (Doucet MS 6911).

Derain's niece Geneviève Taillade posed for the figure of the goatherd in this painting.

PORTRAITS

45 *Female Head c.*1920
oil on canvas 32.5 × 23.8 cm
Kunstmuseum, Berne (fig. 85)
Provenance: Mr and Mrs
    Walter Bangerter Collection
Exhibitions: 1975, Berne,
    'Zehn Jahre Sammlungs-
    gewachs'

This study of a head or portrait of an unknown woman has the same intensity as the *Portrait of Madame Carco* (cat. 47). Although it is an intimate work and delicately modelled, it is related to the more strongly modelled and far more stylized heads of 1920, such as that which was once in the collection of Lucien Descaves (Sutton, 1959, p. 45). The humane sense of the pathetic in all these works is related to the melancholic qualities of Derain's studies of women just before the war, although here it is understated and less generalized. There is a mystical quality in this head emerging from the dark background which is based on traditions of tenebrist painting.

46 *The Artist in his Studio*
1920–1
oil on canvas 116 × 89 cm
Estate of Pierre Matisse (fig. 84)
Provenance: Fukushima
    collection, Tokyo
Exhibitions: 1935, London,
    Leicester Galleries, 'Fifty
    Years of Portraits'
    (92); 1947, Chicago (22)

This complex portrait with its 'traditioniste' reliance upon Renaissance and sixteenth-century Flemish painting is a precursor of Derain's *c.*1939 *The Painter and His Family (see* cat. 55) and in the 1930s was known as *L'Artiste et sa famille.* Madame Derain at one time identified the figure in the background as herself and the small figure in the foreground as a servant. If it is indeed Madame Derain in the background, she is included in the guise of a model posing. Her bare shoulders, the white drape tucked under her arms, associates the pose with a nineteenth-century orientalist model in the manner of Delacroix or Ingres. This figure is closely related to the studies, both drawings and paintings, which Derain made in the early 1920s of women with their hair dressed in a large chignon seen from the back (see cat. 9 and the *Portrait of Madame Renou*, 1924, Private Collection, Paris).

The figure in the foreground is the same little boy who posed for Derain's *Le gosse assis* (Musée du Petit Palais, Geneva) and is treated in a similar way, with the same tilted head and wistful look. The stiff vertical bouquet at one end of the table is like that in the *Portrait of Madame Derain in a White Shawl* (Tate Gallery, London) which Derain painted either during or just after the First World War, reusing a canvas he had painted in 1913. The still life in the middle of the table composed of a spoon, pipe, and fruit compares closely with cat. 21. A tiny *Still Life* in the Raeber Collection in Basle is a study for the still-life element of *The Artist in his Studio* and includes a flat dish which appears in another early study for this painting, a gouache study for the portrait as a whole (fig. 82), which was exhibited in the Lefevre Gallery, London, in 1928. This portrait gouache does not include the child or the woman but in all other particulars is similar to *The Artist in his Studio*. The table in front of the artist with the still-life elements on it, the pose which Derain takes, his right hand curled toward him and held above the palette which is

in his left hand, the cravat, the hat, the shadow cast against the canvas, the green curtain behind, all of these are directly comparable to *The Artist in his Studio*.

This gouache marks Derain's development of a more complex portrait type, as can be seen by comparison with an earlier self-portrait, in which he appears in a similar though not identical pose, in a white cravat but no hat, which from 1917 had been in the John Quinn Collection in New York (fig. 82). The Quinn self-portrait, which is now in the Minneapolis Institute of Arts, is in the severe 'Gothic' style of *Le samedi* (fig. 28) and *Les buveurs* (fig. 29). It is a work of the directly pre-war period and is based on a still earlier self-portrait of about 1911–12 (Priv. Coll., Paris) in which Derain had aped the curvilinear damp-fold style of the twelfth century and added an inscription in magiscule, 'André Derain Peintre', in the manner of fifteenth-century French portraits.

The comparison with Derain's pre-war portraits points up the humanity of *The Artist in his Studio*, in contrast to the impersonal severity of many of the directly pre-war paintings. The child holding fruit harks back directly to Derain's painting *L'Offrande* of 1913 (Kunsthalle, Bremen) but has lost the liturgical stiffness and the strong stylization of the earlier figure. Derain's profound interest in Renaissance painting in the early 1920s led to a gentler treatment of the human image, as well as to a grander and more complex conception of portrait painting.

47 *Portrait of Madame Carco*
   1921
oil on canvas 34 × 24 cm
Kunstmuseum, Zurich (fig 86)

Provenance: Galerie Paul Guillaume, Paris

The sitter for this portrait was the wife of Derain's friend, the poet, novelist, and art critic Francis Carco. Derain had known Carco well in both Montmartre and the Quartier Latin before the First World War. After 1918 they rejoined each other in the café life of the Boulevard Saint Germain in which both Madame Derain and Madame Carco took part. Derain's portrait of Carco's beautiful young wife is influenced by Romano-Egyptian as well as Renaissance painting and carries with it the pathos of the antique model. Francis Carco's brother, Jérôme Carcopino, was a political and literary historian of Roman antiquity, and Derain may have found the Carco circle sympathetic to his own interest in Roman painting and sculpture. Derain eventually owned two Fayoum portraits, one male and one female.

After the war Derain made many studies of female heads, including paintings and several etchings published by Galerie Simon in 1920. Several of these are loosely based on antique models, but none is as closely inspired by Egyptian painting as this work. The *Portrait of Madame Carco* was reproduced in the journal of the Galerie Paul Guillaume, *Les Arts à Paris*, in May 1926. It might be compared with another picture which was reproduced in that journal some six years earlier in November 1920, Derain's classicizing *Portrait of Mlle L* (location unknown).

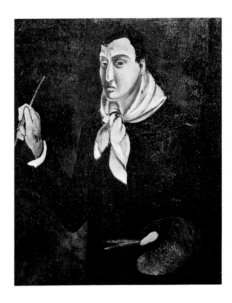

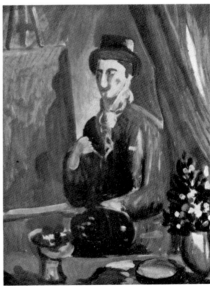

82. *Portrait of the Artist*, gouache, from catalogue of 'Exhibition of Works by André Derain', March 1928, Lefevre Galleries, London.

81. (top) *Self-Portrait*, c. 1913–14, Minneapolis Institute of Art.

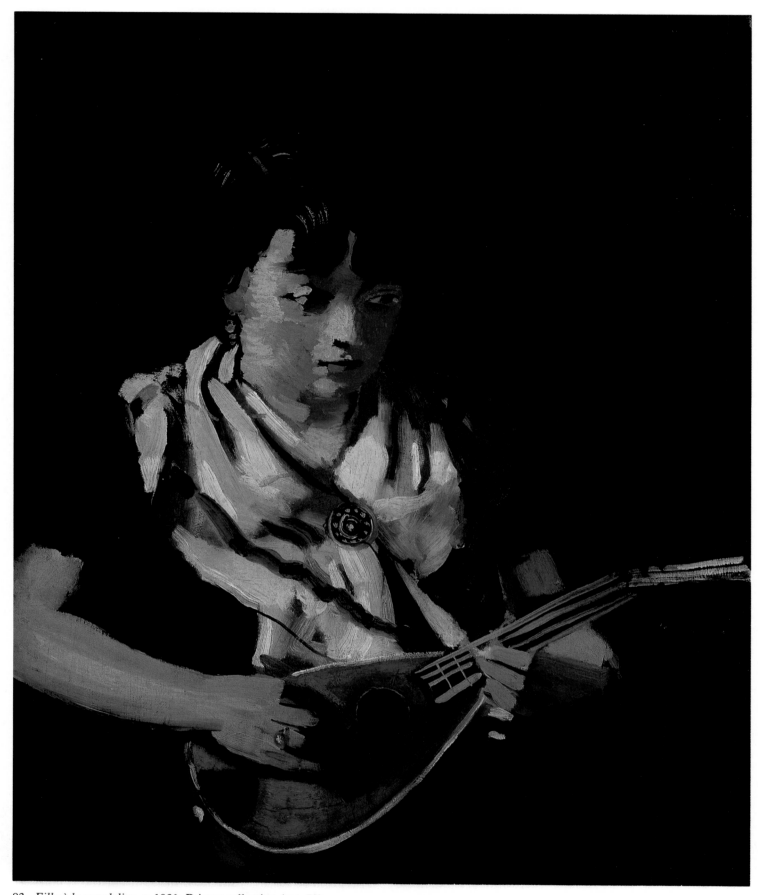

83. *Fille à la mandoline*, c. 1931, Private collection (cat. 52).

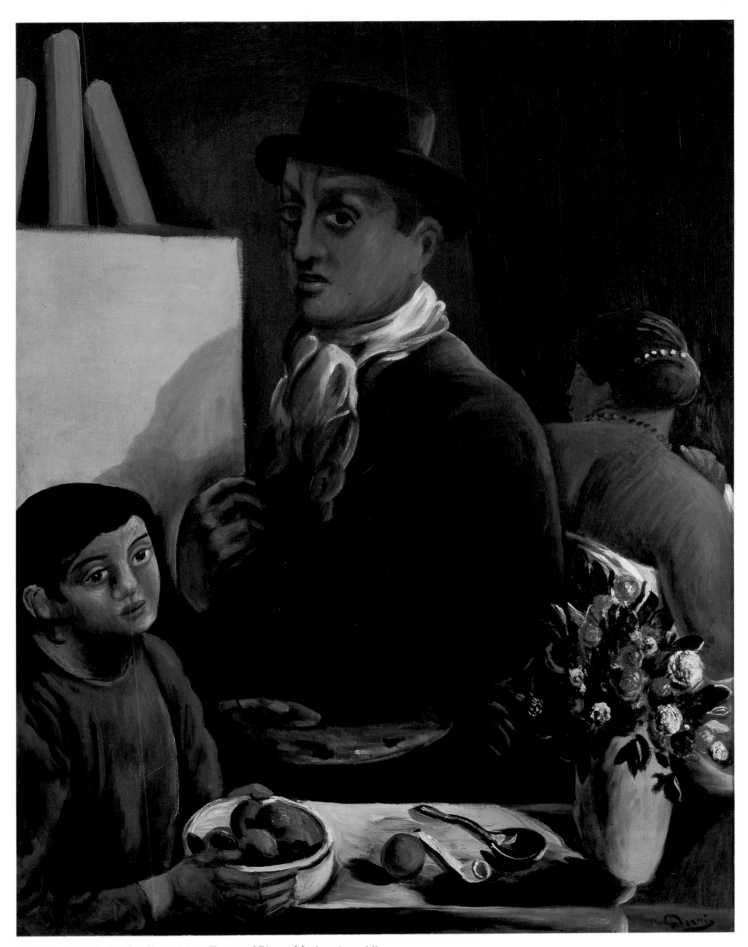

84. *The Artist in his Studio*, 1920–1, Estate of Pierre Matisse (cat. 46).

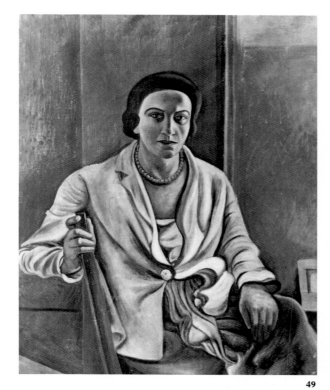

49

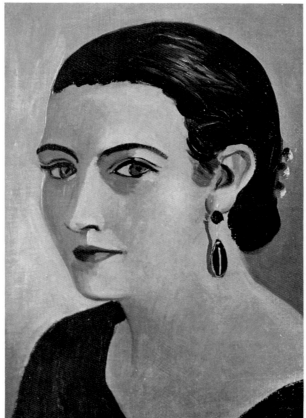

48

48 *Portrait of Madame Derain*
1922
oil on canvas 37 × 26 cm
Collection André Derain fils
Exhibitions: 1981, Tokyo,
Nagoya (20)

Madame Derain was Alice
Marie Géry, born in the heart
of Paris at the Quai de l'Hotel
de Ville in 1884. Her father was
Limousin and her mother was
Basque. Her formal education
was not extensive – she was
largely self-taught – but she had
a quick intelligence, wide
interests and was well-read even
as a young woman. Her cousins,
who knew the young Spanish
artistic and poetic society in
Paris, introduced her to Pablo
Picasso, and through Picasso
she met Montmartre bohemian
society. She painted a little
herself and earned some money
by selling her works to a
postcard company. One
evening in Montmartre, Derain
came into the restaurant where
Alice was dining with Picasso
and joined them at the table. At
this time Alice was married to
Maurice Princet, a young
mathematician who earned a
living as an insurance actuary
but who followed the lectures of
Henri Bergson at the University
of Paris and who transmitted to
the artists of Montmartre his
own enthusiasm for Bergson's
theories of time, space and the
'fourth dimension'. Alice
divorced Princet and married
Derain in 1907.

Alice's experience of life
among the studios of Paris since
her teenage years and her innate
good sense were to prove
invaluable to Derain. Impatient
with practical matters, he relied
on Alice to act as an
intermediary, and Kahnweiler
often paid Alice for canvases
which she would arrange to be
delivered to his gallery. During
the First World War she took
over her husband's affairs and
arranged the loan of paintings
to exhibitions, as well as the sale
of works to the Norwegian
dealer Walther Halvorsen and
the setting up of a one-man show
with the young Parisian dealer
Paul Guillaume.

She was a very striking
woman whose elegance made
her a favourite of the greatest
fashion designer of the time,
Paul Poiret. As Clive Bell
records in his memoires of Paris
after the First World War, *Old
Friends*, Alice and André
Derain held a kind of court
among the poets and painters in
the cafés of the Boulevard Saint
Germain in the 1920s (Bell,
1956, p. 175). Although the
Derains tended to avoid the rich
and fashionable set which
Derain's dealer Paul Guillaume
cultivated, Alice often visited
the Guillaume couple. She liked
Paul Guillaume and was
grateful for his devotion to her
husband's affairs. She was
always happy to welcome the
'bande à Derain', either in Paris
or in the country. Like her
husband and many of his
friends, Alice was a discerning
collector, and her rich collection
of antique 'santons', crèche
figures from the eighteenth and
early nineteenth centuries, were
an inspiration to Derain's book
illustrations, particularly to
those for *Amie et Amille*
(cat. 127).

In the late 1940s and the early
1950s, when Derain tended to
retire from a wide circle of
friends, Alice still led a very
active life between Chambourcy
and Paris and on frequent
holidays in the Midi and in
Spain. Derain had become
increasingly suspicious of both
dealers and collectors, and Alice
had found herself once again his
intermediary. After Derain's
death Alice surrounded herself
with his most trusted friends,
Georges Braque, André
Dunoyer de Segonzac, Robert

Dignimont, who advised her on the arrangements she made for the protection of her husband's work and the interests of his son. With the help of Jean Adhémar, Madame Derain selected from among Derain's prints a major donation to the Bibliothèque Nationale. She also donated several important works to the nation including *Le retour d'Ulysse* (cat. 2) and *L'Age d'or* (cat. 4).

49 *Portrait of Madame Derain*
c.1922
oil on canvas 92 × 73 cm
Collection André Derain fils

50 *Portrait of Vincent Muselli*
1925
oil on canvas 61 × 50 cm
Private Collection, Paris
    (fig. 46)
Inscribed 'A Vincent' and
    signed lower-right corner
Provenance: Emile Vautheret
    collection, Lyons; Galerie
    Schmit, Paris
Exhibitions: 1955b, Paris
    (59); 1976, Paris (32)

The sitter is Derain's friend, the poet Vincent Muselli (1879–1956). Muselli had been trained as a Latinist by the Jesuits at Le Mans and was a leading classicist among the poets of his generation. His poems play with great subtlety on classical forms and themes, and the excellence of his verse is based on a thorough understanding of the tradition of pastiche in late Roman literature. This expertise and the fluid, evocative verse to which it led were much admired by Derain. Muselli's first major collection of poems was *Les Travaux et les Jeux*, first published in 1914 but republished in 1929. The later edition was illustrated with forty lithographs by Derain (*see* cat. 119). Muselli was a friend of Francis Carco, of Jean Poulihan, and of André Billy, who wrote a description of him

which relates well to Derain's portrait: 'Muselli has one of the finest manes I have known, a thick, black, curly mane under which his forehead seems enormous' (Silvanie, 1957, p. 13).

There is a tenderness in Derain's portraits of his close friends which is carried in the light, fluid brushwork and gentle modelling of the facial features, as well as in the distinct and sympathetic characterization of the sitter. This portrait might be compared with a portrait painted four years earlier, that of Georges Gabory, the young poet who was a protégé of Muselli and Derain in the 1920s (Private Collection, Great Britain), and another, made nearly seven years later, of the painter Robert Dignimont (Private Collection, Paris). In all these portraits the manner of painting is quite different from the suave, classical virtues of such grand portraits as that of Madame Guillaume (fig. 47).

51 *Le gitan* c.1926
oil on canvas 101 × 81 cm
Musée d'Art Moderne de la
    Ville de Paris
Provenance: bought from the
    artist in 1936
Exhibitions: 1947, Zurich, 'Art
    français' (208); 1947,
    Switzerland, 'Quelques
    oeuvres des collections de la
    ville de Paris' (25); 1952,
    Rotterdam, 'Maîtres français
    du Petit Palais' (47); 1966,
    Paris, Musée des Arts
    Décoratifs, 'Les années 25'
    (15); 1974, Turkey,
    Czechoslovakia, 'Art français'

The revival of the Spanish baroque in French romantic painting is the foundation of this picture. But, although the type of figure is Spanish, *Le gitan* is as closely related to the works of Gericault or Manet as it is to Ribera.

Derain's romantic genre figure succeeds the harlequins of the early 1920s, and the smooth Renaissance-inspired finish of those earlier works is replaced by the soft, loose brushwork and dramatic light effects of Spanish Caravaggist painting. As in the work of Ribera, local colour is applied at points of light upon a dark canvas. This work also seems to be allied to the theories of light and form which Derain explored in his notes at the beginning of the decade. Extreme tenebrism was a recurrent force in Derain's work, and this painting might be considered as much in the development of Derain's dark still-life paintings of the late 1930s, or the light-on-dark nudes of the Second World War period, as in the development of his painting of genre figures.

52 *Fille à la mandoline* c.1931
oil on canvas 72.5 × 59.2 cm
Private Collection (fig. 83)
Provenance: Paul Guillaume
    collection, Paris; W. Averell
    and Marie Harriman
    collection, New York
Exhibitions: 1931,
    Pennsylvania Museum; 1932,
    New York, Marie Harriman
    Gallery, 'French
    Paintings'; 1933, St Louis,
    Newhouse Gallery; 1934,
    San Francisco, The
    California Palace of the
    Legion of Honour; 1947,
    Chicago; 1976, Paris
    (41); 1981, Tokyo, Nagoya
    (42)

This work, inspired by Corot's lute players, is contemporary with Derain's views of St Maximin (cat. 37) in the manner of Corot's landscape painting. The influence of Courbet's pictures of servant girls is also apparent, particularly in the creamy white and blue scarf over the model's shoulders (*see*, for example,

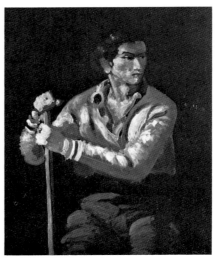

51

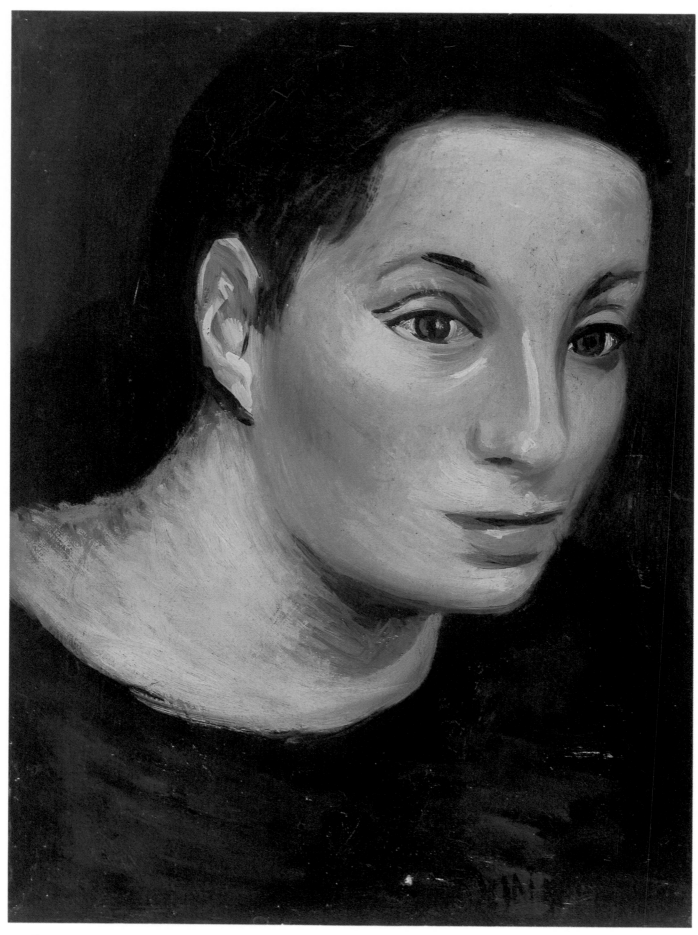

85. *Female Head*, c. 1920, Kunstmuseum, Berne (cat. 45).

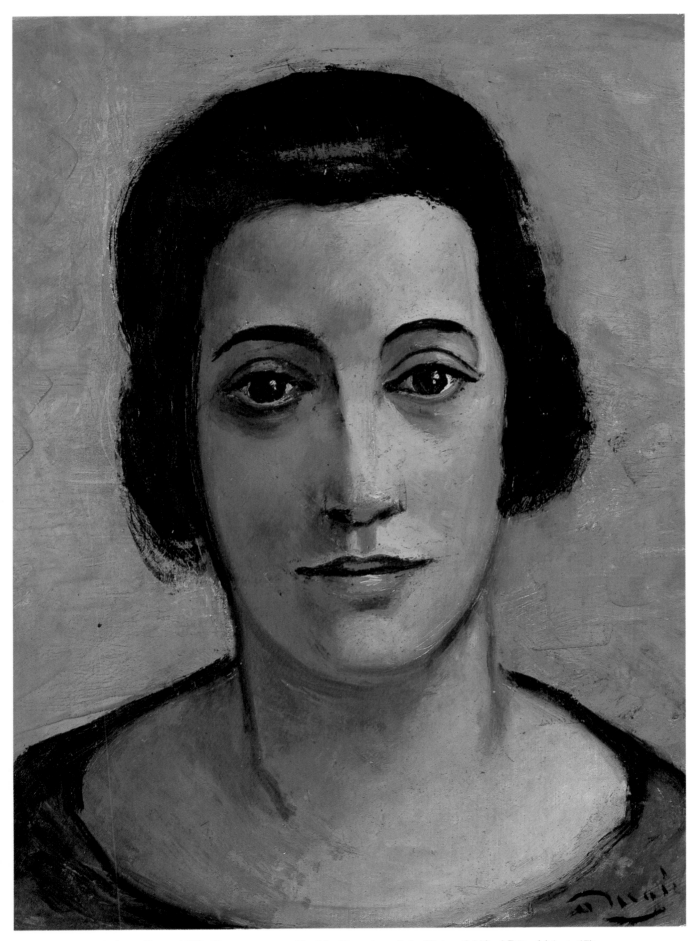

86. *Portrait of Madame Carco*, 1921, Kunstmuseum, Zurich, Donation of the Heirs of Alfred Rütschi (cat. 47).

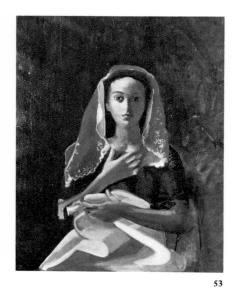

53

Courbet's *Sleeping Servant*, Lefevre Gallery, London). The brushwork and the emergence of the figure from a very dark background associate this work with Derain's earlier painting, *Le gitan* (cat. 51).

Derain asserted in his treatise on painting that the way to paint is either with a scale of black and white or with two or three pure colours, but that it is the internal scale of a picture, the ratio of its opposing surfaces, that gives it expression: 'one can add colour that doesn't count, but that's a matter of taste' (Doucet MS 6887, f. 42v). In this work, however, ten years after his treatise was written, colour, tone and 'the size of surfaces' are all of equal importance, each subtly influencing the other. Particularly striking is Derain's care with the colour and underpainting. The lower-left three-quarters of the painting, underpainted in a rich terracotta, is divided along a diagonal from the upper-right quarter, which is underpainted in olive green. The border between the two adds to the intensity created by modelling the dark side of the face not in light and dark but in a bright terracotta, like that of the underpainting. This manner of modelling in colour is comparable with the portrait of Derain's niece, *Geneviève à la pomme* (cat. 54), painted a few years later.

Genre figures were a favourite theme of the contemporary Ecole de Paris, within which Derain was much admired. Often, however, in works such as those by Kisling, these painters strained after sentiment, 'tristesse', and the works were repetitive and mawkish. Unlike those of the Ecole de Paris, Derain's genre figures have nothing to do with 'modern life' but refer directly to romantic tradition.

53 *Geneviève à la mantille*
  c.1937
oil on canvas 94 × 75 cm
Private Collection, France

Madame Derain collected fine pieces of old lace which her niece would occasionally wear to church. This portrait of Geneviève in her late teens casts the young woman as a Renaissance Madonna. Derain owned a painting of the *Virgin and Child* attributed to Mabuse (Jan Gossaert), a work which appeared a few years later in a portrait of another young woman, Carmen Colle (Private Collection, Paris).

The deep folds of white cloth which Geneviève holds associate this work with the *Still Life* with rolled paper (cat. 29). As in the still life, not only tone but sweeping counter-curves interest Derain, and the lines of the drapery, with the position of the arms, set up a continuous series of opposing angles which lead to the face. The hands posed at an angle, one above the other, might be compared with Geneviève's hands in *The Painter and his Family* (cat. 55) where one is directly above the other, adding to the stable columnar effect of that standing pose. The strong architecture which rises through the centre of the figure to the face is made even more pronounced by the loose, broken silhouette below the level of the mantilla, where the elbows particularly show several pentimenti.

54 *Geneviève à la pomme*
  1937–8
oil on canvas 92 × 73 cm
Private Collection, France
  (fig. 89)
Provenance: Estate of the artist
Exhibitions: 1954–5, Rome, Villa Medici, and Paris, Grand Palais (99); 1957, London (63); 1964, Marseilles (53); 1964, New York (28); 1974, Albi (24); 1976, Paris (54)

Derain painted his niece, Madame Geneviève Taillade, many times, and she recalls at least twenty-four portraits. The portrait of Geneviève in the Albright-Knox collection, Buffalo, N.Y., *Girl Peeling Fruit*, which is very similar to *Geneviève à la pomme*, was begun at the same time as this painting. According to Madame Taillade, Derain painted them simultaneously and continued them both for some time after she had finished her poses.

Geneviève Taillade was born in Paris in 1919, the daughter of Suzanne Géry, Alice Derain's sister. When she was eight days old she was taken by her aunt to Derain's studio in the Rue Bonaparte where both Derain and Braque, neither of whom had ever seen a new-born, both reacted with such horror that it became a legend in the two families. A few months later, however, Geneviève had become sufficiently presentable for Derain to paint the first portrait, a full-faced baby in a close-fitting bonnet, now in a private collection in Paris. Suzanne Géry was alone with her daughter, and from 1919 to 1924 they lived with her father who had retired to Bougival (Yvelines). When François Géry died, they moved to Derain's house at Chailly-en-Bière where they lived until 1928. In that year they moved into the new house in the Rue du Douanier where they lived with Alice and André Derain until 1935, travelling with them to the Château Parouzeau. There are two portraits from this period in the Musée de l'Orangerie, *La nièce du peintre* and *La nièce du peintre assise*.

Derain took a close interest in Geneviève's education at her catholic college, St Germain des

Prés, but apart from his insistence upon the prime importance of Latin, his ideas were fairly traditional. Her education revolved around the piano, with a little Italian for singing and German so that she might have a foundation for 'northern' languages such as English. In 1935 Suzanne and Geneviève moved with the Derains to Chambourcy. In 1943 Geneviève married Robert Joseph Taillade, with Georges Braque as her witness. After the war she lived with her mother, her husband, and eventually her two children in the pavilion next to Derain's house at Chambourcy. As Alice and Suzanne became elderly and frail, Geneviève and her family moved into the big house in order to care for them more easily.

Geneviève à la pomme, painted when Geneviève was eighteen, is based on a Renaissance portrait type associated with youth. It might be compared with the early sixteenth-century double portrait by a Venetian master in the Museo del Palazzo di Venezia in Rome (Pope-Hennessy, 1966, ill. 146, p. 137) in which a dreamy young man, his face half in shade, leans on a ledge with an apple in his hand. The direct influence of Raphael on Derain's portraits of his niece at this time is striking, and *Geneviève à la pomme* owes a great deal to Raphael's self-portrait now in the Uffizi. The complicated play of light and shadow in this painting, however, subverts the modelling of the forms by its stark contrasts, leaving a very shallow space in which the figure and the still life are drawn. This is particularly noticeable around the head where a line of light on one side and the sharp line of black hair against flesh on the other brings the face forward as a mask.

Derain worked with scores of large-scale photographs of the paintings in museums and great collections all over the world. Thirty years after his death there were well over a hundred of these still in his studio, including details of Piero della Francesca's *Dream of Constantine* (S. Francesco, Arezzo) which are a likely source for the dramatic lighting of *Geneviève à la pomme*.

55 *The Painter and his Family*
c.1939
oil on canvas 176.5 × 123 cm
Tate Gallery, London (fig. 88)
Provenance: Galerie Schmit, Paris
Exhibitions: 1940, New York (2); 1947, Chicago (19); 1954–5, Paris, 'André Derain' (91); 1967, Edinburgh, London (86); 1974, Albi (31); 1976, Paris (58); 1981, Tokyo, Nagoya (57); 1984, Melun (18); 1989, Cologne, Rein Hallen der Kölner Messe, 'Bilderstreit: Widerspruch, Einheit und Fragment in der Kunst seit 1960' (147)

Pictured with the artist in his home at Chambourcy are his wife Alice, reading in the foreground, his niece Geneviève, holding a small dog, and his sister-in-law, Suzanne Géry, entering the room from behind a dark curtain, the three women who, as Derain put it in a letter to Pierre Lévy, made up the '*côté féminin*' of his life (letter of 11 January 1950). Derain's life also included a menagerie of sorts: Geneviève had several dogs, and a peacock and hen roamed about in the country garden with the ducks and geese before the war. Derain represents himself in the act of painting a still life, a compote of fruit against a white linen table-cloth, a frequent motif of the period.

The painting is, however, so stylized and such a carefully orchestrated group of references to different traditions of portrait painting that we are left doubting the portrait's 'realism' or 'actuality'. Each element, for instance, takes on a symbolic significance, as in the seventeenth-century Dutch tradition of artists' 'emblem' portraits. The example to which Derain turns first, however, is that of Nicolas de Largillière, whose great series of portraits of famous artists spanned thirty years and epitomized the grand manner of the turn of the eighteenth century. Several of these were reunited in a celebrated exhibition of his work at the Petit Palais in 1928. In Derain's painting, the sweeping extended curves and the build-up of shallow space from a close overlapping of planes reveal the influence of the seventeenth-century master. Although Largillière's portraits were often elaborately composed and rich in allusive detail, they included an intense characterization of the artist's face. The face of Derain might be compared with that of the painter *Jean-Baptiste Forest* in Largillière's much copied masterpiece in the Musée des Beaux-Arts in Lille, as well as to later eighteenth-century portraits such as Angelica Kauffmann's portrait of Winckelmann now in the Kunstmuseum in Zurich. The major compositional structure of Derain's painting – opposing diagonals, one along the easel, the other through the artist and his niece – is a mannerism of the years around 1700. A work in the Louvre by Largillière's contemporary François Desportes, *Self-portrait as a Hunter*, may well be the source of this composition, as it is undoubtedly an influence upon other works by Derain of the same period (*see* cat. 3).

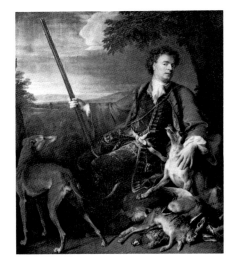

87. *The Artist as Hunter*, by Desportes, Musée du Louvre, Paris.

133

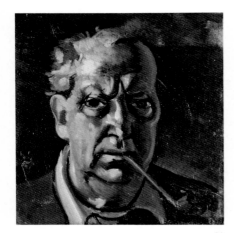

56

The traditions reflected in Derain's picture are by no means exclusively French. The table which spans the full width of the painting and stands between us and the artist is a seventeenth-century Dutch device. Perhaps the best-known example of this is Gerrit Dou's *Self-portrait* (1647) now in the Staatliche Gemäldegalerie in Dresden. Dutch painting also provides the inspiration for the figure of his wife Alice, reading in the half light and seated in the artist's line of sight, as he combines still life and portrait. Alice's pose is a combination of two Renaissance themes, the Virgin reading and the Virgin seated before St Luke who paints her portrait, but these had already been combined in Holland in the seventeenth century, and perhaps Derain was inspired by Michiel van Musscher's *Portrait of the Painter Michiel Comans II and his Wife* (1669, Amsterdam, Rijksmuseum). The complex play of light in Derain's picture is also an indication of the importance of seventeenth-century Dutch painting to Derain's work in this period. The light which strikes Geneviève is so direct that it simplifies rather than defines her features, in contrast with the gentle illumination of Alice's features modelled in light and shade.

Geneviève takes up the classic 'muse' pose behind Derain like the muse in Ingres' *Portrait of Cherubini* in the Louvre. Her mother, entering from the obscurity behind the curtain, takes up an equally familiar position well known from the work of Titian and Velázquez. Her relation to the main group is equidistant with ours, sealing the group between herself and us in a close intimacy. Her appearance is in keeping with the sober reverie of the other

figures, and the few vessels she carries seem to symbolize the ritual nature of what is taking place in the dark area between the artist and his canvas.

Similarly, in such a setting, the dog which Geneviève carries takes on a symbolic function as an attribute of her fidelity to the family and her uncle's fidelity to his art. The peacock, whose head is surrounded by a folded white cloth, as it is occasionally in lavish still-life paintings of the late sixteenth century, resumes its traditional role as a symbol of both worldly glory and the mystical glory in paradise. The black cat Derain had recently used as an attribute of arcane knowledge in an engraved self-portrait (cat. 77). The parrot to which the artist attends with such seriousness represents a special kind of knowledge. The parrot, according to Aelian, is excellent among birds and has an intelligence much like our own in its talent for imitation.

This portrait has developed directly from Derain's earlier work *The Artist in his Studio* (cat. 46) but has grown in complexity, not only of composition but of theme. As in seventeenth-century emblem portraiture, everything in this work speaks of Derain's views on painting. It is something of a manifesto. 'The mission of art is to equalize time', wrote Derain (Derain, 1935, pp. 940–2). He despised the cult of originality and took into his own work the finest of past painting, which in this period he thought to be the painting of the seventeenth century. This was not a naive emulation but a re-formation subsequent, as he said, to 'the assimilation and digestion of experiment and knowledge'. In the mid-1930s another issue in painting arose in which he had to take a stand. Some of the young artists who

most admired him, foremost among them Alberto Giacometti, were deeply committed politically and eager to put their art publicly into the service of the struggling masses. To Derain this was impossible and inconsistent with the purposes of art. The domestic circle, the *côté féminin* at Chambourcy, was a symbol of the artist as a private man.

56 *Autoportrait à la pipe c.*1953 oil on canvas 35.5 × 33 cm Private Collection, Paris Provenance: estate of the artist Exhibitions: 1954, Paris (105); 1959, Geneva (56); 1974, Albi (49); 1976, Paris (76); 1980, Chambourcy, La Maison de Derain

This painting is thought to be Derain's last self-portrait.

PRINTS

All prints are from the collection of the Bibliothèque Nationale, Paris.
'JA' refers to the number in the catalogue which Jean Adhémar prepared in 1955 for a memorial exhibition of Derain's prints (Jean Adhémar, Julien Cain, Jean Valery-Radot, *Derain*, Paris, Bibliothèque Nationale, 1955).

57 *Baigneuse c.*1923 Etching 40 × 30 cm Atelier Stamp JA3

58 *Femme appuyée sur le genou c.*1923 Etching and drypoint 39.5 × 29 cm Atelier Stamp second of two known states of this print JA4

59 *Nu debout* c.1935
Etching 39 × 29 cm
Atelier Stamp
JA5

60 *Nu couché, la tête en arrière*
c.1933
Etching 24 × 29 cm
Atelier Stamp
JA6

61 *Femme au bord de la mer*
c.1923
Etching 21 × 12 cm
touched with pencil
JA7

62 Four prints of a suite of
nudes published by H. M.
Petiet 1929
Lithographs 53 × 40 cm
Femme nue se coiffant
Femme nue se baissant
Nu de dos
Nu couché
JA90

63 *Nude* (one leg folded under
the other, arms behind back,
head thrown back) 1929
Lithograph 53 × 40 cm
Atelier Stamp

64 *Nude* (one arm over head,
other hand catching a raised
foot behind) 1929
Lithograph 53 × 40 cm

65 *Nude* (seated sideways,
leaning forward, that is to the
left, head in crook
of arm)
Lithograph 34.5 × 44.5 cm
signed lower right

66 *Nude* (seated, back view)
Lithograph 63 × 20 cm
signed lower right
stamp of editor H. M. Petiet
marked 31/60

67 *Nude* (turned away, arms
raised, sketch)
Lithograph 46 × 35 cm
signed lower right
stamp of editor H. M. Petiet
marked 31/60

68 *Nude* (bending, one leg
raised, reaching forward with
right hand)
Lithograph 42.5 × 31.5 cm
signed lower right

69 *Small Nude* (in a chamber)
Drypoint 10 × 6.0 cm
Atelier Stamp

70 *Nu de dos*
Engraving 22 × 18 cm
JA100

71 *Nu assis, bras levé* 1929
Lithograph

72 *Nu assis sur une chaise* 1929
Lithograph

73 *Vénus marine* c.1935
Etching 30.5 × 11.5 cm
Atelier Stamp
JA104

74 *Odalisque* c.1935
Etching 11.5 × 29.5 cm
Atelier Stamp
JA105

75 Nine Artist's Proofs for the
illustrations to Vincent
Muselli, *Les Travaux et les
Jeux* (cat. 119; illus.) 1929
Lithographs 16.5 × 10.5 cm
(sheet size 29 × 22.5)

76 Four Experimental Prints
for a project known as *Les
Luminaires* c.1930
JA106

Decorated Frontispiece
Etching (frame) touched with
pencil (figure) 41.5 × 31.5 cm
Atelier Stamp
Inscription outside plate: LES
LUMINAIRES COELI
HOMINISQUE FOEDIA [sic]
Man in a Constellation (illus.)
Etching touched with pencil
28 × 24.5 cm
Atelier Stamp
pencil drawings of homunculi
outside the plate mark
*Constellation and Seascapes with
Sailing Boats*

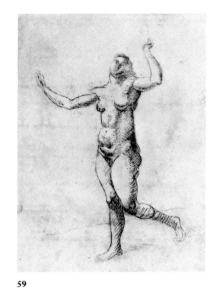

59

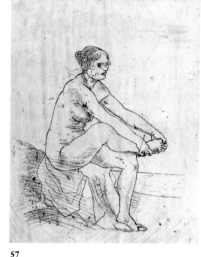

57

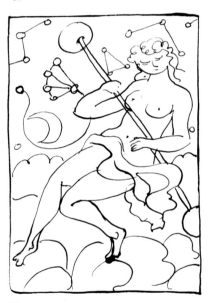

75

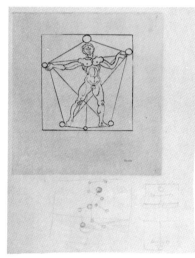

76

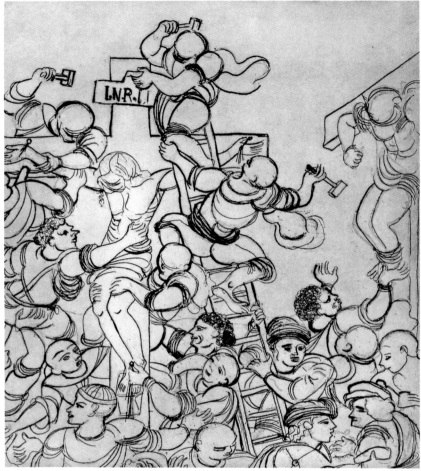

78

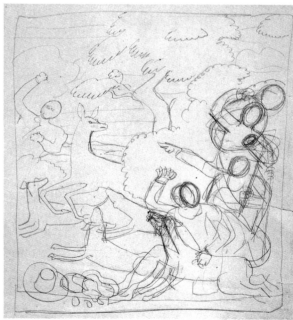

85

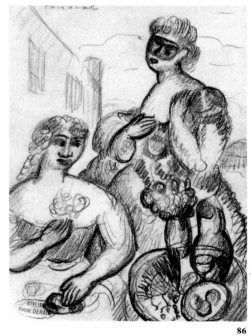

86

Etching touched with pencil
29.5 × 39.5 cm
Inscription outside plate: Le Cygne
Constellation
Etching touched with pencil
27.5 × 24.5 cm
Atelier Stamp
On reverse: drawing in red pencil of planetary system with astrological signs

77 Suite of Prints for a project known as *Le Bestiaire c.*1929
Engraving
JA94
Le cadran solaire, 9.5 × 8.5 cm
L'oiseau et la tête de mort,
   10.5 × 5.5 cm
La pointe du clocher,
   11.5 × 6.0 cm
L'oiseau, 5.0 × 10 cm
Le fumeur (self-portrait),
   10 × 7.0 cm
La croix, 11.5 × 6.0 cm
Le grand duc 10.5 × 6.5 cm
Le hibou, 9.0 × 6.0 cm

78 *Crucifixion c.*1935
Etching 36.5 × 31.5 cm
JA107

79 *Landscape*
Lithograph touched with
   gouache
On reverse: drawing in gouache
   of a theatre design

80 *Femme aux boucles d'oreilles*
   *c.*1945
Lithograph
Atelier Stamp
JA120

81 Three Artists' Proofs for the illustrations to *Contes et Nouvelles de La Fontaine* published 'Au dépens d'un Amateur' in 1950.
The lithographs for this book were printed by Mourlot in 1949 but drawn on the stone in the early 1930s. These proofs may date from before or after the Second World War.
14 × 9.0 cm

Standing Male Figure
Group of Three Figures
Solitary Scholar

82 Two of five states of *Le pont neuf*. A further state of the print was used as an illustration to *Paris 1937*, published by Daragnès for the International Exhibition in that year. 1937
Etching
JA110

83 *Le morin* c.1911
Etching and drypoint
29 × 35.5 cm
signed lower right
Inscribed No 8 (not Derain's hand)
This is the most ambitious of Derain's early prints. It was not widely sold until after the Kahnweiler auction of 1923.
JA49 (as *Paysage dans le goût italien*, c.1913–19)

DRAWINGS

All drawings are in a private collection

84 *Two Heads*
pencil 30 × 20 cm
Atelier Stamp

85 Study for *La chasse au cerf*
pencil 32 × 41.5 cm
Atelier Stamp on reverse

86 *Carnaval* (*Isabella*)
Pencil 15.8 × 12.4 cm
Atelier Stamp

87 Study for *Arlequin et Pierrot* (fig. 3)
Pencil 33.9 × 23.8 cm
Atelier Stamp

88 *Nude*
Pencil 40 × 30 cm
Atelier Stamp

89 *Two Nudes* (reverse of *Nude* above)
Pencil 30 × 40 cm

90 *Nude*
Pencil 63 × 47.5 cm
Atelier Stamp

91 *Nude*
Pen and ink 63 × 48 cm
Atelier Stamp

92 *Nude* (reverse of *Nude* above)
Pencil 63 × 48 cm

93 *Nude*
Pencil 59 × 48.5 cm
Atelier Stamp

94 *Nude*
Sanguine 43.5 × 37 cm
signed lower right

95 *Nude*
Sanguine 63 × 48 cm
Atelier Stamp

96 *Nude*
Pencil 28 × 22 cm
Atelier Stamp

97 *Nude*
Pencil 27 × 21 cm
Atelier Stamp

98 *Nude*
Pencil 28 × 20 cm
Atelier Stamp

99 *Standing Nude*
Pencil 29 × 21.5 cm
Atelier Stamp

100 *Reclining Nude*
Pencil and Pen and Ink
17 × 28 cm
Atelier Stamp

101 *Nude*
Pencil 31 × 25 cm
Atelier Stamp

102 *Nude*
Pencil 63 × 48 cm
Signed lower right

103 *Reclining Nude*
Pencil 14.1 × 21.9 cm
Atelier Stamp

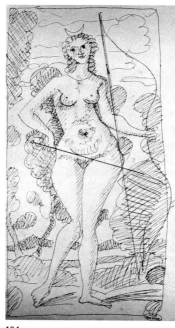

104

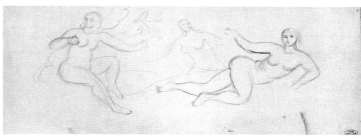

105

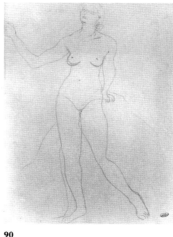

90

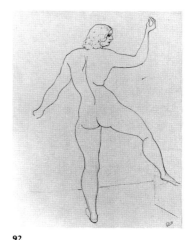

92

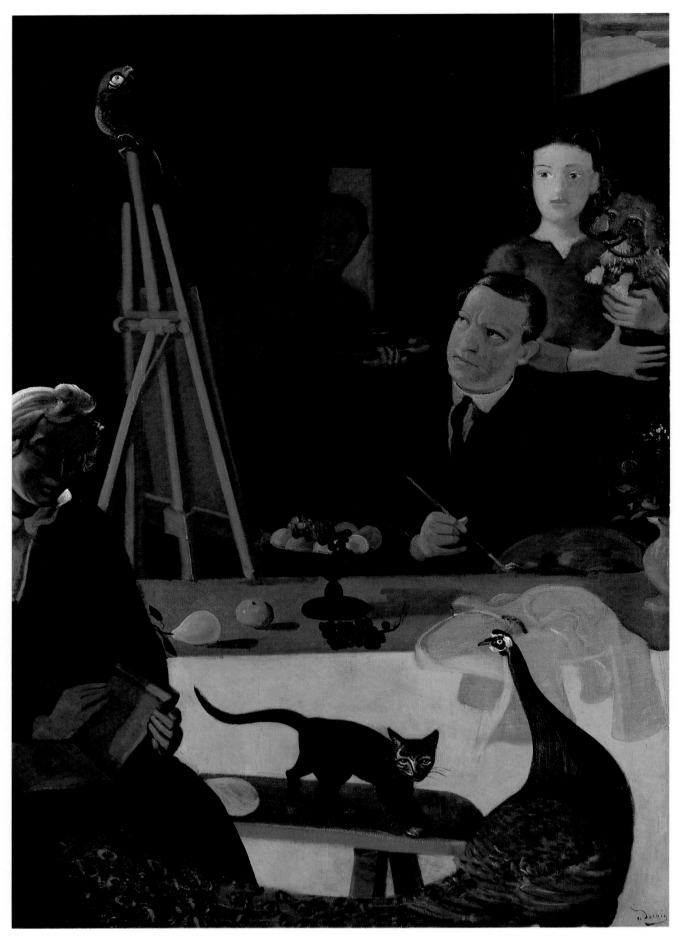

88. *The Painter and his Family*, c. 1939, Tate Gallery, London (cat. 55).

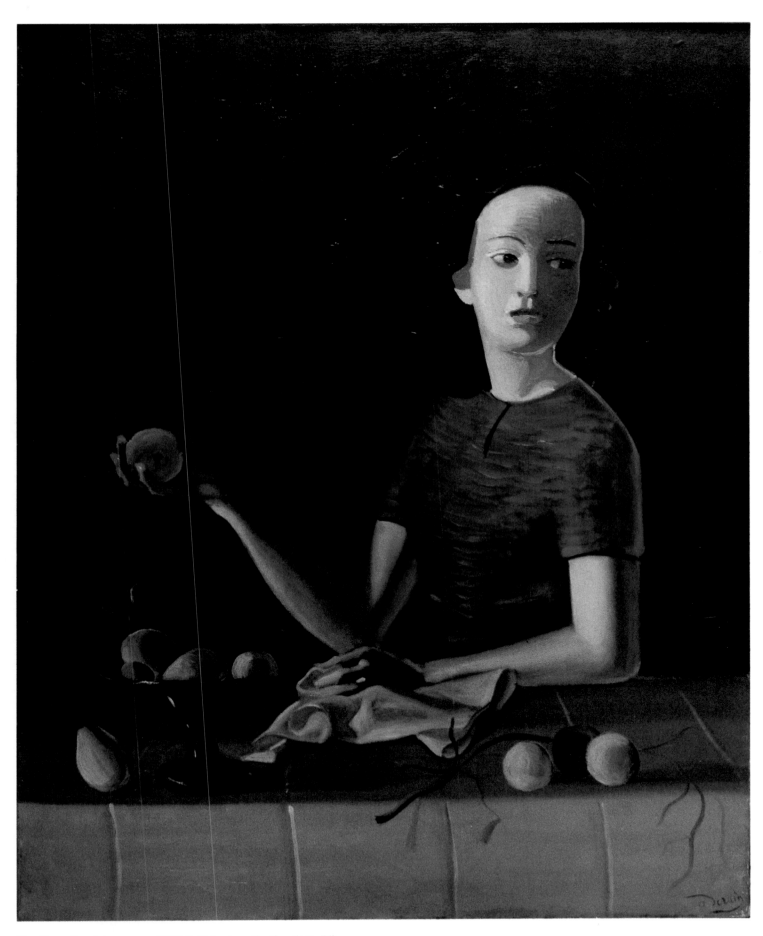

89. *Geneviève à la pomme*, 1937–8, Private collection (cat. 54).

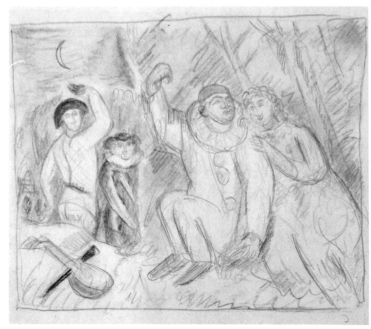

106

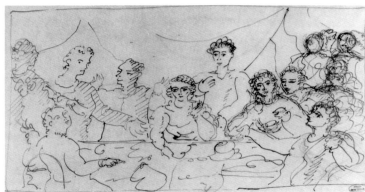

107

104 *Diane*
Blue ink 45.1 × 34.9 cm
Atelier Stamp

105 Study for *La clairière ou le déjeuner sur l'herbe*
Pencil 22.2 × 60.3 cm
Atelier Stamp

DRAWINGS FROM THE MUSÉE D'ART MODERNE DE LA VILLE DE TROYES, DONATION DENISE AND PIERRE LÉVY

106 *La comédie italienne*
Pencil and colour pencil
15 × 18 cm
lower right: a
lower left: a.d.

107 *Le banquet* (study for *Le retour d'Ulysse*)
Ink on tracing paper
23 × 44.4 cm (inner frame)
25.4 × 51.7 cm (sheet size)
Atelier Stamp

108 *Composition. Scène idyllique avec 5 personnages (Bacchanale)*
Ink wash
27 × 47 cm (inner frame)
38.4 × 56.9 cm (sheet size)
signed lower right

109 *L'Arlequin*
Pencil on tracing paper
51.8 × 34.8 cm
signed and dedicated lower right: 'à Paul Guillaume A Derain'

110 *Nu féminin assis, vu de dos*
Sanguine 43.6 × 35.8 cm
signed lower right

111 *Nu féminin debout* (*de face*)
Pencil 62 × 49 cm
signed lower right

112 *Nu féminin assis*

Charcoal 62 × 47.5 cm
Atelier Stamp

113 *Nude*
Pencil 63 × 48 cm
Atelier Stamp

114 *Male Nude*
Sanguine 63 × 48 cm
Atelier Stamp

115 *Seated Nude*
Pencil 34 × 27 cm
Atelier Stamp

116 *Torso*
Sanguine 62.5 × 48.5 cm
Signed lower right

ILLUSTRATED BOOKS

117 *La Cassette de plomb*
Georges Gabory
1920
Editions Galerie Simon, Paris
printed by François Bernouard
edition of 155
(108) signed in blue ink
contains two etchings
Bibliothèque Nationale, Paris

118 *Le Nez de Cléopâtre*
(fig. 45) Georges Gabory
1922
Editions Galerie Simon, Paris
printed by A. Birault
edition of 112
signed by Derain and Gabory
contains ten etchings
Bibliothèque Nationale,
Paris

119 *Les Travaux et les Jeux*
Vincent Muselli
1929
J. E. Pouterman, Paris
printed by Coulama
d'Argenteuil
lithographs printed by Mme
Dûchatel, Paris
edition of 111
(81) signed by Derain and
Muselli, initialled by
Pouterman
contains forty lithographs
Bibliothèque Nationale, Paris

120 *Héliogabale (ou l'anarchiste couronné)* Antonin Artaud
1934
Denoël et Steele
illustrations from six drawings by Derain
Bibliothèque Nationale, Paris

121 *Le Voyage en Grèce* Cahiers édites par la Société Neptos, Paris
1935
frontispiece, *Enlèvement de Dionysos par les pirates*
Bibliothèque Nationale, Paris

122 *Le Satyricon* (fig. 55) Petronius, translated by Héguin de Guerle
1951
published 'au dépens d'un amateur' (Sickles)
printed by Fequet et Baudier
engravings printed by Georges le Blanc
contains 33 engravings of the 36 which were made in 1934 for Ambroise Vollard who initiated the project
also contains wood-engraved decorations and endpieces after designs by Derain
edition of 280
framed prints: Musée d'Art Moderne de la Ville de Paris
opening: Taylor Library, Oxford

123 *Les Héroïdes* (fig. 56) Ovid, translated by Marcel Prévost
1938
La Société Les Cent et Une
printed by Guillaume Budé
etchings printed by Roger Lacourière
wood engravings after Derain's designs printed by Pierre Bouchet
edition of 101
(34) signed by Princess Schakomskay and Princess Carbuccia (vice-presidents)
contains fifteen illustrations after a suite of etchings printed in sanguine ink in an edition of ten for the Société Les Cent et Une
Taylor Library, Oxford

124 *Pantagruel* J. F. Rabelais (text established by Abel Lefranc 1922)
1943
Albert Skira, Geneva
Printed by Georges Girard
Woodcuts printed by Roger Lacourière
edition of 275
contains 158 woodblock prints
Taylor Library, Oxford

125 *Contes et Nouvelles* La Fontaine
1950
published 'au dépens d'un amateur' (Sickles)
printed by Fequet et Baudier
lithographs printed by Mourlot Frères
edition of 200
contains sixty-seven lithographs from the early 1930s, printed for Vollard who initiated the project
Taylor Library, Oxford

126 *Anacréon (Odes Anacréatiques)*
1953
Cercle Lyonnais du Livre
printed by Fequet et Baudier
edition of 200
this is an example printed especially for the Bibliothèque Nationale
contains 59 lithographs, some set in text
Bibliothèque Nationale, Paris

127 *Amie et Amille* mystery play of the fifteenth century, translated by Elenin Bourges
1957
Nouveau Cercle Parisien du Livre
printed by Fequet et Baudier
lithographs printed by Mourlot Frères
edition of 180
contains 22 colour lithographs
Taylor Library, Oxford

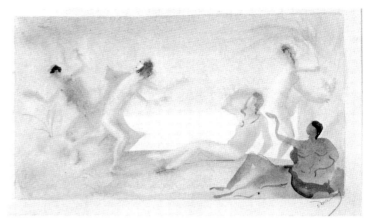

108

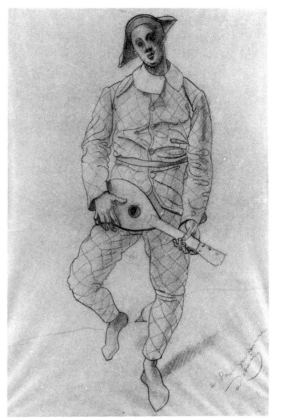

109

BIBLIOGRAPHY

Primary Sources

The documents cited in the text as manuscript notes belong to a collection of papers which were recovered from Derain's house at Chambourcy soon after the artist's death. They were deposited by his family in the Bibliothèque Littéraire Jacques Doucet, Paris. Citations are identified by the manuscript number assigned to the document by that library and the folio number within that manuscript. A few of the manuscript notes deal with practical matters, lists of paintings, guests to be invited to private views, but the majority of them are poetic or theoretical writings. A number of them are notes from Derain's reading, compilations of the results of his research into a variety of subjects, experiments with signs, letters, and language, and experiments in musical notation and composition. Also included is his unpublished treatise on painting 'De Picturae Rerum', written between 1919 and 1921. Nearly all of these documents are undated, but using only dated documents among them, they can be seen to span at least the period 1903–33, and there is a great deal of internal evidence for dating some of the notes in the late 1930s and after the Second World War.

Substantial selections from these notes have been published. See Rosanna Warren, 'A Metaphysic of Painting: The Notes of André Derain', *The Georgia Review*, vol. XXXII, no. 1, Spring 1978, 94–149, in which a large part of Derain's treatise on painting is published in English translation. See also Gabrielle Salomon, 'Les Notes d'André Derain', *Cahiers du Musée National d'Art Moderne*, vol. 5, 1980, 343–61, in which most of the text of the three manuscripts of the treatise on painting are published.

There are two large collections of letters. Those from Derain to Vlaminck, edited by Maurice Vlaminck, were published as *Lettres à Vlaminck*, Paris, 1955. This collection of letters covers the years 1900–17. The letters are from three distinct periods: Derain's military service, his painting trips to the south of France during 1905–8, and his service in the First World War.

The largely unpublished correspondence between Derain and Kahnweiler is in the archives of Daniel Henry Kahnweiler, Galerie Louise Leiris, Paris. It extends over the period 1907–24, with a single letter dated 1927. There is also some slight correspondence with Madame Derain after the artist's death. A few of these letters were published in the exhibition catalogue, *Donation Louise et Michel Leiris, Collection Kahnweiler Leiris*, Paris, Musée National d'Art Moderne, 1984, pp. 37–8.

Published statements by the artist include the following:

Derain, André, 'Hommage à Jacques-Emile Blanche, peintre splendide et critique admirable', *Signaux de Belgique et de la France*, Paris and Brussels, September 1921, pp. 243ff. (repr. in P. Lévy, *Des Artistes et un collectionneur*, Paris, 1976, pp. 142–7)

——, 'Quand les Fauves . . . quelques souvenirs', *Comoedia*, Saturday 20 June 1942, pp. 1, 6

Crevel, René, 'Ou va la peinture?', *Commune*, no. 21, 22, 24, May, June, August, 1935. The quotations from this work are in the May issue, pp. 940–2.

Collection Comoedia-Charpentier, *Peintres d'Aujourd'hui: Les Maîtres*, Paris, 1943 (unpaginated)

Principal Monographs

1920 Henry, Daniel (pseudonym for D. H. Kahnweiler), *Derain*, Leipzig

1921 Carrà, Carlo, *Derain*, Rome; English edn 1924

1923 Faure, Elie, *Derain*, Paris
Salmon, André, *André Derain*, Paris

1929 Basler, Adolphe, *A. Derain*, Paris
Salmon, André, *A. Derain*, Paris

1931 Basler, Adolphe, *A. Derain*, Paris

1938 Svrcek, J. B., *André Derain*, Prague

1949 Leymarie, Jean, *Derain, ou le retour à l'ontologie*, Paris

1958 Sandoz, Marc, *Eloge de Derain*, Paris

1959 Hilaire, Georges, *Derain*, Geneva
Sutton, Denys, *Derain*, London

1960 Papazoff, Georges, *Derain mon copain*, Paris

1961 Segonzac, André Dunoyer de, *A. Derain*, Neuilly-sur-Seine

1964 Diehl, Gaston, *Derain*, Paris

1965 Cailler, Pierre, *Catalogue d'oeuvre sculpté d'André Derain*, Geneva

1966 Carrà, Massimo, *Derain*, Milan

1970 Lévy, Denise, *André Derain*, Paris

1976 Kalitina, N., E. Georgiyevskaya, A. Barskaya, *André Derain*, Leningrad

Other Published Sources

For exhibition catalogues, see the list of Selected One-Man Exhibitions.

Apollinaire, Guillaume, *Chroniques d'arts*, ed. L. C. Breunig, Paris, 1960 (all original articles by Apollinaire quoted in the text are republished in this collection)

Bazin, Germaine, 'Le Reveil des traditions sensibles', *L'Amour de l'art*, no. 7, July 1933, 175–84

Bell, Clive, *Since Cézanne*, London, 1922

——, *Old Friends*, London, 1956

Breton, André, *Les pas perdus*, Paris, 1919

Charensol, G., 'Paul Guillaume, curieux homme et homme curieux', *Plaisir de France*, December 1955, p. 15

Claudel, Paul, *Art poétique: Connaissance du temps, traité de la connaisance au monde et de soi-même, developpement de l'église*, Paris, 1907; Paris, 1984

——, *La Physique de l'Eucharistie*, Paris, 1910 (repr. in Paul Claudel, *Oeuvres complètes*, vol. 5, Paris, 1961)

——, *L'Annonce faîte à Marie*, serialized in *Nouvelle revue française* between December 1911 and March 1912; first performed at the Théâtre de l'Oeuvre, Paris, December 1912

Courthion, Pierre, *Courbet*, Paris, 1931

Dorival, B., '*L'Age d'or* de Derain', *Revue du Louvre*, vol. 3, 1964

Dûchartres, P.-L., *Commedia dell'Arte*, Paris, 1924

Giacometti, Alberto, 'Derain', *Derrière le miroir* (an occasional publication issued by Galerie Maeght), Paris, 1957

Gimpel, R., *Journal d'un collectionneur*, Paris, 1963; English edn, trans. John Rosenberg, London, 1966; London, 1986

Horne, Jeannette, 'Two New Monumental Derains and his other Recent Paintings and Drawings', *Art News*, 12, November 1938, pp. 12, 19

Jacob, Max, *Le cornet à dés*, Paris, 1916

Lee, Jane, 'Painting as Divination, A Still Life by André Derain', *The Stanford Museum*, vol. XIV–XV, 1984–5, 2–8

——, 'L'Enchanteur pourrissant', *Revue de l'art*, vol. 82, 1988, 51–60

——, 'Derain's *The Painter and his Family*', *Burlington Magazine*, vol. CXXX, April 1988, 287–90

——, 'The Prints of André Derain', *Print Quarterly*, vol. 7, 1990, 36–58

Léger, Fernand, *Courbet*, Paris, 1929

Lévy, Pierre, *Des Artistes et un collectionneur*, Paris, 1976

Matisse, Henri, 'Notes d'un peintre', *La Grande Revue*, vol. LII, December 1908, 731–45

Moréas, Jean, *Pélerin passioné*, Paris, 1891

Oberlé, Jean, *La Vie d'artiste (souvenirs)*, Paris, 1956

Parke-Taylor, Michael, 'André Derain: les copies de l'album Fauve', *Cahiers du Musée National d'Art Moderne*, vol. 5, 1980, 363–77

Pope-Hennessy, John, *The Portrait in the Renaissance*, London, 1966

Rey, R., 'Derain', *Art et décoration*, February 1925, 33–44

Rivière, Jacques, *Etudes*, Paris, 1912

Salmon, André, *La Jeune peinture française*, Paris, 1912

——, *La Jeune sculpture française*, Paris, 1919

——, 'André Derain', *L'amour de l'art*, no. 6, 1920, 196–9

——, *Quatrième centenaire de Raphael, propos d'atelier*, Paris, 1922

——, *Derain* (Les peintres français nouveaux, no. 15), Paris, 1924

——, 'André Derain, peintre français', *L'Art vivant*, no. 39, August 1925, 570–3

——, 'Derain', *Chroniques du jour*, no. 1 (n.s.), March 1929 (unpaginated)

——, *Souvenirs sans fin*, Paris, 1956

Signac, Paul, 'D'Eugène Delacroix au Néo-Impressionisme', *Revue Blanche*, May, June, July 1898; repr. as a book, *D'Eugène Delacroix au Néo-Impressionisme*, Paris, 1899

Silvanie, A., *Vincent Muselli, L'oeuvre poétique*, Paris, 1957

Westheim, P. 'Über das kunstlerische Situation in Frankreich', *Das Kunstblatt*, September 1922

ACKNOWLEDGEMENTS

The works of Derain are © ADAGP, Paris/DACS, London, 1990.

We would very much like to thank the following for their help in facilitating the loan of works to the exhibition: Michel Hoog, Musée de l'Orangerie, Paris; Philippe Chabert, la Musée d'Art Moderne de la Ville de Troyes; the Pierre Matisse Gallery, New York; Michel Kellermann, Paris; Robert Stoppenbach of Stoppenbach & Delestre, London, all lenders to the exhibition, listed separately, including those who have asked to remain anonymous.

We would also like to thank the following for their kind assistance in the research for this publication: Geneviève Taillade for her help, information, loan of pictures and photographs, and particularly for making available the family documents which inform the author's account of events during the Occupation, and for the precise details of her own and her aunt's biographies; Michael Parke-Taylor of the Art Gallery of Ontario, a generous colleague upon whom the author has relied heavily for information concerning exhibitions and collectors in the United States; Michel Kellermann, who is preparing the catalogue raisonné of Derain's works; Robert Stoppenbach, Manuel Schmit and Colette Giraudon for their valuable advice; the Galerie Louise Leiris for access to the Kahnweiler Archives; Françoise Chapon in the Bibliothèque Littéraire Jacques Doucet, with whom the author examined Derain's manuscript notes; Madame Woimant and Antoine Coron in the Bibliothèque Nationale; Leland Bell, Christopher Green, Richard Shone and Sarah Wilson for support and advice; and Catherine Henry for her hospitality, advice and particularly for her valuable opinions on the work of André Derain.

Lenders

Art Salon Takahata, Osaka City; Berne Kunstmuseum; Bibliothèque Nationale, Paris; the Museum of Art, Carnegie Institute, Pittsburgh; the Cincinnati Art Museum, Ohio; André Derain fils; the Detroit Institute of Arts, Michigan; Hokkaido Museum of Art, Sapporo; Michel Kellermann; Kunsthaus, Zurich; Galerie Adrien Maeght, Paris; the Estate of Pierre Matisse, New York; Musée National d'Art Moderne, Centre Georges Pompidou, Paris; Musée d'Art Moderne de la Ville de Paris, photos © Spadem 1990; Musée de l'Orangerie, Collection Jean Walther and Paul Guillaume, Paris, photos © Réunion des Musées Nationaux; Musée du Petit Palais, Geneva; Musée d'Art Moderne de la Ville de Troyes, Donation Denise et Pierre Lévy; Ryoko Company Ltd, Tokyo; Galerie Schmit, Paris; the Tate Gallery, London; The Taylor Institution Library, University of Oxford.

Photographic Acknowledgements

Prudence Cuming Associates; Patrick Goetelen; Beatrice Hatala; D. le Nevé.

INDEX